PRAISE FOR GIRLS WRITE NOW'S 2015 ANTHOLOGY

"As a journalist, I believe in the power of storytelling: to shed light, to move people, to effect change... and I believe girls need to be able to take control of their stories and launch them into the world. Girls Write Now helps to harness that magic and make it happen."

— JUJU CHANG, EMMY AWARD-WINNING CO-ANCHOR OF ABC NEWS *NIGHTLINE*

"From an elderly wrinkle of an abuela shuffling around her Spanish-only kitchen, to a Pulitzer Prize-winning ebullient lesbian playwright, to a mohawk-clad Jewish pianista fronting a rock band at CBGB, my own women mentors changed my life one drop of wisdom at a time. I hold the baton. And I cannot wait to pass it onto this talented group of young dreamers and writers. I have a feeling I'll get much more than I give in my time with Girls Write Now."

— QUIARA ALEGRÍA HUDES, PULITZER PRIZE-WINNING AUTHOR OF *WATER BY THE SPOONFUL*

"*Voice to Voice:* Girls Write Now's 2015 anthology gives hope — not only for the empowerment of female human beings, but also for that of language. Not for nothing do reactionary extremists consider a little girl who can read and write the most dangerous creature in the world!"

— ROBIN MORGAN, NEA-WINNING POET, ACTIVIST, AND FORMER EDITOR-IN-CHIEF OF *MS. MAGAZINE*

"Telling the truth is hard enough, but to do it with writerly finesse takes bravado, self-knowledge and fortitude. These young women have already figured that out. Just read their stories, you'll see."

— JULIE SALAMON, AUTHOR OF *WENDY AND THE LOST BOYS* AND *CAT IN THE CITY*

"Girls Write Now gives rise to a vibrant young generation of women writers whose work is inspiring, and proves that while we hold onto our own individual identities, our life's dreams and struggles are universal."

— AWISTA AYUB, AUTHOR OF *KABUL GIRLS SOCCER CLUB*

"Writing, by definition, can be a lonely passion, but pairing these girls with a caring mentor, and, ultimately, with each other, it transitions solo work into a community of passions, and a synergy of writing. I can't think of a more inspiring effort to rally around."

— JESSICA BARRACO, AUTHOR OF *THE BUTTERFLY GROOVE: A MOTHER'S MYSTERY, A DAUGHTER'S JOURNEY*

"I vividly recall being a Brooklyn teenager, cramming notebooks full of story ideas and profound thoughts on the world, and having no idea what to do with my precious words. Bravo to Girls Write Now for providing these amazing young women writers guidance and opportunity, and to the mentors who give their time and wisdom to support and shape their words into art."

— VICTORIA BROWN, AUTHOR OF *MINDING BEN (GRACE IN THE CITY)*

"Girls Write Now is fighting the good fight. Inside this anthology you will find the work of women who will change the world with their words."

— SUSANNAH CAHALAN, #1 *NEW YORK TIMES* BESTSELLING AUTHOR OF *BRAIN ON FIRE: MY MONTH OF MADNESS*

"Girls of color often contend with others speaking for them, about them, at them. How wondrous that Girls Write Now has given these girls the discovery tools to speak for themselves, and just as importantly, to be heard by us. Girls' lives matter, and we are lucky to have this collection of personal stories."

— BRIDGETT M. DAVIS, AUTHOR OF *INTO THE GO-SLOW*

"Girls Write Now rightly gives voice to young women who might not otherwise be heard."

—DENISE DIFULCO, WRITER AND JOURNALIST

"How powerful to read these works in which young women find their individuality, as well as their community, through their writing."

— NICOLE HAROUTUNIAN, AUTHOR OF *SPEED DREAMING*

"This anthology is a testament to the power of community, one in which each writer brings her own unique vision to a fold where she acquires mastery of the craft and blossoms."

— BEENA KAMLANI, SENIOR EDITOR OF VIKING PENGUIN RANDOM HOUSE, WRITER AND TEACHER

"A living bouquet of voices — come along on the journey of Girls Write Now through their poetic writing."

— LILY KOPPEL, *NEW YORK TIMES* BESTSELLING AUTHOR OF *THE ASTRONAUT WIVES CLUB*

"The verve and power in these young women's voices is invigorating and heartening. This book tells the story of how tomorrow's leaders are coming to be."

— CATHERINE LACEY, AUTHOR OF *NOBODY IS EVER MISSING*

"Girls Write Now mentees are a reservoir of raw talent begging to be cultivated and harnessed. They speak of a world that is broken and demand we listen, and when we do we find reason to hope. No one is better equipped to do this than Girls Write Now. Read this anthology and then, please, pass it on to a friend."

— LYNN LURIE, AUTHOR OF *QUICK KILLS*

"Girls Write Now knows that finding one's voice is as much about discovering who you are as an artist as it is about learning who you are as a person. These pages are a moving testament to the raw power of creativity and the untarnished genius of youth."

— KIMBERLY MCCREIGHT, *NEW YORK TIMES* BESTSELLING AUTHOR OF *RECONSTRUCTING AMELIA*

"By showcasing this medley of voices — by turns tender, funny, strident, brimming with intelligence and righteous anger — Girls Write Now has proved just how essential an organization it is."

— YONA ZELDIS MCDONOUGH, AUTHOR OF *YOU WERE MEANT FOR ME*

"Warning: there is so much heart, intensity, guts and sheer talent in these pages, you're going to need to remind yourself to breathe."

— LYNN MELNICK, VIDA: WOMEN IN LITERARY ARTS AND EDITOR OF *PLEASE EXCUSE THIS POEM: 100 NEW POETS FOR THE NEXT GENERATION*

"A powerful antidote to hopelessness and despair. Even as the voices of Girls Write Now reveal the broken heart of the world, they are healing that heart with their medicine of talent, resilience, clarity and passion."

— SYBIL ROSEN, AUTHOR OF *RIDING THE DOG*

"One of the most important lessons my mentor Paula Vogel taught me was this: we individual writers rise when we all rise together in a circle. Girls Write Now is a beautiful anthem to this idea of circles rising together. What an astonishing circle of young women writers pushing the written word further into this next century."

— SARAH RUHL, PLAYWRIGHT AND AUTHOR OF *100 ESSAYS I DON'T HAVE TIME TO WRITE*

"Girls Write Now teaches young women that their voice, their story is worth something. What a lesson to take into the world! Open this book and you will hear the future. On every page there is written hope." — HANNAH TINTI, EDITOR OF *ONE STORY;* AUTHOR OF *THE GOOD THIEF AND ANIMAL CRACKERS*

"As a woman, a writer, and a board member of Girls Write Now, I have long had a front row seat in witnessing the fearless, funny, moving, unexpected and brilliant output of our girls. (At one Girls Write Now reading, a well-known publisher I was sitting next to was so blown away she asked, 'When can I sign her up?') The world routinely censors the voices of these girls — 93% high need, 94% girls of color — by privileging white male writing in every medium and genre there is; this book is an opportunity to take an axe to that ivory tower by journeying, with our girls as your guide, into the myriad worlds their writing has wrought."

— KAMY WICOFF, BESTSELLING AUTHOR OF *WISHFUL THINKING*

"Girls Write Now helps young women blessed with the gift of story express the deepest, smartest and most wonderful part of themselves on the page."

— TAIIA SMART YOUNG, AUTHOR OF *FAMOUS! HOW TO BE THE STAR OF YOUR SHOW: A TEEN GIRL'S GUIDE TO EMBRACING HER FABULOUS SELF*

"Reading these surprising, bold, profound and inspiring pieces is like moving back the curtains on a sunny day. Buy this book. Share it with your daughters, mothers, nieces, sisters, aunts, friends. Girls Write Now is a gift to the world, and to all girls and women who need the confidence and support to write their truth."

— CLAUDIA ZULUAGA, AUTHOR OF *FORT STARLIGHT*

Voice to Voice:
The Girls Write Now Anthology

ABOUT GIRLS WRITE NOW AND OUR ANTHOLOGY

For 17 years, Girls Write Now has been championing the power of a girl's voice, the importance of her ideas and words, and the need to share her stories on a global platform. By pairing the next generation of women writers with professional writing mentors in a supportive community, Girls Write Now is nurturing, and showcasing the stories that need to be told. Our program activities culminate each year with the publication of our award-winning anthology, which includes the best writing from the mentees and mentors in the program. For many girls, this is the first time seeing their work in print, and that experience has a profound effect on their image of themselves as writers. This year's theme for the Girls Write Now Anthology is "Voice to Voice," and in your hands are the original poems, essays and fiction from nearly 70 mentee and mentor pairs who have been working all year writing, editing, and refining their work. Each writing piece went through a process that explores what it is to find your voice, share your story with the world, and look to other voices — even in today's noise. Quite simply, these voices will resonate with the reader and successfully engage in today's cultural conversation. Our 2015 mentees emerged with this body of work that demonstrates just how essential and powerful these voices are in advocating for change and a better world.

Through weekly pair sessions — often conducted in bookstores, Internet cafes and libraries across New York City — as well as workshops, portfolio-building seminars, and readings, our girls are gaining the skills and confidence necessary to share their stories both on the page and on the stage, from Lincoln Center, to the White House, to the United Nations. You will learn about each pair and how their working relationship and growing friendship profoundly affects their work as well as their lives. Girls Write Now is proud to share with you the voices of today and all that they teach us.

— ANTHOLOGY EDITORIAL COMMITTEE

AWARDS FOR GIRLS WRITE NOW

Girls Write Now has been distinguished twice by the White House and the Presidents Committee on the Arts and the Humanities as one of the top after-school arts and culture organizations in the nation. Our girls have earned hundreds of Scholastic Art & Writing Awards, and 100% of our seniors go on to college.

In the past year alone, Girls Write Now was recognized by the Nonprofit Excellence Awards as one of New York City's top 10 nonprofits, by the New York City Council's $1 million STARS Citywide Girls Initiative, by NBCUniversal Foundation's 21st Century Solutions with a grand prize $100,000 Social Innovation grant, and by Diane von Furstenberg as a "People's Voice" Nominee. Our girls — 93% high need and 94% girls of color — performed at Lincoln Center and the United Nations, published original work in *Newsweek, Elle India,* and our award-winning anthology.

This year, Girls Write Now teen writers won a total of 52 Gold and Silver Keys and Honorable Mentions, including one National Gold Medal, from the Scholastic Art & Writing Awards. A broad array of publications and recognitions are listed with all of the pair profiles in the anthology.

Our annual anthology has received the Outstanding Book of the Year award by the Independent Publisher Book Awards and has earned honors from the International Book Awards, The New York Book Festival, the National Indie Excellence Awards and the Next Generation Indie Book Awards. The anthology has also received Honorable Mention from the San Francisco Book Festival and the Paris Book Festival.

PARTNERS

Alliance for Young Artists & Writers
AOL Makers
Barnard College
Book Riot
Bust Magazine
Bustle.com
Children's Book Council
Chime for Change
Flavorpill
Fletcher & Co
Hachette Book Group
HarperCollins
Hive Learning Network New York City
Huffington Post
Hunter College
Independent Publisher
Knopf
Little Brown & Company
Macaulay Honors College at CUNY

McNally Jackson Mentoring Partnership of New York
News Corp
Of Note Magazine
One Teen Story
Open Road Integrated Media
Outbrain
Parsons The New School For Design
Penguin Random House
Poet-Linc at Lincoln Center
Poetry Society
Poets & Writers
Poets Out Loud at Fordham University
Queens Library
Riverhead Books
Rona Jaffe Foundation
Scholastic
She Knows
She Writes Press

Simon & Schuster
SPARK
StoryBundle
Student Science
Theatre Communications Group
The Feminist Press
The New School
THINK
Kelly Writers House, University of Pennsylvania
VIDA: Women in Literary Arts
Wall Street Journal
Women's Media Center Live
Writers House
YesYes Books
Young to Publishing Group

ANTHOLOGY SUPPORTERS

We are grateful to the countless institutions and individuals who have supported our work through their generous contributions. Visit us at www.girlswritenow.org to view the extended list.

Girls Write Now would like to thank Amazon.com, which provided the charitable contribution that made possible this year's anthology.

The anthology is supported, in part, by public funds from the National Endowment for the Arts; the New York State Council on the Arts, a State Agency; and the New York City Department of Cultural Affairs, in partnership with the City Council.

Voice to Voice: The Girls Write Now 2015 Anthology

Girls Write Now, Inc.

247 West 37 Street, Suite 1800

New York, NY 10018

info@girlswritenow.org

www.girlswritenow.org

Printed in the United States

ISBN 978-0-9962772-0-4

THE
GIRLS WRITE NOW
2015 ANTHOLOGY

VOICE TO VOICE

Foreword

MARIANE PEARL

Girls ́ ideas, wisdom and vision are a precious gift to those who listen. Girls Write Now showcases this by introducing us to a new generation of women writers in Voice to Voice: The Girls Write Now 2015 Anthology.

Women and girls have been deprived of their voices ever since anyone can remember. Based on traditional, religious or cultural justifications, the act of depriving half of humanity of their right to interpret and tailor their own lives according to their beliefs has resulted in a solid and complex system to keep women away from power.

But as human beings, we need our stories, we need to make sense of our lives and of the obstacles that confront us. In my opinion, giving this right back to women and girls is an essential factor in redeeming them the most fundamental human dignity. Even though we have seen more changes in the last 50 years than in many centuries combined, we also have a better insight into how much girls are suffering still — just because of their gender. From self-esteem issues to incest, the number of crimes against girls is horrifying.

But, by giving girls their own voices, and not necessarily as victims, we also understand and slowly realize their unfathomable power to transform their own lives and that of others. Then we need to listen as girls reveal the impressive reservoir of resilience, perseverance and compassion that we need so urgently for our own survival as a species.

Reading is an essential part of life and there is great joy to be found in relating to an apparent stranger's story and emotions. There is great joy in feeling part of a whole and nourishing our inner lives with others' experiences. Girls Write Now gives us the chance to share these young girls' feelings and experiences, carefully narrated from the heart, intimate enough to touch the universal, this anthology is a read for all generations, cultures and for anyone who has an interest in the future. I genuinely believe in the power of stories and yours are beautifully crafted, sensitive and smart. The power of the written word can change lives by changing the way we think.

— MARIANE PEARL, Managing Editor of Chime for Change
and author of *In Search of Hope: The Global Diaries of Mariane Pearl;
A Mighty Heart: The Inside Story of the Al Qaeda Kidnapping of Danny Pearl.*

Introduction

TIPHANIE YANIQUE

There is an old-timey bit of advice that young people used to hear a lot: "Pull yourself up by your own bootstraps." It's a weird saying. First of all, what is a bootstrap? And even if we know what bootstraps are, I can't see how it would be physically possible to pull yourself up by them! But it's a really weird bit of advice because it seems to suggest that a person can be successful all by herself. In reality, nobody makes it alone. We need mentors to pull and push and encourage us along. 'I will help you,' mentors say. 'You are worth helping.' Mentorship says, 'what you are doing is valuable.' Individual hard work and creativity is important, but it is never the whole story.

At Girls Write Now, mentorship is the whole point. Young women are creating writing that is sad and funny, fierce and sweet. As a keynote speaker for the Girls Write Now CHAPTERS Reading Series, I heard the girls perform their work. They write comedic stories about how to get the best gift for your birthday and tough poems about domestic abuse. These girls work on their writing with the help of professional women writers. Some of them were even once mentees! Which says a lot about the lasting impact of the organization.

Sometimes we don't know who our mentors are. Sometimes mentors work behind the scenes. Among my first mentors were my teachers. I didn't realize it was mentorship, but it was. My first grade teacher told me: 'You read with such expression.' I hadn't even realized I was doing that. I certainly hadn't realized it was something worth commenting on. But now I see that my becoming a writer might be located in that early moment, and so many early moments like that. Sometimes mentorship is that simple. At the reading, one mentee interspersed a lyric story with a more lyric video. Her piece made commentary on the value of mentorship, saying that one teacher was great because she challenged her students. Challenging her students made her "dangerous."

The mentors in this anthology make encouraging comments but they go further. They do brave, dangerous work. They challenge their mentees. The young writers in this anthology are brave (they read in front of audiences!) and strong (they write poems about difficult things) and they are creative (they work hard to make their stories, poems, and essays as good as they can be). The world is tough and complicated and so girls have to be brave, and strong and creative. But at Girls Write Now, mentors demonstrate that girls don't have to be all those things all by themselves.

— **TIPHANIE YANIQUE,** author of *Land of Love & Drowning*

Table of Contents

GWN 2015 ANTHOLOGY

RACHEL AGHANWA

YEARS AS MENTEE: 1

GRADE: Sophomore

HIGH SCHOOL:
Queens Gateway to Health
Science Secondary School

BORN: Brooklyn, NY

LIVES: Queens, NY

Sara and I set some very large goals to complete by the end of the year (one included finishing a novel). I didn't realize how hard it would be getting started, or the other challenges we've faced. Writer's block, deadlines and, believe it or not, my horrible spelling were all things that sound like it would hinder our progression but it did the opposite. For all these months I've gotten to know Sara, she taught me that no matter how stuck you may be on a blank page, you're always just a twenty minute timer away from a breakthrough.

SARA POLSKY

YEARS AS MENTOR: 1

OCCUPATION:
Writer and Editor

BORN: New York, NY

LIVES: Queens, NY

Rachel and I both began the year hoping to write novels. But facing the blank page is always daunting, and more so when what we're hoping to put on the page is something as large and complicated as a novel. So instead we went back to building blocks, writing and revising smaller pieces. Watching our work evolve reminded me that writing is a process that needs time, and that that's both the hard and the fun part.

BLACK

RACHEL AGHANWA

Here is a piece displaying the insecurities I felt and the views I held as a small child because of the color of my skin. This really hit home because I've always felt uncomfortable writing about myself or my own race.

"Black is just a color," I've heard people say.

Technically, they're wrong. Black is the presence of ALL colors. But black is deeper than "just a color."

Black is my roots, the vines of my family tree twisting their way across the Atlantic Ocean on a straight path to the motherland. Black is my complexion, the skin tone stretching over the canvas of my body, encasing every crevice on the surface. Black is beautiful, and black is what makes me, me.

> "Black is the presence of ALL colors. But black is deeper than "just a color."

But as a child, black was a curse.

Black meant I wasn't as pretty as the other girls in my class. Black meant chemically damaging my hair since the age of five just to get that pin straight perfection of the girls with an ivory complexion. Black was the crayon I never used in my 64-pack crayon box because my friends always said to me how dark and ugly it was.

And to my current disappointment, I thought black meant failure.

Black was also the color of the television screen when you lost a video game, and in big white letters, it would say "you lose" or "game over" depending on what game I decided to play.

My whole life, I felt like I wasn't important enough to speak so that people would listen to me, due to my skin tone. I felt as if my color was an obstacle I could never overcome.

I went through a period of self-hatred, beating myself up, trying to fix myself even though I was nowhere near broken. I would straighten my hair constantly, burning it to the root, just to be "pretty enough." I would cry endlessly when girls of all colors used to berate me because I wasn't light enough or I was "too African to actually be considered black."

It took me a while of self-inflicted mental torture to realize that being black was not hindering me, but actually propelling me.

When I visited Nigeria with my mother and my brother, I remember our driving past a billboard that read "black is not a color, but is actually an attitude."

That was the day I realized, why should I hate myself over something I have no control over? Why should I see what I am as a curse instead of a blessing?

After I finally came to terms with myself, I looked around and realized that my story was a sad one told twice over. There are many other girls with my skin color that went and are still going through this disheartening journey I struggled through as a child.

But my mission now is to release all the black girls from the shackles society has weighed down on them, and bring them to finally see how beautiful they are.

Black is beautiful, and black is me.

Barter Systems

SARA POLSKY

I'm not usually a poet, but as I looked for shorter pieces to work on during our pair sessions this fall, I began drafting poems. It was a wonderful surprise to discover a new form to write in and the beginnings of a voice as a poet.

The tooth fairy and I began corresponding
when I was seven. Well, when I say "corresponding,"
I mean that I asked for things and she took them,
my notes and my teeth, my paper and enamel offerings,
and sometimes, overnight, she'd respond with
a gift, a hand-drawn picture or a miniature pillow
just the size for dollhouse people. T.F., as I called her,
was willing to barter. And I was able, then,
to hold in my mind both fact and belief:
that T.F. was at once real and not real;
that it was actually my mother who sewed
the world's smallest pillows in the middle of the night;
that if only I could put my wants into words,
I could trade for them, one by one, before morning.

CHENELLE AGNEW

YEARS AS MENTEE: 3

GRADE: Senior

HIGH SCHOOL:
High School of
Telecommunications
Arts and Technology

BORN: Brooklyn, NY

LIVES: Brooklyn, NY

**PUBLICATIONS
AND RECOGNITIONS:**
Scholastic Art & Writing
Award: Honorable Mention

Eccentric, exquisite, energetic — all of that wrapped up and tied with a bow is my mentor, Mary Pat Kane. Having been mentored for two years by such a remarkable person has given me the honor of what I'd call being great by association. Mary Pat Kane has allowed me to grow not only as a writer but as a thinker, and an overall individual. My experience at Girls Write Now has become worthwhile because I had such an amazing friend, listener, and mentor to share it with.

MARY PAT KANE

YEARS AS MENTOR: 4

OCCUPATION:
Writer

BORN: Rochester, NY

LIVES: Brooklyn, NY

My mentee is a treasure, a joy, and fun, too. She is a strong and incisive writer, growing more so weekly. In the two years I've had the good luck to work with Chenelle, I'm astounded at the wisdom she possesses for her young years. She is the calm knowing one in our relationship! I will miss her terribly when she goes off to college. I see nothing but a bright and successful future for her. Chenelle has much to offer the world community, and I know she will do that. Her voice and spirit are true. Thank you dear friend. God speed — you are on your way.

Why We Write

CHENELLE AGNEW AND MARY PAT KANE

Last year my mentee Chenelle and I decided to work together on a piece for the Girls Write Now CHAPTERS Reading Series — a "Voice to Voice" piece, if you will. We chose several themes and both of us wrote about them, then we interspersed our sections. This is the first time this piece is in print. We hope you enjoy it.

CHENELLE'S VOICE

It all started in the sixth grade
When I first noticed that those words were called poetry on my page.
At first I thought that it was just a phase.
But then my writing startled me into amazement.
At first it was a secret in which I used to hide.
My friends would ask what I'm doing, I'd say 'nothing.' I lied.
Because it was my treasure but not yet my pride.

MARY PAT'S VOICE

I think it came from eighth grade, when I'd write these one-page essays on wide blue-lined paper in my once-readable cursive writing. The nun would tell us to take a topic and I'd write about it and I found it so exciting that in just one page, a story would be told with a beginning, a middle and end, all nice and neat and tied up — unlike life.

C.

Then came along my favorite English teacher, I told her my predicament and she sighed.
But then she said 'this is yours, own it'; and I obliged.
I distanced myself from negativity and pushed my insecurities aside.
Whew! I don't know why that was so hard, it was like:
I was trying to let go of something that kept biting. But I'm glad that I broke the ball and chain that tied down my writing.

M.P.

I wanted my work out in the world, I wanted to be a well-published, highly sought out writer reading all over the country, standing up at Barnes & Noble regularly, making people laugh and cry. People would probably be so enthused, they'd ask me out for dinner afterwards! Or to their next dinner party. But that publishing success never came. Though I'm still always available for dinner and have been known to be fun at parties!

C.

It's a way to avoid all my struggles, it's my way of fighting.

It's my way of expressing my gratitude to what my mother's sacrificing.

And honestly I don't yet know what I aspire to be but I know that I'm going to chase my dreams and not the money.

But I don't know because it seems like dreams are so close yet so far.

But I guess I can do it because look at Paul Dunbar.

M.P.

I hate when they reject you with typos in the rejection letter, that is so tacky, like "let us hurt you just a little more" — like a "double whammy rejection" — and from very major companies. In another city, I published regularly and as I biked through the streets, people would holler out and stop me and we'd talk about the latest story. That was a great feeling, most people don't know what a writer looks like, it was great but the articles paid $20, $30 with photos or when on the front page. I would never earn my living as a writer. I do 'odd jobs' to get by, some odder than others — I can pet your puppy, burp your baby, make your manuscript sing, and I can, should you need it, fix your furnace. I'm real proud of that one.

> "I've been called opinionated; too young to understand, even naïve."

C.

I've been called a trickster but there's no magic up my sleeves.

I've been called opinionated; too young to understand, even naïve.

But I beg to differ, it's not at all what I believe.

I believe that you give so you shall receive.

I believe that my voice is just as strong as my letters so I'm supreme.

I believe that what's in my heart is dear and tight but

I believe that I put all of me in what I write.

It all started in the sixth grade.

When I first noticed that those words were called poetry on my page.

M.P.

I still write all the time, though I get discouraged about if it will ever be read and/or enjoyed. But I simply cannot see a bright yellow flower without celebrating it, nor hear a child's wonderful chortling voice without wanting to tell you about it. And when people are horrid and rude (!), I just have to rant about them!

And, so I write!

ENDING
(CHENELLE AND MARY PAT TOGETHER — LOUD AND CLEAR) — AND, SO WE WRITE — AND, SO, WE WRITE!

SHRIEN ALSHABASY

YEARS AS MENTEE: 2

GRADE: Senior

HIGH SCHOOL: Beacon High School

BORN: Brooklyn, NY

LIVES: Brooklyn, NY

PUBLICATIONS AND RECOGNITIONS: Scholastic Art & Writing Awards: Gold Key, Honorable Mentions (2)

Growing up in an Egyptian-American household has played a huge role in my life. I find myself constantly pressured to win awards, stack on responsibility, and to prove myself to others. When I meet up with Bria for our writing sessions, I feel the stress ease off. Her voice, logical and reassuring, encourages me. "Priorities, Shrien," Bria reminds me. I add my own thoughts to the mix, about working hard and my goals in life. Together, over a cup of coffee, we put our heads together to create writing that exhilarates. Our voices are never suffocated by the responsibility of craft. Writing with Bria has allowed me to continue working hard without suffocating my desires. It can be hard to put yourself first when thinking about future goals, but with my mentor's help, I'm halfway there.

BRIA COLE

YEARS AS MENTOR: 2

OCCUPATION: Media Producer, Freelance

BORN: Ottawa, Canada

LIVES: Brooklyn, NY

PUBLICATIONS AND RECOGNITIONS: Mixed Messages Exhibition, IMC Gallery New York Foundation for the Arts; Fiscal Sponsorship for short film

Working with Shrien has enriched my desire for imagining and retelling memories. In her wildly diverse portfolio, I notice that Shrien expands moments from her past to develop her strong present day revelations. This type of thought dwelling — thinking of moments that are deeply embedded in mannerisms and desires — encourages me to reconnect with my past and think about the present. Shrien is generous with her character descriptions, which is a sign that she has a compassionate observations of others. I adore our conversations; we share our interests and explore themes, broad and nuanced. With gratitude to Shrien, I am refreshed to continue writing.

Thahab

SHRIEN ALSHABALSY

Thahab is a piece I was able to read at the Metropolitan Museum of Art. It illustrates a parent's love for their child, as well as the excitement of joining a family as an infant. Sometimes it's easy to forget how important you are to others, so this piece serves to highlight this.

My father said that I was born with eyes of gold. When he pushed back my dark brown hair, he saw those eyes and took in a sharp breath and leaned over my weary mother, whispering,

"Look, Bahiti, look at her eyes."

My mother cracked open her eyes, pushing her thin fingers through her hair and sitting up in the bed.

My father cradled me closer, humming as he leaned toward my mother.

My mother reached her hand out, touched the side of my cheek, and smiled.

"Like the suns in Egypt," she whispered, and my dad nodded, eyes full of unshed tears.

"Thahab." My father whispered, pacing around the room as my mother drifted off into a sleepy oblivion.

Gold.

———

No one really remembers anything about being a baby. But I could swear that I remembered Father's soft fingers under my small neck that night we came home from the hospital. Momma sat in the back seat, her light fingers dancing at the tip of my nose and drawing invisible shades on my cheeks with the pads of her fingers. Momma and Father describe that night differently. Momma says that Grandpa Bomani sat at the driver's seat, blasting his favorite Arabic music. Grandma was leaning halfway out the window, a cigarette decorating her fingers. Whirring past the bright delis and loud streets, momma and father agree about one thing. They say that the air was crisp when they drove me home that night. That although Momma swore Grandma was smoking, and Father swears she wasn't, the ocean sea that wafted across the highway was cool. Father and Momma sat in the backseat with

> "...drawing invisible shades on my cheeks with the pads of her fingers."

me stirring slightly against Father's barrel chest. He hadn't let me go since leaving the hospital. Momma always tells me laughingly that once I was born, I was like an extra arm Father had adopted. Back then Momma and Father lived with Grandpa Bomani, my Momma's father. Grandma Samma was father's momma, a laughing old woman who lived by herself since my grandpa died.

Grandpa dropped Grandma off at her big house where she lived all alone. My mother said that when they kissed her goodbye, she landed three kisses on my forehead and waved, delving into that deep house all by herself.

Momma's favorite part of coming home was opening the door to our apartment. Grandpa Bomani went straight in, flicking on the lights. But Momma said Father and she stood by the doorway, me cradled in their arms. They said nothing, but later they had revealed that they were thinking the same. They had left the apartment with Momma heaving and screaming and seeing red. Now they were entering the apartment with something that would change their life forever. I was a new addition to test their relationship, to test their life. Suddenly there was someone else to think about, someone who needed them and expected them to be there. Momma stepped through the door first, rushing into my new baby room and fixing it up. Father stayed by the doorway with me still in his arms, his amber eyes searching the tiny apartment. Everything seemed so much bigger. His eyes picked up the splinters that could appear on the floor and hurt my tiny hands. His sight set on the radiator that went too hot in the winter and could burn me. He cradled me closer to his chest, and to this day I still remember the fast beat of his heart against my eardrums. I still remember.

Perth

BRIA COLE

*My mentee Shrien's piece "Thahab" expresses a significant moment
with her family. Her piece inspired me to remember a time when my younger
sister was born, and I had recently undergone surgery. My father
was a calm presence to all of us.*

There's a pinch to my right. My hand drifts towards my ear, pushing my head upright to lessen the tension in my neck. I feel my ear enlarged with some fabric. My hand floats, unsure whether to prop my temple upwards, to catch my ear as it dips again, or to roll my rubber ball.

A tall body steps through a beam of light. I am suddenly aware that I am sitting in the middle of a bedroom. Pale, dusty beams bounce evenly along narrow wooden floorboards. This person smirks through a grizzly beard — today, I can remember his solid jaw line. I grunt and kick, what is my head doing? He carefully toes into the sun cast territory, sock covered toes roll, stretching shadows with each step. I feel my head tilt again with piqued observation. He tugs at the fabric around his thigh, and crouches to the ground. In the middle of his hairy face, I recognize a nuzzling feeling and a sign of a voice. I squeal and wiggle for DAD! With a gently furrowed brow, he brings his finger to his mouth in an exaggerated mouth gesture... Shhhhhh.

Someone in the room is taking a very long rest. I was set down on the floor from a bed. I lean towards my crouching man. Once on all fours, I lose my inertia and bump my head on the boundary between morning sun and the room. When I am about to huff a choking, tearful protest, Dad slides his hand under my right ear and curls a hair on my left. This curl is a puppet string that lightens my whole head. I can't feel his fingers. My hands immediately reach up to my forehead, exploring the tangles between cotton and hair. I know now, from pictures, my head was bandaged. With a broad hand hooked under my left arm, my legs stretch out, dangle in the air, and rest against a strong torso. His hand draws a line from under my cheek to his face. His chest is vibrating, I watch his eyes change shape, his cheeks are moving and his beard is bouncing. His hold of me tilts me slightly upwards to my right, straightening my spine for good posture. He points to his mouth — something is repeating — and then he points out the window.

> "I lose my inertia and bump my head on the boundary between morning sun and the room."

The light is a nuisance. A grunt and my forehead plops onto a shoulder. Again his face is moving in front of mine. His finger points to his lips and I follow his point. Shimmering balloons are floating, tied to a chair. My ear is heavy. An involuntary tilt rests my left ear across his arm shelf. When I listen to music, I can only recall the feeling of timber from my father's baritone hum as he paces me through the room. He sways me, and dips me to my mother's cheek; she smiles, her arm curled around my baby sister. We lay together.

MISBAH AWAN

YEARS AS MENTEE: 2

GRADE: Junior

HIGH SCHOOL:
The Young Women's
Leadership School
of Astoria

BORN: Pakistan

LIVES: Queens, NY

**PUBLICATIONS
AND RECOGNITIONS:**
Scholastic Art & Writing
Awards: Gold Keys (2)

I feel as if this year has truly been about the voice. This year, I articulated my thoughts aloud in a small diner at the corner of 30th Avenue in Queens, NY with my newbie mentor. It was comforting and acted very much as a release. Free writing periodically helped to strengthen my writing lens by seeing things from a different angle. It helps me zoom in, find comfort in my voice, and then eventually be able to zoom out and talk my way through the edits to finalize a piece such as the one I submitted to this anthology. I am grateful for that, because of my mentor. She has challenged me to write whenever I get the chance and didn't pressure me into forcing a piece out because a piece forced is rarely a piece genuine of my voice. Thank you, Frankie.

FRANKIE THOMAS

YEARS AS MENTOR: 1

OCCUPATION:
Writer and Writing Tutor

BORN: New York, NY

LIVES: New York, NY

**PUBLICATIONS
AND RECOGNITIONS:**
Special Mention in the
2013 Pushcart Prize An-
thology; 2013 Best of the
Net Award; *The Hairpin*
and *The Toast*

You're welcome, Misbah! But also: thank you, Misbah. I'm supposed to be the mentor here, but my mentee teaches me something new every day. I can only aspire to be as organized, ambitious, and idealistic as she is, and she makes me want to strive to be a better writer. I treasure our pair sessions, because the moment we step into our little diner in Astoria, Queens, something magical happens. For one magical hour, we aren't daughters or sisters or girlfriends or employees or students — we're writers. Real, serious, professional writers, supporting and celebrating each other's work. How many people get to be so lucky?

Apple Is a Religion

MISBAH AWAN

Capitalism drives this piece. However, it initially started as a Facebook status my good friend wrote back in September 2014. A few lines were taken from it and our conversations were molded into this story to fit the plot. I tried to use a similar voice as was used in Brave New World by Aldous Huxley. It also shows my hypocrisy, as I am also an Apple user. Whether this writing piece was a hit or miss, I plan to rewrite this work again. It isn't finished yet. But then again neither is Apple, with their new and improved products.

It is warm out. I am writing, sitting at this red and white tiled pizzeria. Every so often, you can hear the clerks shout insults to the brightly lit TV screen behind my back. I look out of the anamorphic frame of the store's walls and I see the city lights (stars are lost to these urban dwellers) and the cars passing by. The ting! when someone walks in or out has become somewhat comforting. It has taken time, indeed. But my ears have learned to appreciate the sound. I scratch my lead pencil against the lined paper in the journal gifted to me two months ago. I am writing about Apple quietly, crouched over my words so that no one can see. I would be sent to Hell if I were seen.

The iconic building still stands. It is a clear glass rectangle on Fifth Avenue surrounded by the usual all-too-eager tourists, mothers who want their children to take a picture of the good side of their face for their next Facebook profile picture, and gilded smiles on Apple employees faces when welcoming teenagers smacking their gum loudly and debating between getting the iWatch 4.0 or the iPhone 360. It is not their fault, however. Nobody is, in fact, at fault here. Not at all. Their enthusiasm is justified, especially at night when the building looks like a brightly lit glass lantern, holding more than 700 people crowding together and checking out the new stocks inside. If you were to walk a few blocks down, you would probably come by a long line of hungry people waiting for the Halal Guys, an inexpensive and famous gyro cart owned by Afghans and Arabs, to take their order. That, too, still stands. A business success of many years.

But first, I will entertain you with the inside scoop for Apple.

Over the main entrance of the glass building, by the words, there is a bitten apple glowing faintly. That is their logo, the apple of Eden, mysteriously alluring; unnecessary but attractive, promoted by greed. If you need an Apple product to reassure you of your self worth, you are in a dire situation, friends. Apple promises eternal happiness but only allows transient. Once in, you are met with the words LIVE A BETTER DAY. Walk past the bold message, you have to be careful as you step down the spiraling staircase, which, too, is glass.

The enormous room on the ground floor is decorated with changing slides on the walls. Babies coo at it after every four seconds. It is stuffy inside, but bearable. People sit, exhausted from waiting long hours for their phones to be delivered. They need to hire better employees, not ones with a haughty attitude. The T-shirts of the workers are blue, their hands occupied, carrying an iPad mini with them to note down customers' orders. "Wait two seconds and I'll get right back to you," said Patty. Well she looked like a Patty, with her blonde hair pushed back into a messy bun and a red bandana tied around her head. I've noticed her a few times there. She usually tries to strike up conversation with foreigners. She tends to go on about her Indian husband and how they'll one day make cute interracial babies together. She says she feels elated when around him, that he is the one. After all, he did buy her the iRing. It can even take your pulse! In actuality, she does not seem happy at all. She seems pale, her bags darker each day. I feel sad for her.

"They do not realize one glaring thing, as they infiltrate this glass lantern building in floods."

I feel sad for everybody here. We've come to an age where writing is more strange of an activity than gluing your eyes to a dim screen for long periods of time. Everything is so artificial here. The lighting, the elevator music, the people's behavior. They are all so odd. They do not realize one glaring thing, as they infiltrate this glass lantern building in floods. They do not realize this: Apple is a religion.

Apple is a religion. Advertisements prove it to be so: THIS PRODUCT WILL CHANGE YOU IN REVOLUTIONARY WAYS. THIS PRODUCT WILL ENLIGHTEN YOU. THIS PRODUCT WILL MAKE YOU A BETTER PERSON. They are, as my past lover once told me back in November, a business with really good marketing schemes. They deify each new product they release as if it were necessary for life. I suppose my situation, however, is even more of an enigma than that of consumers.

Funnily enough, I sit in this pizzeria — with its red and white tiled patterns and screaming matches behind my back — still awaiting anxiously for X to reply back. However, there is humor in my own corruption, in my own stupidity. Alas, I am also a flawed human.

The Hairdresser's Commute

FRANKIE THOMAS

I wrote this during the Girls Write Now Persona Poetry Workshop.
It's inspired by a chat with my hair stylist, who has
the world's worst commute — and the world's best attitude.

There is no excuse for bad hair! I swear
I'm not mad at you or anything, but when I see
dark roots or fried-out bleach jobs or, God forbid,
a mullet, well, it's hard to bear. Listen.
This is what I do to get here every day,
okay? Just listen — you're gonna flip.
Can I swear? You're gonna freaking FLIP.
This is how much I care:
I live in Staten Island — no, listen — way out there
at the south end, so I gotta drive — it's a 45-
minute drive — to the ferry station, and the ride
on the ferry is half-an-hour. Then to Morningside
it's an hour on the 1. Today I tried
to transfer to the 3 instead — that was fun.
The crowd, I swear, I couldn't get through the door!
But if I stay on the 1 the whole time I get bored.
I like to be on my feet. Facts!
(Okay, sweetie, tilt your head back.)
You think that's bad, though? — back in beauty school
I had to carry my own mannequin all the way,
back and forth, every day, with the stand in my hand.
It was heavy. Now I'm saving up — a lot, two grand —
for a two-day master course in cutting men's hair. Oh, no,
I'm licensed, I'm graduated, I don't need to go,
and some other people here don't, but man,

if you want to cut hair, and the classes are there,
why wouldn't you go? I don't understand —
why wouldn't you do everything you possibly can
to keep improving at what you do?
Wouldn't you?
(Take a look in the mirror. How did I do?)

LIBRANECE AYALA

YEARS AS MENTEE: 1

GRADE: Junior

HIGH SCHOOL:
Herbert H. Lehman
High School

BORN: New York, NY

LIVES: Bronx, NY

My growing relationship with my mentor, Alyssa, is and continues to be one that constantly opens my eyes — to new perceptions, of literature and of life, to the kind of writer, student, and woman that I want to become. Though we come from different walks of life, Alyssa and I have so much in common, and more than anything else, it's reflected in our writing.

ALYSSA PELISH

YEARS AS MENTOR: 1

OCCUPATION:
Freelance editor and
writer; part-time writing
consultant at Columbia
University

BORN: Eau Claire, WI

LIVES: New York, NY

**PUBLICATIONS
AND RECOGNITIONS:**
Slate and *Harper's*

I love my weekend writing sessions with Libranece. There's something about writing together that opens people up to each other in a way that just plain talking doesn't. Coming to know Libranece in her own words, a bit more each week, makes my world better — not to mention more interesting. Writing with Libranece reminds me how many stories we carry with us.

My Mother

LIBRANECE AYALA

This poem was originally a journal entry that I wrote during a session with my mentor. Seeing how emotional and passionate it turned out to be, I decided to make a few revisions and share it with others. I was inspired by my mother, the person who inspires me the most.

My mother.

My mother is many things, but weak, she is not.

My mother stands on mountaintops during hurricanes, she swims across brutally cold seas.

My mother has been stabbed in the throat on multiple occasions, and still, she manages to breathe.

If you kick my mother down a flight of stairs, she will stand tall, and climb up two.

My mother has been given countless reasons to resort to bitterness and misery, yet her smile resembles the brightness of a thousand burning suns.

My mother has been let down, kicked down, put down, and beat down; but she is always up.

My mother is many things, strong is one of them.

My mother will only shed tears when she is angry, and even maintain a smile when she is melancholy.

She will pick you up and place you on top of the sun, even when she's having difficulties getting herself out of the mud, at the bottom of the earth.

My mother is sweet, and she is kind. She is giving, and loving.

My mother likes to please others, even if she won't admit it to anyone, or herself.

My mother puts up a front to people on the outside, and portrays herself as a woman with a cold heart that is incapable of welcoming new people. But the very truth is, her insides are warmer than May and her intentions are pure.

My mother likes to make others happy, despite the fact that she hasn't been anything close to content in over a year or so.

My mother is a "people pleaser."

She'll tell you otherwise. She will tell you that she isn't friendly and that she enjoys her isolated and confined lifestyle.

But I know, and she knows, she is clearly stuck in a rut.

Isolation is a defense mechanism for someone who has been damaged too many times, to let new people too close into their lives.

So she resorts to isolationism, and she will tell you that she is happy but she is not.

She may smile from time to time, and she does laugh, sometimes uncontrollably.

She still reads and spends hours in the kitchen and carries on as usual, and I think that that is strength.

And I think that she is only strong for the one thing in her life that is not corrupted: her daughter.

My mother.

My mother is wise and she is courageous.

She is ambitious and she is so goddamn independent, my father must have been intimidated by it.

She is beautiful and she is intelligent.

She is loyal and she is selfless.

She is broken.

She is broken.

She is broken.

But no one, other than me, would ever know.

A Weather Map of the World

ALYSSA PELISH

This short piece grew out of a question that Libranece posed during one of our weekly writing sessions. Her prompt, "Pinpoint the last time you felt completely happy," is not an idea I would typically begin with — but the way she phrased it caught my fancy. And she, for her part, got an answer she said she hadn't expected.

The question, as Libranece has printed it in black pen on a loose leaf sheet of notebook paper, is to "pinpoint the last time you felt completely happy." Pinpoint, as if our moods comprised a weather map, and each separate instance a squall or sun-shower we've passed through.

But this may not be such a bad analogy. There is, as Wallace Stevens would have it, "major weather," the mental climate we live in for much of our lives. This is the steady consternation of my father. The profound grey of my good friend. My own abiding inwardness. And then there are the emotions we visit. Or perhaps they're visited upon us. Flashes of surprise, spikes of fear, mudslides of sobbing. And bursts of happiness. Like heat lightning, they appear, on the weather map of our moods.

If my map these days is broadly a steady state — little roiling or storming — then I could indeed pinpoint those bursts of happiness across it. These are different from a patch of contentedness, or a long exhalation of relief. They are shorter. You could catch them in your hands like fireflies, almost. They are those briefest of moments when the sun appears from behind a cloud and I can feel it on my face. On a weather map of the world, they are silver pushpins.

AYANNA BAILEY

YEARS AS MENTEE: 1

GRADE: Sophomore

HIGH SCHOOL:
Urban Assembly Institute of Math and Science for Young Women

BORN: Brooklyn, NY

LIVES: Brooklyn, NY

I learned from Naz that you won't always get something right on the first try. You have to keep practicing and working at it and eventually you will improve. Her voice is genuine and strong and she helped me realize that you have to show emotion to have a good piece.

NAZ RIAHI

YEARS AS MENTOR: 5

OCCUPATION:
Founder, Bitten: a food conversation

BORN: Tehran, Iran

LIVES: Brooklyn, NY

I love so many things about working with Ayanna. She's charming and engaging and has taught me a lot about listening and striving to improve. But I've also discovered that in encouraging her to question her perspective, I've come to question my own perspective and presumptions — a great reminder that no matter my age or experience, I can always improve myself, especially when it comes to being open-minded and empathetic.

The Voice

AYANNA BAILEY

My sister inspired me to write this piece because
I wanted to show her how strong she is.

The things I have to say
they need to be heard
What frightens me most
is that I might sound absurd

My kids were taken away
and you ask me to say
Why have things
turned out this way?

I was unable to take care
of the ones I loved most
Sometimes I see them at night
but it's like I've seen a ghost

I carry a broken heart
for my careless mistakes
Sometimes I feel
my heart as it breaks

I've had my faults
yes, I know I'm not ideal
The emotions inside me
make my life so surreal

Without them I feel empty
like a body without a soul
I'm out of my mind
and my life's a black hole

These tears I cry
are not a fabrication
They are the sad tears
of my desperation

I may not look like it
but I really do care
Not having them next to me
is so hard to bear

I will do anything,
whatever it will take
No matter how many
smiles I have to fake

On Things That Happen Some Cold Autumn Nights

NAZ RIAHI

*Ayanna and I worked on writing poems about autumn and
exploring the different perspectives illustrated by the same subject.*

It was the talk, the walk, the tea.
It was the break of leaves beneath my feet.
It was this place, this space, this feeling.

Maybe of being bad.

Maybe.

It was autumn in New York and I shivered on the couch until you lit the fire.
And it was maybe the last kind thing you did, but that was all it took.

It was the lake already showing signs of freeze
It was the dogs and their bark and their howl and their pleads
It was the wine, the cigarettes, and that sad sad song.

It was me being bad. And not yet seeing.

That for you the grass is greener. Always is.

It was autumn in New York and I was lost just enough to be thrilled.

It was not yet snow, but gray all over.

It was cold to the bone, and we were nowhere.

It was autumn in New York. That is all.

ROMAISSAA BENZIZOUNE

YEARS AS MENTEE: 1

GRADE: Junior

HIGH SCHOOL:
Hunter College High School

BORN: New York, NY

LIVES: Queens, NY

**PUBLICATIONS
AND RECOGNITIONS:**
Scholastic Art & Writing
Award: Honorable Mention

Robin's unique voice and endless support encourages me to continue writing, and reassures me that everything is going to be alright. Every pair meeting makes us both feel happier and more inspired, and Robin's open-mindedness and willingness to try new things makes any creative venture exciting and worthwhile. In addition, our personalities and ideas seem to sync as we can comfortably discuss pretty much anything. I'm a little more organized than I was after meeting Robin (well not really, actually, but I'm trying, ish). Robin's writing is awe-inspiring, and I feel lucky to have such a great mentor to collaborate with.

ROBIN WILLIG

YEARS AS MENTOR: 1

OCCUPATION:
Chief of Staff, Center for
Reproductive Rights

BORN: Far Rockaway, NY

LIVES: Brooklyn, NY

Romaissaa recently asked me what my impression was of her when we met. I remember: she was very pretty, had a shy smile with a mouthful of braces, and wore a hejab. Maybe it was "hejab, braces, pretty." She knows processing her hejab is a "thing." While I've known and worked with people of various religions and rates of observance, she is my first "hejabi." Through writing together, I am learning what that means to her — and to others. I am still learning about Romaissaa; perhaps we both are. She inspires, challenges, and teaches me: she is so much more than "hejab, braces, pretty."

Memorial Day

ROMAISSAA BENZIZOUNE

After writing this, which conveys the feelings I had after hearing about my uncle's death years ago, I put it on the back burner. With the help of the Girls Write Now Workshops, I gained the confidence to go back and make edits, playing with structure and style. I feel this poem is not only a personal piece but also one of progress.

Tomorrow is Memorial Day. It's been five years and so I'm a little late
to my favorite uncle's funeral, but if I catch the next flight at 5:35, Eastern time, and
run down the concrete blocks across the ocean-sized streets,
> *run, there are no traffic lights, don't worry, just*
> close your eyes and hold my hand and run
dodge the mules and wailing cars and rolling, glowing orbs of sweet oranges, and
float through gray smoggy fumes of gasoline and cigarette smoke, maybe I can
make it to my grandmother's house
run up the spiral stone steps and catch my whole family there, mid-sob, and prop
my mother against her sister and her sister against her grown son and her son
against my mother's 12 brothers and the brothers against my tree trunk grandmother so that nobody falls.

Maybe if I catch the next flight at 6:40, Eastern time, I can still get my mother on
the plane,
make sure she eats a steaming plate of yellow couscous heaped with buttery vegetables and red sauce, maybe she will cry and laugh as she pops a soft, rolling chick-
pea into a mouth so accustomed to bagels and pizza, quinoa and Greek yogurt,
and she won't forget how
her 13 brothers and sisters used to scramble around the table, how
her mother and father would make each of the children little balls of yellow couscous
> 13 balls of couscous
and maybe she will thank me for bringing her back home, even if it is a little too late.

Today is Memorial Day and it's been exactly five years

and so I'm a little too late for my favorite uncle's funeral. It's been seven years since
he ran across the street with me, told me to

run, there are no traffic lights, don't worry, just
close your eyes and hold my hand and run

seven years

since we ran to my grandmother's house under the smothering sun

and he asked me what I wanted and promised me that he would take me to the
beach one day

Maybe if I catch the next flight at 7:30, Eastern time, I can sprint down Casablanca
and stop to pick up Minoosha, the stray cat I cried over eight years ago, and
maybe I will reach his house
— a thick yellow finger of an apartment building,

smelling like the olives he picks and seasons in batches — maybe I will knock on
his door and it will start to rain even though the sun is shining, illuminating each
raindrop so that it looks like slivers of crystals falling through the air

and maybe he will open the latch-string door and pick me up one more time and
rub his thick brown mustache smelling of olives and cigarettes, and ask me what
I want.

Ice Water

ROBIN WILLIG

This piece came out of the Girls Write Now Persona Poetry Workshop,
and in taking on the voice of another — in this case, my mother — it helped
me to connect to how our art is not just a representation of ourselves,
but indeed, brings "Voice to Voice."

You are annoyed by me, I can tell

I like my water with a lot of ice

I tell you this every day,

but you fill my glass with a pitcher that has grown tepid,

lingering and sweating on your rolling cart

while you walk around the dining room.

I would get it myself if I could.

But I am not in my kitchen, nor my home
where I grew four children from nothing
where I fed and clothed them, cleaned and cooked nightly
helped with homework,
sewed costumes for Halloween and plays.

And also worked,
analyzing blood samples and cultures in the lab,
telling you if you had mono or syphilis or HIV or strep

I held answers then
With test tube and microscope and centrifuge
You waited for me
In a room of red bucket plastic seats
Scratched and dirty
While I spun and studied
And did not dawdle
knowing these answers determined the rest of your day
perhaps the rest of all your days

I held answers then, and I gave them to you:
Dispassionate, quick,
with a precision you did not fathom.

I didn't plan on 91.

Didn't plan to lose my hearing, ability to walk, or drive
or roam freely through the streets.

No one depends on me now but myself.

I like my water cold, so cold that it blazes a path down my throat, to my stomach
You might see it if you looked at me
A blue streak racing through a body that is no longer mine.
It is the loud thumping music that rises and falls as the cars go down Emmons Avenue.
Loud beyond the need to hear
Cold beyond the need to taste.

I can feel
still.

ARNELL CALDERON

YEARS AS MENTEE: 2

GRADE: Senior

HIGH SCHOOL:
NYC iSchool

BORN: New York, NY

LIVES: New York, NY

When I first met Morayo I was more confused than excited because having another person read and listen to my writing was foreign to me. And then the confusion became something I looked forward to. I never really believed much in my writing, and I think that the right people teach you how to be gentler towards a craft you have been doing for a long time. Morayo, being one of those people, taught me the meaning of integrity for the sake of my characters. It was not until our relationship formed that I realized that there was nothing to fear.

MORAYO FALEYIMU

YEARS AS MENTOR: 3

OCCUPATION:
Campus Director, Citizen Schools

BORN: Miami, FL

LIVES: Elizabeth, NJ

Working with Arnell has helped me grow as a writer. Not only do we write about similar themes, but we also have the same aversion to the editing process. Over the past two years, however, I've pushed Arnell to revisit and finalize her pieces. She's done the same for me. I owe my submission to the VONA/Voices writing workshop to her. I'm doubtful that I would have had the confidence or stamina to complete those pieces if not for Arnell.

Trujillo

ARNELL CALDERON

*Throughout the late 1970s to early 1980s, the women in my family lived
in a small town in Honduras called Trujillo. This town was
where people would keep caskets on their roofs in preparation for death;
my intention was to explore the town.*

In Trujillo, it was not the creator who understood love the best, nor the healer, nor the cleaner, but the alterer. Alterers of all sorts: alterers who picked the fruit flies off the bananas, alterers who yanked weeds out of the soil and, most importantly, alterers who made clothing. But because Trujillo was lonelier than the people in it, who understood love the best did not matter.

Before Trujillo was Trujillo, it was filled with indios who would later be killed. Then it would become a place where morenos would try to avoid their own potential murder, then to a place where they would put caskets on the roofs. The caskets made the soil better and the bananas better, but for the Trujillanos, all the caskets made was a mystery. Despite the fact that your typical Trujillano felt lonelier in any place other than Trujillo, they would not consider themselves Trujillanos for the simple reason that they did not know what a "Trujillano" was, but they knew that that was all they were to people.

> "Trujillano felt lonelier in any place other than Trujillo..."

The caskets (made by the Trujillanos themselves) were what kept Trujillo alive. While Trujillo was not necessarily altered by the pickings of fruit flies off of bananas or fabrics into dresses, what altered Trujillo was something Trujillanos spent most of their lives figuring out, and while some had ideas about what the town was about, their unfinished answers were not enough.

The Wife

MORAYO FALEYIMU

*This work is inspired by the Girls Write Now Persona Poetry Workshop.
I wanted to take the figure of the ultimate betrayer, Judas, but have
someone else seek his pardon. The poem that follows is his wife's attempt
to present their side of the story.*

They said you betrayed Him.
He, the one you kissed like a brother.
He, who sat at the table to break bread
and drink wine with his fishers of men.

History raised him up off the cross.
His deeds live on.
As do yours.

His name lives on — as does yours.
They spit it from their mouths like shards of broken teeth.

Judas Iscariot.

The coat of Judas is drenched scarlet
You shoulder the weight, alone.

But weren't your brothers fallible, too?
Peter the Denier. Doubting Thomas.
Why do they serve Him in Heaven
while we wait, thirsting,
outside the gates?

Did God not choose you as well?
Choose you to betray? Choose you to be reviled?
Were these not your crosses to bear?

Come close. I want to say to you this:

It was you, Judas Iscariot,

who made Jesus into the Christ.

Not Mary or Joseph or even God Himself.

It was you, half of my heart — my beloved

You the man who made a Son.

Can they not revere how God undid your work?

How cruel.

To be denied entry to the gates of Heaven

Recast as Adam and Eve after the fall.

RACHEL CHANDERDATT

YEARS AS MENTEE: 1

GRADE: Senior

HIGH SCHOOL:
Brooklyn Technical
High School

BORN: Brooklyn, NY

LIVES: Queens, NY

**PUBLICATIONS
AND RECOGNITIONS:**
Scholastic Art & Writing
Award: Silver Key

Two short girls walk into a coffee shop anxious to write but most of all grateful for each other's company. Rhoda is a spunky lady that I can see myself becoming. Taking risks and doing the unexpected is a big part of what she is about, and the part that I love the most is that she'd do it with a smile. As a writer, she's shown me how to bring life to characters through dialogue and description, making them come to life on the page. Not only has this helped my writing, but it allows me to want to write more. Having Rhoda as a mentor is one of the best privileges I could have ever asked for.

RHODA BELLEZA

YEARS AS MENTOR: 1

OCCUPATION:
Editor, Paper Lantern Lit

BORN: Los Angeles, CA

LIVES: Brooklyn, NY

Rachel brings so much joy into my life. Her writing matches her demeanor: honest and raw, thoughtful and deeply challenging. "She" mentors "me." I live my life by her example; her strength and optimism make me remember that I can overcome any challenge and live my life the way I want and need to.

Random House

RACHEL CHANDERDATT

*Single motherhood has always fascinated me although it wasn't in
my own familial ties. In the subway I watch, in awe, those superhero moms
with invisible biceps lifting strollers with sleeping babies up flights of stairs.
The love a mother has for her child is something I learned from my own
mother. It's a sacrificial type of love where another person, a being
you made, becomes your gravity, without which you would spiral out
of control. This piece is dedicated to all the mothers.*

I dropped my heart beneath the current; my home became the ocean. The rays of sunshine eased the pain as my eyes drifted off.

The sea is always changing, rearranging by force, unable to make a choice of its own. Dependency isn't a good thing, not always. You walk, I follow. You ask, I answer. You push, I pull.

Push. Pull. Push. Pull. Push. Pull.

The waves hit my body sharp and hard as they knocked the breath right out of my lungs, bringing me to an abrupt awakening. What seemed like hours was probably only seven minutes at most. My mind awakens before my body; the detachment is what scares me the most. When did my mind stop caring what my body did? When did the utter disregard begin?

My feet move without my brain saying a word, and the cold from the hardwood floor runs up my spine and seeps into my bones before I even have the chance to exhale.

On Carlton Street, the sidewalk is dampened by an early rain, and now the newly fallen autumn leaves cling to it in desperation. Where am I? Mario had told me to take the G train to Church Avenue, but I just can't seem to find it.

This hand-me-down stroller seems to grow heavier with every step. Looking up, I see a girl clutching a few textbooks and a bag and ask her where the train is.

"Make a right and walk straight down, can't miss it," she says without even slowing down.

New Yorkers aren't as rude as everyone says. They just have a different way of going about things. I can't blame them. A city like this swallows you up and spits you back out. Primitive qualities are required. I should've thought of that as I boarded the airplane to this wasteland. I can still hear the roaring engines now...

Difficult doesn't even begin to describe how it felt to leave my family behind at those security gates. The look on my father's face as I walked through the archways of the terminal gates is one that's imprinted on my heart forever.

A small breeze stirs up as I see the glowing green ball of the train stop. Nearing closer to the stairs, a pigeon walks towards me. He is lost and confused; his flock flew without him and he lost the shared path. He is alone. A stranger in an unfamiliar land.

Living in Cuba was the complete opposite of the concrete jungle of New York. Nothing beat Sunday mornings growing up. My mother would wake me up early for mass by bribing my six brothers and me with the smell of her arroz con dulce wafting throughout the house. Little did she know, we actually enjoyed the service.

Sunday mornings in New York, I'm woken by the crying newborn rather than my mother's soothing voice. My warm breakfast is replaced by cold cereal that's reminiscent of cardboard. The pastor's sermon is instead conducted by the man at the head of the train.

"Esperanza." The woman at the WIC counter calls my name, but it doesn't sound like my own, twisted and convoluted it holds no power. Just another ethnic name among the masses, too difficult to pronounce.

"That's me." I step up to the counter with unsure motions as she inspects Ashton in his stroller sound asleep.

"Take this certificate to the store to purchase the designated items on this list. Make sure you get these specific things otherwise it will not work. Sign here and here. Do you understand what I'm saying." A statement not a question.

Before I had a chance to say anything else, she called another name among the masses.

What would my father say to his daughter if he saw me in this condition?

The brisk wind hits me once again as I brave the outdoors. Getting used to the cold is impossible when I grew up with the sunshine in my very bones.

> "Getting used to the cold is impossible when I grew up with the sunshine in my very bones."

Despite the inability to navigate the monstrosity of the MTA, I manage to make my way back home. Ashton, sound asleep in his stroller, remains my rock as the wind continues to howl around me.

This is the part where I am supposed to make dinner and set myself up for the rest of the week. But I'm startled by the ring from the far left corner of the kitchen.

That phone has never rung before. Those knotted spirals remained silent next to the microwave. Before my body can listen to my mind telling me to reach for it, the answering machine beats me to it.

The beep surprised me with a voice I knew all too well.

"Eszze," the pause in his voice coincided with the stopping of my own heart. A flood of memories were interrupted by the voice once more.

"We need to talk about Ashton. You can't keep me away from my own son."

The cracks in the once smooth voice were almost believable.

"Goddammit. I'll take you to court and get full custody." The possibility of what could've been love left his voice, and I remember why I left.

Bicycle Built For Two

RHODA BELLEZA

I wrote this piece because too often, the complexity of female relationships is reduced to catty fights and over-the-top portrayals of jealousy in pop culture. Our bonds are so much more terrifying and beautiful than that. We are lovers, sisters, mothers and daughters.

To set the record straight, Enaida doesn't hate men — she just hates that I've been with one, or two or 20. I've never told her my number. She asks nearly every day and goes on about being a strong black woman, that she can handle it, that shit isn't gonna phase her because she's a survivor.

"You're half Filipino too…"

"Sur. Vy. Vor." She cuts me off and repeats it, every syllable loud and hard, like she thinks I'm deaf.

"I know," I tell her. I don't doubt she's lived through nightmares. Not for a second.

She stops pacing and changes tactics. She slides onto the couch, our knees touching, her hand on my thigh. This girl, this beautiful girl, with her earthworm lips and her light brown eyes — touching me, wanting my love — and all I am is distracted. The corner of the cushion pops up whenever someone sits down.

But when she puts her mouth close, that voice lowers to something teasing and soulful: Do you still think of him? Are you happy here? Do you love me? I could drown in this voice. Her finger plays with my hoop earring and I understand why men are terrified of women.

I know if I pause a second too long she'll erupt, which I do and she does. She yells and stomps through our apartment and I want to turn inside out, squeeze myself gone. When my dad would come home I used to clear out a me-sized space out in storage closet, and between the vacuum and the plastic Christmas I'd hold my breath, close my eyes, and pray to God to make myself disappear.

But now I'm the asshole with my eyes closed like I'm meditating, there and back again on some heady trip, while Enaida throws pillows and tears down towers of folded laundry.

"You're cold," she says as she jabs a finger in my chest. That's one thing that stays the same across men and women: both of them think you're cold. They don't realize every silence is preservation. It spares a million tiny heartbreaks — theirs and mine. It's kindness.

"I don't know what to say." I've grabbed her hand and I'm on my knees. She tires to yank it away but I squeeze it tighter, kiss her fingers that smell of sweet tobacco.

"Start with the truth," she says.

> "It spares a million tiny heartbreaks — theirs and mine. It's kindness."

I nod, running the back of my hand against the inside of her thigh. The squeezing and grabbing I have to ease into. If I do it all at once she'll stiffen up and lock her knees together, remembering some other time that might make her cry much later, in the bathroom when she thinks I can't hear. So I take it slow and breathe warm breath into the lap of her dress. When I'm pressed against her I remember trips out of the city and into the Redwoods. I think of sleeping on the earth, fern against my skin, a canopy of trees that made everything dark and cool.

ASHLEY CHRISTIE

YEARS AS MENTEE: 3

GRADE: Senior

HIGH SCHOOL:
The Urban Assembly
School for Law and Justice

BORN: Brooklyn, NY

LIVES: Brooklyn, NY

**PUBLICATIONS
AND RECOGNITIONS:**
Scholastic Art & Writing
Award: Honorable Mention

Like a flower, this relationship between Chana and I continues to bloom. The last three years we have spent together has made a huge impact in my life as both a writer and a person. Chana has become more than just a mentor to me, she is my friend.

CHANA PORTER

YEARS AS MENTOR: 3

OCCUPATION:
Writer, Yoga Teacher

BORN: Takoma Park, MD

LIVES: Brooklyn, NY

**PUBLICATIONS
AND RECOGNITIONS:**
This year I received a
commission to adapt a
play for the stage

Working with Ashley is a constant source of delight. Over our years together our relationship has deepened into a profound friendship, built on mutual admiration, trust, and fun. I will miss her next year, but I know we'll stay in each each other's lives for a long time to come.

He Is Your Father

ASHLEY CHRISTIE

*Capturing this moment allowed me to speak to my father
and allow him to be a part of my life. It also
allowed me to communicate my emotions to the world.*

I walked into the bleached blue cafeteria with grey tiled floors and anxiously looked around. The tiny windows looked out into a gloomy courtyard surrounded by barbed-wire fences. Lined in rows close enough that people could eavesdrop on one another's conversations, the rusty tables and chairs were bolted down to the ground as though they might try to escape, too. "Row A, Table 3," the officer shouted as she slammed my paper on the desk. I took a seat and squirmed when I felt the cold metal. Suddenly I felt the heat of his hand touch my shoulder. I looked up and there he was, staring at me. He smiled and I forced a smile back. My stomach dropped and the muscles in my throat tightened. His army green linen jumpsuit felt stiff on my face as we hugged uncomfortably. I closed my heavy eyes and inhaled, the scent of his cologne filled my nose.

I was three years old when my father was arrested. My memory of him is so blurred. My mother always reassured me, "Even though he is not physically here with you, when he was, you two were inseparable." When she said this, I would roll my eyes. Here I was 13 years later visiting him at Green Haven Correctional Facility.

> "I was three years old when my father was arrested."

"Brittany you look so different since the last time I saw you. Your hair got longer!" he said. "It's not my real hair," I replied coldly. He began to ask me about school and how things were at home. I gave him closed-ended responses with no explanations to follow. As we made small talk, he held my stiff hand and tenderly massaged it. My father suddenly asked, "Do you want to hear a story?" Unsure of what he was about to say, I nodded my head. "When your mom and I had to go to work," he began, "we would leave you with your aunt Beverly. When I came to pick you up, you were sitting right where I left you. You was so scared of her!" His eyes glistened and his voice got lower. "But when I came to get you, Brittany, you ran to me." He smiled faintly. I felt my eyes well up and I excused myself and went to the bathroom.

I rushed into an empty stall with my hands over my mouth trying to block the smell of disinfectant. The tears started falling too quickly for me to wipe away. I cried for the relationship we never got to have. I cried because of the tears in his eyes. I cried because of the emotion in his voice and the strength that he held my hand with. That little girl that he told me about reminded me that I do love him. I had a father, finally I understood that.

Though the pain of his being absent for most of my life continued, I found the courage to visit him weekly and slowly even forgive him. I realized that the actions that led to his arrest were separate from the love that he had for me. During this first visit I found myself becoming a more open-minded person beyond that bleached blue cafeteria. I learned to empathize with others and be aware of the different circumstances and perspectives we all come from.

A few months ago, I walked back into that bleached blue cafeteria. While I waited for my father, I noticed a chubby, bald baby sitting across from me. She was holding her father's finger in her mouth. He sang to her and she smiled. Her smile was so contagious I smiled back. That little girl and I aren't so different. Just like her, I need my father. The scent of my father lingered. I looked up and he was watching, too.

Seep (EXCERPT)

CHANA PORTER

This is the opening of my science fiction novel, Seep, *which I have been writing during my years with Ashley. She influenced me to think about writing for both teenagers and adults.*

Dani pulled on his dark brown body suit in the chilly basement bathroom. Upstairs the party raged on, the lilting highs of street opera mashed with choral throat singing. Dani affixed his leaf headdress. He heard a bottle shatter on the floor upstairs. A high-pitched voice rang out with laughter. The party kids seem to get younger all the time, he thought. Same faces, different people. Dani studied himself in the mirror. His lean, androgynous body was only a slightly lighter brown than his bodysuit. It wasn't a perfect match but synthetics were priced very high. In the dim light of the party and the haze of drugs, he would look perfect. Dani took a deep breath and steadied his hands. This was what made him feel older. The gaiety, the frivolity in which he used to Seep seemed distant. Each performance felt like that last one. Dani dipped a long finger into a small jar of black paste. Expertly, he rubbed the unctuous paste on his eyelids, creating a smoky Cleopatra slant to exaggerate his eyes.

There it was again, that feeling in his chest. A fluttering akin to fear. Dani was proud of this performance. It had taken months to construct and tonight would be its first and only presentation. It was just pre-show jitters. He snorted.

"One would think I would get used to this," he murmured to his reflection. Dani had performed his transformations guided by the Seep many times, in all kinds of venues, for all kinds of audiences. He'd been touring on this last bout for months. The performance tonight at the Go-Go, Detroit's oldest and fiercest collective, was as close to a homecoming as he would have. The Go-Go was the closest thing to a home he had, and Dani liked it that way. There was a great thump on the ceiling, like a speaker falling over. Laughter rang out again, mixing in with wild singing of something like The Internatio-nale. He loved his brothers and sisters in anarchy at the Go-Go; he loved leaving them and returning to them. He especially loved nights like tonight, when he'd come home bringing something beautiful. Perhaps later Ilana would come down from her little turret and they'd sleep under the stars by the fire pit like they did last Solstice. The night spread out before him like a great carpet.

"Laughter rang out again, mixing in with wild singing..."

So why did he feel so, so wormy?

CINDY CHU

YEARS AS MENTEE: 1

GRADE: Senior

HIGH SCHOOL:
Hunter College High School

BORN: New York, NY

LIVES: Queens, NY

**PUBLICATIONS
AND RECOGNITIONS:**
Scholastic Art & Writing
Awards: Silver Keys (3)

When I first met Iris, I was nervous because I had no idea what to expect. However, I soon came to realize that she is an exceptionally understanding mentor who has an amazing way with words and great taste in writing. Iris has expanded my perspective of writing by introducing me to a plethora of new poets and forms of poetry. Also, her support and encouragement has helped me get through a brutal college application process. I'm grateful for Iris and her invaluable guidance in writing and advice on life.

IRIS CUSHING

YEARS AS MENTOR: 1

OCCUPATION:
Graduate student in
English Ph.D. Program,
CUNY Graduate Center

BORN: Tarzana, CA

LIVES: Queens, NY

**PUBLICATIONS
AND RECOGNITIONS:**
Process Space Residency
through the Lower Man-
hattan Cultural Council;
Published in *Fence* and
Barrelhouse; literary
criticism in *Hyperallergic,*
the *Boston Review* and the
Poetry Project Newsletter

My weekly meetings with Cindy keep me connected to the joy and wildness of writing poetry. Getting to know Cindy's precise and imaginative way of using language to engage with the world has given me exciting new perspectives on things like description, voice, and narrative — I'm so thankful to her for sharing that gift with me! Amidst seemingly endless deadlines, meetings, and professional obligations, it's truly refreshing to take time every week to enjoy writing, reading and imagining together.

Qixi

CINDY CHU

*This poem was inspired by bedtime stories my grandmother told me
when I was a child, cultural superstitions, and my mentor's encouragement
to make the ordinary seem surreal.*

I once played amongst knotted trees
And brambled briars. Those were the days
When calm, crystalline sky met tense earth,
Where the ever-changing sands of time
Reached unwilling equilibrium; this is why branches
Are emblazoned with embossed leaves,
Fingers grazing the base of the atmosphere.

If that explanation fails to suffice, I will
Expand until I am less dense than air —
Only then will I be able to reach for
Heaven's secrets and spirit them away
To fashion a tapestry of the finest silk
Embroidered with a flood of leaves,
Inundating you with memories of where
You last left me. Then, and only then, you will see.

Under the light of the pregnant moon,
You told me I was radiant. And, like the weaver-girl
To your cow-herder, part of me fell in love with you
That night — the galaxy a delicate ribbon,
An auspicious red thread binding our fates
By their fingers; playing cat's cradle and getting
Entangled, enmeshed, entrenched, that sorrowful
En, en, en, the sound of sobbing.

We realize the galaxy is a river of milky tears, one we cry

Year after year. All that is left is for us to forget,

To accept that the heavens have a plan for us,

A great proposal for the state of the universe,

That doesn't involve *us*. If that hurts,

You have remembered our ends of bridges touching,

And, for that, I will never, can never, forget you.

Child in a Room, Edouard Vuillard, 1900

IRIS CUSHING

This piece grew out of an ekphrastic poetry experiment that my mentee Cindy and I practiced side by side one day. Cindy's quiet, inquisitive way of observing the phenomenal world informed the inner "voice" that speaks in this poem.

You live in these little shapes.

The matching upholstery of two chairs,

celadon green stitched with olive and burgundy paisleys.

Your day is made of small squares.

The brick fireplace long ago swept clean

lends a weight and formality to the west side of the room,

although it doesn't have a purpose, which the curtain does.

What purpose does a curtain serve?

To hide you in a stiff brocade fold between

itself and the window. The lead glass window,

another thing without a texture.

Your skin and the glass. Glass is a kind of slow liquid —

settling in its frame so gradually

only future generations will detect a flow.

Where do your own textures begin?

You have hair, you have fingernails.

The bottoms of your feet are just staring to grow

lines and ridges. But there's a presence inside you

that is nothing like the things of this room or world.

The wallpaper is a false field.

Repetitive and tame in a way no real field is.

What purpose does the bed frame serve?

You press your face and hands

into its white-painted wrought-iron bars

and see behind eyelids of flame:

a blacksmith pulling the bars into shape,

dropping the hot and heavy edifice into cool water. Hissing.

This soft bodily space is where you sleep.

Sleep, does it have a texture?

The fibers of the carpet bristle through

the wide weave of your child-stockings.

CORRINE CIVIL

YEARS AS MENTEE: 3

GRADE: Senior

HIGH SCHOOL:
Young Women's Leadership School of East Harlem

BORN: New York, NY

LIVES: New York, NY

COLLEGE:
Columbia University

SCHOLARSHIP:
QuestBridge Scholarship

I thought my last year with Robin at Girls Write Now was going to be ruined by college applications and senioritis. Instead, this has been our best year. Meeting with her is the highlight of my week. We write and chat as she drinks coffee and I sip water. I honestly could not ask for anything better. She was one of the first people I called when I got into Columbia University, and we are closer than ever! There is no such thing as our "last year as a pair." Where did I get that idea from?

ROBIN MARANTZ HENIG

YEARS AS MENTOR: 6

OCCUPATION:
Freelance Journalist

BORN: Brooklyn, NY

LIVES: New York, NY

PUBLICATIONS AND RECOGNITIONS:
Finalist, Nonfiction Literature Arts Fellowship; New York State Council for the Arts The Deadline Club Award; Best American Science & Nature Writing, 2014 edition

Corrine sometimes arrives at the coffee shop where we meet at the same time that a friend of mine is leaving. The friend is usually someone who has heard about Corrine — I talk about her a lot — and who wanted to stick around to meet her. When that happened one rainy spring afternoon, it let me view Corrine as a stranger might. And I could see how much she's changed from the sweet, chatty girl I first met three years ago, into a young woman with intelligence, confidence, and a strong voice that will carry her through the years ahead.

The Race

CORRINE CIVIL

At the Girls Write Now Persona Poetry Workshop, poet Rachel Eliza Griffiths
spoke about poems she wrote about Toni Morrison characters — the same
ones I spent hours thinking about in tenth grade. I realized my poem had to
be about the person on my mind the most lately.

I started running to run away from him.
Every night I sat and planned my escape.
What would it be next?
A punch or a kick or a slap.

When I finally got away, I kept running,
Out of Alcalá, my feet created the olas that kept the tides of the Atlantic flowing.
He never chased me.

Once I reached New York, I kept on running,
Except I was running in circles,
From home, to the school, to the gym and back around again.

At home I healed the wounds he left,
At the school I healed my students' wounds,
At the gym I healed my heart from loving.
Every mile on the treadmill was a mile from the truth.

I slowed down to focus on a new man,
Cariñoso, simpático,
But eventually I sped up and ran away from him too.
I realized that no one could keep up with me,
That my impatience and refusal to let anyone be happy were just manías that ever
one was going to have to accept,
Because long ago I had to grow up and accept them too.

While running I never grew tired, just wiser.

The need to impart this wisdom in young women consumed me,

This race was no good without leaving a mark.

I tried to teach my students how to be strong,

So they didn't have to run like me.

But when I got sick, the broken girls who I stood in front of each day in a classroom,

The girls who feared my stern lectures and tough love,

Had to teach me what strength was,

They approached me, eyes wide and wet,

They told me that I didn't have to be so hard,

That I didn't have to run from my problems because nature will always overcome even the strongest among us,

That I was going too fast in a short, unpredictable race.

I took in their words the way they took in my lessons.

They whispered what someone should have screamed at me by the starting line,

And still, I don't know if I can admit that my manías are flaws.

Now that I can't run anymore, I'm not so sure what's left.

Seeing Green

ROBIN MARANTZ HENIG

My mentee Corrine and I start each pair session with a free write, sometimes using prompts to get us going. One time we set ourselves the task of including three items: a stolen ring, a sinister stranger, and a recipe with a significant mistake. I only managed two out of three.

Wasn't this just the best birthday ever? I was so happy to be at this restaurant with Peter. I was surprised he had asked me out, actually — I mean, it's a Tuesday night, and everyone has a lot of homework to do. And I was surprised he suggested this restaurant, which was so perfect: all dark and loud and it just seemed, I don't know, festive or something.

So how did Peter know that this was exactly the right place to take me? And did he even realize it was my birthday?

It was easy to talk to him. He wasn't like the other boys, who really only wanted to talk about themselves. Not Peter. He was really curious about me, like he actually wanted to know what I thought about things. And we agreed on so much! We both loved the Harry Potter books, but kind of hated the movies. How often does THAT happen?

It took a while to get a waiter, and the guy who finally showed up kind of glared at us, like he was annoyed about being there at all. I saw his heavy hands gripping the order pad, and I was kind of grossed out by the hair that curled at the base of each finger. Even the pinkies.

And there, on his right pinky, I saw something that made me give a little gasp.

He was wearing a ring that looked just like my father's. The ring my father said he lost at the gym last week. The ring that had come from HIS father. The ring he was looking for everywhere. The ring he said was irreplaceable.

I looked from the waiter's disgusting hairy pinky and up to his face. Then I looked at Peter.

"What's the matter?" he asked. "Do you want to order, or what?"

"I . . . I . . . um, I don't know what I want yet," I stammered. I looked up again at the waiter's face. He gave me a sinister sneer, almost like he was reading my mind, almost like he was daring me to accuse him of stealing the ring on his pinky. I realize mind reading isn't possible, but, I don't know, that's how it felt.

> "He gave me a sinister sneer, almost like he was reading my mind, almost like he was daring me to accuse him..."

The waiter went away. I leaned over the table.

"Peter," I whispered, sounding more melodramatic than I meant to. "That guy. That waiter. Did you see the ring he was wearing?"

"Yeah, unusual, huh? I don't think I've ever seen a stone cut exactly like that. Or that color. What color is it? Sort of green?"

"Yes, sort of green. Emerald green. I think that's a ring he stole. From my father."

Peter's eyes got wide. "You think this waiter knows your father?"

I felt myself getting kind of sick. This was turning out to be a really bad birthday.

KAYLA CORBIN

YEARS AS MENTEE: 2

GRADE: Sophomore

HIGH SCHOOL:
The Young Women's Leadership School of Queens

BORN:
St. Charles County, MD

LIVES: Queens, NY

PUBLICATIONS AND RECOGNITIONS:
Scholastic Art & Writing Awards: Honorable Mentions (2); Winner of The Young Women's Leadership School of Queens Essay Compeititon

Very simply put, Liz has pushed me to be better. She's never the type to talk at me, she talks to me. We both always learn from each other. Her voice is kind, encouraging but over all it's real. She doesn't sugar coat, nor does she bash me. She is the perfect balance of sugar and spice wrapped up in one curly haired package. Liz is a fixture in my life, a helping hand and one of the most realistic people I know. How to define us — the most realistic pair of creative minds that share a mutual desire for growth.

ELIZABETH DURAND STREISAND

YEARS AS MENTOR: 1

OCCUPATION:
Entertainment Journalist

BORN: Charlottesville, VA

LIVES: New York, NY

PUBLICATIONS AND RECOGNITIONS:
US Weekly; Usmagazine.com; Yahoo; Founded and hosted the 1st annual Gossip Awards

When it really comes down to it, with Kayla, I don't feel like a mentor who "mentors" a mentee. I leave our sessions as educated and inspired as (I hope) she does. A career in writing inevitably includes successes and failures. Working with Kayla, my failures have been put into context. She offers up an unusual level of insight accompanied with the perfect level of optimism. Her voice is a balancing force and a beacon of light in my own career, which has been an unexpected bonus.

Pickles

KAYLA CORBIN

Pregnant people love pickles. At least they're said to enjoy them, but what if they like pickles more than they love their kids? When I thought of this concept, I flushed out everything that's taboo about being a constantly pregnant, suburban housewife. The funny thing is, I don't even like pickles.

Every day I wake up, pull my hair back and make breakfast. Eggs and toast for James (my husband), pancakes for Emily (my oldest), waffles for Thomas and Peter, fruit oatmeal for Kristen, as well as Winnie, and lastly plain dry cereal for my youngest Ethan.

He always picks the cereal up, smiles and puts it in his mouth. As if it were clockwork, he immediately spits it back out, practically mocking the fact that I take so much time to delicately put the Cheerios in the bowl. He makes it obvious to me that I am no Betty Crocker. So in total I make breakfast for seven kids, that's including my husband.

When I'm carpooling for soccer games, brushing Winnie's hair, or tucking Ethan in at night, I wonder how people can feel so much love for their kids. I wonder why I can't love my kids the way I once knew my mother to love me. Yet I'm too ashamed to say that children are a burden to me. This is probably the reason that I'm pregnant with my seventh child, besides the fact that my husband has the sexual tendencies of a jack rabbit. This is the third time in five years that I'm pregnant. For heavens sake, I'm always pregnant! I've been pregnant so many times, I have nothing left to crave; but I so badly want to crave something, anything..... anything that will fill this void. So to compensate for my lack of cravings, I eat pickles.

I don't even like pickles to be honest, I've actually grown to despise them, but a pregnant woman always seems to crave pickles and I needed something to crave. I eat pickles instead of drinking or using crystal meth. So when my oldest daughter Emily told me she was pregnant at 21 and didn't want to keep it, I ate a whole jar of pickles. I honestly didn't want to keep any of my children, but my guilt never presented me any other option. Of course being who I am, I offered to raise Emily's kid. So now, in four months, I will be a new "proud" mom and in another six months, I will be a "proud" mom again. So if anyone who reads this invests in the stock market, invest in pickles because I have a feeling I'm not the only one with this problem.

THE BIRTHDAY GIRL

ELIZABETH DURAND STREISAND

*For me, "Pickles" was the story of a woman struggling to reconcile the type
of mother she thinks she should be with the type of mother she fears she is.
It was dashed off in one fiery blaze during a workshop, but kindled
and smoked in the corners of my mind long after.*

I'm snug as a bug in a rug looking up at my mom. She pulls her hair (which she
insists is the color of dishwater even though it's obviously dark blond) into a ponytail,
revealing the white shock just above her right ear. I have the exact same one. It's
called a highlight and women on the Upper East Side pay hundreds of dollars for
them, but ours are — as my mom puts it — "au naturale." We really are a lot alike.
Which reminds me, my feet are freezing. Our feet are always freezing. Even when it's
the middle of summer in New York City and our apartment is so hot that we put on
bathing suits, we wear them with wool socks. "That's because we're practical," my
mom always says.

But right now I can't do anything about my ice cube toes, so I just try to get comfortable as she floats around the room.

"Mom?" I whisper.

She shushes me with the flick of an index finger, and places something shiny on a
large tray. When she sets it down, a metallic chink echoes through the room and suddenly my entire body feels like a block of ice. This must
be what they mean by the phrase "scared stiff."

> "...a metallic chink
> echoes through the
> room and suddenly my
> entire body feels like
> a block of ice."

I silently count backwards from 10. I learned this
from my dad. He usually makes it to seven and then
starts screaming again. I make it to four and then I stop
because it is my fourth birthday today. I decide that —
even though I am most certainly in a lot of trouble —
turning four is still way better than three. On my third birthday I didn't get to see my
mother at all, but now we've been hanging out for six minutes. I know because there's
a digital clock on the wall. My mom glances at it as she glides around the room in her
sea-foam green pants, never stopping and never making a sound. This, I realize, is
what she calls "being in her element."

My heart thumps against my icy chest because I've never gotten to see her "being in her element" before. She brushes some sticky hairs out of my face and wipes a damp cotton ball over my cheek. She's really much more beautiful than she gives herself credit for — but more than that, she's gifted. So what if my friends' moms can bake cookies that don't break off the tray in little blackened crumbles? My mom can do so much more than that. She tosses the cotton ball in the trash can and my body warms the slightest bit. It's the same way I would have tossed it.

"This is going to sting," she warns before pulling a mask over her nose and mouth and settling her gaze on me. And then excitement overpowers my fear as she stabs a needle into the shredded tissues that used to be my cheek — and it really does sting — and then my stitches begin.

SAMORI COVINGTON

YEARS AS MENTEE: 2

GRADE: Sophomore

HIGH SCHOOL:
Millenium Brooklyn
High School

BORN: Brooklyn, NY

LIVES: Brooklyn, NY

**PUBLICATIONS
AND RECOGNITIONS:**
New York Writers Coalition

This year, I decided to focus on science fiction. My mentor and I practiced writing science fiction stories as well as reading them. We both realized that science fiction is a tough subject to write about, but no one is right or wrong.

BROOKE BOREL

YEARS AS MENTOR: 2

OCCUPATION:
Science writer, journalist,
and author

BORN: Topeka, KS

LIVES: Brooklyn, NY

**PUBLICATIONS
AND RECOGNITIONS:**
*Infested: How the Bed Bug
Infiltrated Our Bedrooms
and Took Over the World,*
from the University of
Chicago Press

This year, Samori wanted to focus much of her writing on science fiction. We started out trying to define for ourselves what science fiction actually is — something with which even the most famous writers in the genre struggle. From there, we read a lot of short science fiction stories, talked about what made them sci-fi, and tried to diagram their structure to understand why they are so compelling. And of course, we also wrote storeis of our own to see how our unique voices feel and sound in this fun genre.

The Trial

SAMORI COVINGTON

I was watching TV one day and thought it would be a cool idea to write a superhero science fiction story. The main character, Kaleb, takes a jog in the park and faints. This is Kaleb's story. He doesn't know if the person who saved him is good or evil.

It was a bright, sunny day in Central Park. Kaleb was jogging while Mariah was walking her dog wearing all leather and texting with what looked like a hologram cell phone. Jogging backwards, Kaleb tripped, hit his head on the concrete, and passed out. Mariah rushed to his side.

Fast Forward

Kaleb woke up in an all-white room that had a double mirror, with eleven other people. He felt dizzy and everyone stared at him as he coughed. Not to mention that his hands were turning magenta. A man named Johnny got up from his seat and introduced himself to Kaleb. They got to know each other a little better and Johnny revealed that he had been in this hospital for three months. Johnny showed Kaleb a worn picture of his son, around the age of 12, and his two-year-old. He was very anxious to get home to his family. The room stirred as a doctor walked in. Kaleb looked up and was completely surprised to see a familiar face, though he couldn't place it.

"Hey, how are you feeling?" she asked him

"Not so good, I feel a little light-headed. Why do you look so familiar?"

"That's completely normal. You passed out while jogging in Central Park. Luckily I was there and was able to squeeze you into a new study for people with your disorder. I'm going to give you some more of this drug — it's a new one, called dodec, and it should take care of your fainting spells."

She connected Kaleb to a new IV of the dodec solution and escorted him to a hospital room.

Kaleb woke up laying in a hospital bed feeling drowsy with several more IVs injected into his arms. He leaned forward ripping the IVs out, groaning at the tad bit of pain. Against hospital policy, Kaleb stumbled up and left his room, wandering down a mysterious hallway with flickering white lights and grey walls in his hospital gown. He stopped at room 132 and saw Johnny. He knocked on the door but didn't

> "She connected Kaleb to a new IV of the dodec solution and escorted him to a hospital room."

get a response. Walking all the way in the room, Kaleb saw Johnny staring aimlessly out of the window.

On a table next to the hospital bed was a vase of wilted roses with a card that said "Get Well Soon." Kaleb looked at the roses, blinked twice, and red beams shot from his eyes. In amazement of what he just did, he looked over and the roses were slowly regaining their color. Kaleb turned to Johnny and blinked.

After leaving room 132, to finally see his family, Johnny told all of his friends about his miraculous recovery, who then told their friends, who then told even more friends. One day, not long after, Mariah heard the nurses gossiping at the desk while she was clocking in. "Did you hear about the patient in room 132? I think his name is Johnny. He went from being ill to having a miraculous recovery. He posted a picture on Instagram, he looked really healthy, and thanked that Kaleb guy in a tag."

Within days, Kaleb had received hundreds of phone calls from all over the world on his Google Glasses — so many that he got a headache and he had to take them off. But eventually, he returned each and every call, and healed them all.

Fast Forward

Mariah had a three o'clock appointment. She called out, "Jane Doe." After several minutes of waiting and no Jane Doe, she noticed that the waiting room was empty. She realized that there could only be one person responsible for this, but she needed proof. She pulled out her Siri hologram and noticed that her clientele has decreased around the same time that Kaleb experienced his change.

Angry, Mariah dialed Kaleb on the hologram phone.

"Hey Kaleb, it's Mariah, from the dodec study. Can you come by the office today?"

"For what exactly? I thought I was cleared," he said.

"You are. I just need to run a few more tests."

"Can this wait until next week? I'm kind of busy."

"It would be better if you came in today."

"Alright, fine. I'm on my way."

When Kaleb walked into her office, Mariah asked him if he knew anything about her decreasing clientele. Things escalated quickly. Kaleb yelled, "I'm just helping people, and without your dodec!" which frightened Mariah. She stepped back, knocking over a vial of dodec solution and inhaling it. She started coughing and her neck turned a light magenta.

Before passing out, Mariah said: "Your patients are not who you think they are … and I'm coming for them."

The Settlement

BROOKE BOREL

Inspiration for this story came from Mars One, a Dutch project that, ambitiously and controversially, is planning the first-ever Mars colony. An intense competition to pick the first colonists is underway. In an interview, one of the finalists, a young astrophysics student named Maggie Lieu, imagines having children on the red planet — the Martian Adam and Eve. Here's my imagining of what their life is like, as well as how they long for Earth and others like them.

Eve turned the knob on the telescreen through every single channel — CLICK CLICK CLICKclickclickclick — but the snowy noise remained.

"UGH nothing works here ever," she said. There was no one to respond. Her pod was empty; her father was working in the communal Martian vegetable greenpod and her mother was on water duty, flash-melting ice at the planet's frozen northern pole. Worse, her oxygen pack allotment was nearly used up for the month, which meant she couldn't go exploring outside, and she had already read the family's only book — Sirens of Titan, by Vonnegut — at least a dozen times. And now there wasn't even a way to watch the Earth reality shows and sitcoms that constantly streamed on Galaticflix, an agonizing taste of a mother planet she had never known.

There were others like her there — millions of teens doing normal things, growing up, going to school, learning to drive cars. None of their parents had signed up for a one-way ticket to Mars. They didn't have to monitor their bone density and vital signs every day, or send data samples to Mars One for analysis. It was not fair. If only she could be them. Or at least talk to them, to learn more about their tantalizing world than Galacticflix could offer.

> "None of their parents had signed up for a one-way ticket to Mars."

TAPaTAPaTAPTAP came a secret knock on the pod door. Eve pulled an oxygen mask that was hanging from the ceiling onto her face and pressed a button that unlocked the outer door. She heard some stumbling, then another TAPaTAPaTAP-TAP; she pushed a second button, which locked the outer door and opened an inner one. A figure in a slick silver spacesuit and bubbled helmet fell through, tripping over a pile of used oxygen tanks.

"Adam, what, UGH," she said, pulling off her facemask and letting it spring back to the ceiling.

He removed his helmet, revealing a wild grin full of crooked teeth, a splash of acne. "I got it," he said.

"You what?!" Eve said, her mood brightening.

Adam unzipped his suit and pulled a black radio from an inner pocket. "I got it, and we have two hours before my parents get back from the solar plant."

The teens settled onto the floor and Eve snatched the radio from Adam's hands. The last time — more than a month ago — hadn't worked. She started dialing through the channels until she found one with a green signal, which throbbed on the side of the radio.

Eve leaned forward, eyes bright, her mouth against the built-in microphone: "Is anyone there? Can you hear us?"

The line was quiet, save for a gentle whooshing sound that Eve couldn't quite place. It stretched for minutes, during which she pictured her voice transforming into radio waves and bouncing through space, landing on a spindly radio tower in one of those brilliant emerald suburban yards she'd seen on the telescreen, her voice filling an empty room.

And then, softly, a voice said: "I'm here."

KARILIS CRUZ

YEARS AS MENTEE: 3

GRADE: Senior

HIGH SCHOOL:
Urban Assembly Media
High School

BORN: New York, NY

LIVES: New York, NY

**PUBLICATIONS
AND RECOGNITIONS:**
Scholastic Art & Writing
Award: Honorable Mention

My genre base has grown and expanded with Lyndsay right there beside me. Lyndsay understood the things and messages I wanted to say. She made it all a little less mumbled and a little more understood. I guess it's time to go and find more creative adventures. This program is only the beginning.

LYNDSAY FAYE

YEARS AS MENTOR: 3

OCCUPATION:
Author at G. P.
Putnam's Sons

BORN: San Jose, CA

LIVES: Queens, NY

**PUBLICATIONS
AND RECOGNITIONS:**
The Fatal Flame

I will miss my unicorn so much after this year, but I can't wait to see what she's going to accomplish. I remember her as a sophomore, very quiet and never wanting to share her writing with the group — now she's so confident that anyone could learn from her example!

Time's Memories

KARILIS CRUZ

This year is our last year of kicking butt together. Over the past three years, I've grown with the help of my mentor Lyndsay. It's sad to go. I really wish I didn't have to go — it feels all too quick. But with the guidance I'm taking with me, this won't be my last huzzah.

I can't remember growing up,

I can't remember the point when adults cursed around me and stopped apologizing for it.

Or when I was allowed to go and get my own food.

I can't remember when I stopped sliding into my mom's bed after having a bad nightmare.

I can't remember when my mom stopped chopping my food into little bites or when my mom stopped checking on me in the bathroom.

I don't remember when things changed.

When I was younger, I'd put my arms in my shirt and tell people I don't have any arms.

I would restart the video games when I was sure that I was going to lose.

I would sleep with all my stuffed animals, so none would get offended.

I had that one pen that had six colors and tried to push them all at once.

I would pour soda in the bottle caps and pretend that I was taking shots.

I would wait behind the door to scare someone, but eventually leave because they were taking too long or I had to go and pee.

I would fake going to sleep, so that my mom could carry me to bed.

I used to think that the moon followed the car.

I couldn't wait to grow up.

Now I'm not so sure.

Because

suddenly you are 21, screaming to all of the songs you used to listen to when you were in middle school when you were sad. And everything is different but everything is good.

Yet you are still 18.

You are trying to catch your breath and this life is coming at you faster than you've
expected.

You have kissed boys who did not show you the love that you needed.

Your parents have given up on you multiple times.

You have loved boys who never acknowledged your existence.

You have broken bones, and they have healed.

You have experienced things that you wouldn't have wished upon your worst enemy.

You have lost friends, and made new ones.

You have had bad hair days and good hair days.

You have failed tests.

You have scars and you have memories.

You have missed people who will never come back.

You've been to the highest highs and to the lowest lows.

You have had your trials and tribulations.

You are young, and you have time to live.

Slow down and things will be OK.

You are 18 and life is going to happen anyway.

eyes like polaroids

LYNDSAY FAYE

*When my mentee Karilis said she wanted to write another memoir poem for
this year's anthology, I was so proud of her. We both used to be scared to
death of poetry, but the way we think of "Voice to Voice" is enabling each other
to be creatively free. I couldn't write poems at all without her inspiration.*

when I was small, I used to try to
      freeze time
I would look at
      sunlight glistening on electric green grass strung with dew-like jewels
      lace cobwebs with their spiders nestled

the particular light through the bathroom window

a cottony bed of baby mice

meadow grasses taller than I was

the wild rose garden down the street

a weeping willow with leaves like long hair

california poppies

and I would think like a polaroid camera

> *click*

> *I have saved you, tiny instant*

> *click*

> *I have recorded you, beautiful picture*

> *click*

> *You are mine now, 3:48 in the afternoon following a rainstorm*

it never worked

not a single time

I always forgot

the next day or the next week

typical, wasn't I?

because my mind wasn't a camera and my eyes weren't lenses

> but if I concentrate, I can still remember that there was a

> blackberry bush lit by blue morning light

> field of violet sweet peas

> plum tree

even if I can't see them

I wish I could still see them

LEILAH FAGAN

YEARS AS MENTEE: 2

GRADE: Senior

HIGH SCHOOL:
Millenium Brooklyn
High School

BORN: Brooklyn, NY

LIVES: Brooklyn, NY

**PUBLICATIONS
AND RECOGNITIONS:**
Scholastic Art & Writing
Award: Honorable Mention

Catherine has taught me that there are people out there that actually care about your voice. I've learned we should all embrace the things that influence our voices because they're an important and essential part of us and who we are as humans and people in society. My mentor has inspired me to speak my mind and take pride in my style of writing. Also, she has taught me to just love life and be appreciative of the people and things I have. As a woman and a person with a voice, Catherine has made me feel like I don't have to sec-ond-guess myself.

CATHERINE LeCLAIR

YEARS AS MENTOR: 1

OCCUPATION:
Associate Editor, Time Inc.

BORN: Bangor, ME

LIVES: Brooklyn, NY

For Leilah, writing is second nature and she does it for herself alone. As someone who often worries about my audience or whether I have something worth saying, Leilah continually inspires me to write just because I want to, and because as a process it is fun and cathartic. When I show up to our ses-sions she is always already writing away with headphones on, and she looks so content. Writing with Leilah helps me let go of the voices that tell me that writing is not worth it be-cause she does that so effortlessly.

Oceanic Confessions

LEILAH FAGAN

This piece is based on my dying love for love itself — and how words can create an indirect voice for a poet who expresses her true feelings through anonymous characters. I believe writing gives a person a voice she wouldn't necessarily have herself. My voice is my writing.

The sounds of mellow tides
Part your lips
And echo out everything
Willing to absorb or contain it
You whisper soft blue cycles
Of waves
And they overlap each other
Against my eardrum
They sound so good
Softly patting against the other
Against the sandy texture
Of your tongue
Against the horizon
Beneath your half-hazy lids
Against the sprinkles of after showers
In the noon sky
12:01 hits.
So do the words
You let slosh their way
To the barely saturated sands
You defy the laws of geoscientific structures
Because to you excess infiltration
Doesn't exist
Runoff isn't a factor

My zone of saturation

Disappears because I

Wait for your tide

I wait for your soft waves

To turn to intense collisions

Because I can still

Feel you

Purify me

With your echoing waters

And, I will forever bask in

You.

Enunciation

CATHERINE LeCLAIR

This piece was inspired by the intersection of our literal and figurative voices, which I experienced when teaching English to immigrant women. I tried to explore tonality and language as they relate to self-expression and agency within our culture.

These women have trouble with my name. "Cat-der-een," the syllables tumble out of their mouths. They are from Haiti but now they sit in a cold and tiny classroom in Boston where I try to teach them English. They are willing their lives to improve one word at a time. First nouns, the useful ones, then verbs in present tense, past and conditional will come later. First asking directions and pleasantries. They'll need these in America.

I love the sound of the women's voices as they wrap their tongues around the sharp edges and hard consonants of English words. They are always laughing. I am always laughing too, but I have not just left the poorest country in the Western Hemisphere in search of a better life. I have the better life. I don't aim to be a stereotype but here I am the White Girl in College volunteering to teach immigrants English. I hope our collective laughter can serve as a prayer for forgiveness.

Who were these women in Port-au-Prince: Were they sassy, well-read, maybe social butterflies? Here many labels mask their voices: they are immigrants, poor, aliens. Their frustrated English is drowned out by all the shouting done by those of us who can wrestle the language much more deftly. Who is left to listen to them? Does anybody here speak Creole?

One lady, her smile is a beacon. "I love America," she says. "Sometimes I think I love it too much." You might, I think. Sometimes America doesn't love you back. I wonder how these women can watch me write words on the whiteboard with such attention and have the energy to copy them into their notebooks with such determination, as if they will study them later. I know that for them, later is an hour-long bus ride home to fall into bed and wake up to work long hours and send savings back to Haiti and somehow find the time to smile.

> "I love America," she says. "Sometimes I think I love it too much."... Sometimes America doesn't love you back."

Their laughs are deep and honest. They are a celebration. I hope some day our collective laughter will ring out like a chorus and slowly it will wash over everyone of us, like the wave at a baseball stadium, and suddenly like an ocean we will all be laughing.

SALLY FERRIS

YEARS AS MENTEE: 2

GRADE: Junior

HIGH SCHOOL:
Professional Performing
Arts High School

BORN: New York, NY

LIVES: New York, NY

**PUBLICATIONS
AND RECOGNITIONS:**
"The Seven-Month Search:
Navigating The New York
City Public School System"
published on Newsweek.com

With Jen, I have made some of my proudest accomplishments. We have worked together for about two years now, and she has become one of my biggest supporters. Jen has taught me to embrace my mistakes, and be as fearless as possible when it comes to writing. Jen is one of the most compassionate and inspirational people I know. Without her, I wouldn't be the writer or person I am today.

JENNIFER DOERR

YEARS AS MENTOR: 2

OCCUPATION:
Writing Instructor at
Legal Outreach, Arts
Administration at The
New School for Jazz and
Contemporary Music

BORN: Baltimore, MD

LIVES: New York, NY

Sally and I have worked together for nearly two years and, in that time, I've watched her present her poetry at her first public reading and have one of her essays published in a national magazine. Experiencing her growth and success is thrilling and inspiring. We are so similar in our creative struggles, in our reluctance to share our gifts. By giving our work to one another, we allow our voices to be heard in a safe space first. Sally is helping me to become as fearless of a writer as she already is.

Genetically Modified You

SALLY FERRIS

I had the idea for this poem after a friend of mine passed away this year. I noticed that after his passing, he was discussed, especially by adults, in a way that cast him in a negative light due to the circumstances of his death. The memory that was being created of him didn't line up with who he truly was. This poem is a commentary on the tainting of my friend's legacy.

buried
by creators of your legacy
teachers and storytellers
their words the soil
accumulating
sealing your place in the ground
fresh earth the perfect place to plant seeds
for a genetically modified
you

harvested and fed to us
by the guardians of virtue
we bit into the fruit
needing your sweet nectar
offended
as an unfamiliar taste introduced itself
making a travesty of our cravings
failing to replace the authentic, forbidden taste of
you

The Sanctity of Contraceptive Choice

JENNIFER DOERR

This memoir piece began as an op-ed I started writing in the summer of 2014 after the Supreme Court ruling that excused Hobby Lobby and several other "closely held" corporations from providing certain contraceptive medications as part of their employee health care plan. My personal story of how I got my name seemed an incongruous starting point, which is precisely why I chose it to communicate what I find a complex and emotional issue that, nevertheless, has a very clear-cut legal solution.

When my mother was pregnant with me, she received a pamphlet in the mail from a local evangelical church advertising the annual March for Life rally in Washington, D.C. Even in those years before my father entered full-time ministry as a United Methodist pastor, my parents were very religious and staunchly opposed to abortion. The full-color brochure my mother received included pictures of Baby Jennifer, a fetus photographed in utero from six weeks to full term. From my memory of seeing the brochure as a child, the photos showed the fetus in profile suspended in the dark, nebulous womb, an eye growing larger in each successive shot, limbs with minute capillaries forming beneath skin, and, in the last few images, complete fingernails, defined nostrils, and wisps of hair. When I was born, my mother chose to name me Jennifer after the fetus as a declaration of her belief that life is sacred and begins at conception.

> "The full-color brochure my mother received included pictures of Baby Jennifer, a fetus photographed in utero..."

The real reason I get emotional at this bit of family lore is not the fact that my pre-birth, pickle-sized self mattered so much to my mother. It is that no one in this country could prevent her from choosing to do what she wanted regarding her family planning options. When she learned she was pregnant with me, Mom had just given birth to my sister five months earlier, and she could have justifiably taken steps to terminate her pregnancy in the early stages with the medications and procedures available at that time. If she had lived in another country she might have been required to abort by the government, since I was her third child. But in the United States, she had the power to make her own choices. Her decision to carry and deliver me was not a government mandate. It was private and sacred.

In my tradition of evangelical Christianity, as well as in many other religious ide-ologies around the world, the human body is considered a house of God, a divine temple. It's no stranger to believe this than it is to comprehend the recent Supreme Court decision that a company is a "person" with religious freedoms. When viewing the Hobby Lobby ruling from a spiritual perspective, the company has essentially been permitted to serve as an unsolicited high priest for their female employees who may or may not hold to its belief systems. The ability to dictate which medicines a woman is able to take or not take has given them unprecedented corporate domain over the holiest of holies: the human body.

Since leaving the evangelical faith I was raised in, I've tread my own spiritual path in ways I'm certain my parents don't always approve of. But my mother, who still keeps that right-to-life pamphlet with my namesake's pictures in her bedside drawer, always tells me that there is a reason I was born, even though I wasn't planned. Maybe that reason is to provide this reminder: there is sanctity in the trinity of a woman, her doctor, and her personal ethic, with no room for the US government or her employers.

JADA FITZPATRICK

YEARS AS MENTEE: 1

GRADE: Junior

HIGH SCHOOL:
Preparatory Academy
for Writers

BORN: Waterbury, CT

LIVES: Queens, NY

**PUBLICATIONS
AND RECOGNITIONS:**
Scholastic Art & Writing
Award: Honorable Mention

At first I was insecure about my writing. I felt that it wasn't "good enough." This year Linda has taught me to be confident with my writing — to never doubt my ability and let my voice be heard. Because of her I had learned that it is better to write something "bad" than nothing at all. Her kindness and words of encouragement allow me to be comfortable with my writing and to be a more confident individual overall. She is an amazing motivator, mentor, woman, and friend and I'm thankful for her.

LINDA KLEINBUB

YEARS AS MENTOR: 2

OCCUPATION:
Freelance Writer and
Journalist

BORN: Maspeth, NY

LIVES: Queens, NY

**PUBLICATIONS
AND RECOGNITIONS:**
*New York Observer; Our
Town Downtown; State-
ment of Record; Short,
Fast and Deadly; The Best
American Poetry Blog;
Grabbing the Apple: An
Anthology of New York
Women Poets*

I am inspired by Jada's drive and determination. She is passionate about social justice and this is evident in her writing. We have worked voice-to-voice when we collaborated on a poem for the Girls Write Now CHAPTERS Reading Series. Jada is ambitious and wants to get the most out of life. We've worked on essays for applications for a summer journalism program and a summer college prep program. Helping her edit her work has allowed me to discover her tenacity, as well as helped me gain confidence in my own work. We both enjoy sharing our voices through the discovery of new music.

Breathe

JADA FITZPATRICK

*I have always had an opinion but kept quiet. I learned through writing
I can make myself heard and stand up against injustices. My mission to make
my voice profound inspired me to write this piece and be the voice
for kids who are forced to remain silent.*

She sits at the small
left-handed desk
her gold-flecked green eyes
glancing anxiously between her
half-finished test and
the watch painted on her wrist.
Her golden wavy locks
frame her gaze that is fixed on a road to self-preservation
and success, but her dark tired eyes can only
focus on the 10 minutes left on the clock.
She tries to breathe, but she can't.

She walks down the blackened streets of New York
she feels a deviant glare fixated on her
drinking in her aura
scrutinizing her svelte figure,
her elongated legs,
her flowing ebony hair,
her thick black eyelashes,
her Caribbean blue eyes.
She walks fast, her heart pounds
sweat rolls down her face.
Just breathe she tells herself.

He is frail with spiked flamboyant green hair

the paradox to his distraught demeanor.
A reject, alone
tears become waterfalls of hate as he stares in the mirror,
eyes bedeviled by the image boring into his soul.
He so deeply desires to be someone else.
In his reflection he searches for approval,
day after day yearning to catch a glimpse of affection,
but instead it pains him,
paints fresh wounds upon the canvas of hate
surrounding his soul.
Just breathe, he whispers.

She steps through the threshold of her home
tragically beautiful with short blue highlighted hair
atop a heart shaped head
bearing a scowling slender face ingrained with
a faint scar that is shaped like a
macaroni noodle.
Tiptoeing her way into her room, praying for peace and solidarity,
her dreams crash when she hears voices
raised in threatening violence and agony.
Just breathe she thinks, but
short shallow breaths barely even escape her lips.

They can't breathe,
she inhales the miasma of anxiety,
she is suffocated by the overwhelming presence of lust,
he is asphyxiated by the hands of hatred and disapproval,
she is choked by the existence of violence.

Why can't they breathe?!
Why is it that the days must drag on?
Must torture instead of let live?
Why must they be
spectacles of the education system's judgments,
of the rapist's eyes,
of the bullies' attention,
of family problems that arise?

Why does society put so much on

their backs? The load too great to distract

them from their "inevitable" fate,

conforming to the standards of approval the world creates.

To choke on a life of pressure and misery

poisoned by the hand of disapproval is no easy feat.

Let them breathe.

For once can the youth of

today inhale the audacious aroma of acceptance?

A praise so often denied to them.

The hands of systematic control

have molded their once free teenage selves

into the bodies of warriors

they must now learn to fight the battle

of self-worth, of acceptance.

They must now bear the arms of perseverance

must wear the mask of persistence

must hide in the trenches of immortality

to survive,

to breathe.

Droid

LINDA KLEINBUB

*My mentee Jada and I worked on a journalism op-ed piece about
compulsive cell phone usage. Her voice inspired me to write this poem.*

Don't bother me, phone

let me work.

I mute you,

still you vibrate

rattling of the little table where you lay.

Don't talk to me, phone,
no more Instagram,
no more Twitter,
no more Facebook, and Tumblr.
Phone, you connect me to
strangers in strange places.

You're my art museum,
my new love interest,
a card game that leaves me
in solitude.
You make me forget
best friends.

Go away, phone
your texting reply bubbles
are ruining my marriage.
Internet that connects the universe,
Internet that leads me astray,
Internet filled with Isis recruiters, and
poetry brothels.

Don't hum, don't bing, don't buzz, phone.
Leave me alone, phone.
Let me get my job done,
begin my journey in the sun,
feel warmth on my skin,
when evening begins, and
fireflies take flight,
I'll dance in the starlight.

MENNEN GORDON

YEARS AS MENTEE: 4

GRADE: Senior

HIGH SCHOOL:
Institute for Collaborative
Education

BORN: Brooklyn, NY

LIVES: Bronx, NY

SCHOLARSHIPS:
Traina Scholarship

**PUBLICATIONS
AND RECOGNITIONS:**
Scholastic Art & Writing
Awards: Silver Key,
Honorable Mention

We write maybe half of the time, which is nice, because writing isn't about making eloquent words string together into elegant sentences, it's about conversations and life and existing. I like that I get to exist with Elizabeth.

ELIZABETH IRWIN

YEARS AS MENTOR: 1

OCCUPATION:
Playwright
(The Public Theater,
Playwrights Realm)

BORN: Worcester, WA

LIVES: Brooklyn, NY

**PUBLICATIONS
AND RECOGNITIONS:**
My Mañana Comes

Mennen is not just a student, a young woman, or a writer — she is a force to be reckoned with. Her curiosity for the world, the stories she wants to tell about it, and her constant thirst for using new media in doing so have inspired me since our first meeting. Though I may have guided her with some aspects of craft or offered her literary critique, she has shown me the many ways in which a voice can speak, reverberate and shout out loud.

I Think Best/Worst in the Dark

MENNEN GORDON

"I Think Best/Worst in the Dark" is a scene from Dirty Jane, *a feature film I'm currently writing about platonic, romantic relationships, high school and an underwhelming amount of cereal. This scene is the beginning of the end for a pair of high school best friends.*

INT. JANE'S BEDROOM - LATE NIGHT

It is dark, we can only see the girls through the blue light coming through their window. Jane is in her bed. Betty and Erica are on a mattress on the floor. Betty is fast asleep.

> **JANE**
>
> Do you ever think about the future?

> **ERICA**
>
> It's human nature to think ahead.

> **JANE**
>
> (Annoyed)
>
> I don't mean "human nature thinking
> about the future." I mean, just,
> like thinking about the future.

> **ERICA**
>
> Okay so, yeah I guess —

> **JANE**
>
> I can't really see it. Like, the
> future's not all there for me. And
> I don't know what that means for
> me, like, as a person, or whatever,
> but it scares the living shit out
> of me, Erica. Like, does everyone
> see the future, and it's just me

who's, like, blocked out and fucked
up in the head?

ERICA

I don't know. Everyone is
different.

JANE

(Small voice)

Can you see your future?

ERICA

If you mean, "Do I have an idea of
who I want to be," then yeah, I
guess I do?

Beat.

JANE

I think I want to stop. Being
friends, I mean. And, it's not you,
okay. And it's not me, it's just
um. Circumstance.

JANE (CONT'D)

Because sometimes you can't see the
future... so I think that means you
have to make it up for yourself.
And, we're going away to college
and everything. We're not going to be
able to see each other all the time
and be together like we were in
high school. We have to think about
the future... And it's sad, and I
want to cry, but I'm not going to.
Because it's just how it is. People
don't stay friends forever... We
can try, but we won't, so if it's
not going to last, we should just
stop now. I mean, I feel like we
would put ourselves through a lot
of pain later on for no reason when
we could just rip the Band-Aid off

now and get it over with.

Beat.

I love you guys.

> **ERICA**
>
> No you don't Jane. You don't
> because you make shit up in your
> head and expect us to deal with it.
> You always have. You don't love us,
> you're just trying to love yourself
> and you think this is how.

Erica rolls over.

> **ERICA (CONT'D)**
>
> But whatever. I'm not mad at you.
> I'm not going to be your friend if
> you don't want me to, because
> relationships don't work like that.
> Once again, Jane makes sure she
> gets exactly what she wants.

> **JANE**
>
> That's not what I'm doing, Erica.

> **ERICA**
>
> I said I'm not mad at you.

FADE TO BLACK.

Unmapping

ELIZABETH IRWIN

This piece is inspired by my mentee's piece, "I Think Best/Worst in the Dark" which focuses on the specific juncture in young people's lives before they graduate from high school. I was impressed by her ability to pull away from a time so close to her and to write a story that, while still authentic, shows a remarkable ability to view the crises of the characters through a balanced writer's lens.

We talk a lot about the future
And what you want and
what you imagine it will be like
and how it will be better and worse
and I want to tell you yes, it will be —
and no, no, it won't —
and don't even worry about —
and —
All these things that I think
I know.
Then I think of myself
at your age.
I see myself
now
all the
joyful surprises
all the stark, hollowing hurts
the zig-zags and curlicues
and gleeful tumble-overs
my path made and makes
looking at it
plotted out

in my words to you.

So I don't want to tell you anything

about how it will be or

warn you a single syllable

or prophecy even a day

I want only to sit beside you

and hear you

hope and wonder and fear

and steam and smile

when you conjure how

your tomorrows will look.

My joy grows in your beautiful speculation.

SHAKEVA GRISWOULD

YEARS AS MENTEE: 1

GRADE: Junior

HIGH SCHOOL:
Marta Valle High School

BORN: Bronx, NY

LIVES: Bronx, NY

What I've learned from Anna is that I should embrace all of the parts that make up my character. She taught me that my writing is an extension of myself, and that I should put a piece of me into each of the words that leave my pen. She's introduced me to different styles of creation, and helped me find my own.

ANNA J. WITIUK

YEARS AS MENTOR: 1

OCCUPATION:
Student and Nanny

BORN: New York, NY

LIVES: Brooklyn, NY

**PUBLICATIONS
AND RECOGNITIONS:**
Poetry and Online editor
of 12th Street Journal;
SinkReview.org;
newschoolwriting.org;
12streetonline.com

Knowing Shakeva has given me such an appreciation for why and how we write. When we meet for pair sessions, so much of what we talk about are the reasons why we keep returning to our pen and page when we feel we must express ourselves. Even when we feel so frustrated with what we perceive as our "lack of creativity," or other people or institutions aren't giving us what we think we need to affirm that we are, in fact, Writers... writing is still what tugs at and nags our souls to keep going, keep doing, keep fighting for.

The ABC's of Beauty

SHAKEVA GRISWOULD

*This piece was inspired by social media and how it affects
how someone perceives themselves. I wanted this piece to show that you
don't need extra things to be beautiful.*

Apple apps and android accommodators always allow likes

and Comments to allude to

their Beauty. But beauty

does not Begin with begging

for Broadcasting on the billboards of

Social Media. Criteria:

I Always allow myself to take a Break from the belligerent

nature of Certain sites.

When you see me, I Begin to bloom as my Creativity courses

through the Cords of my Body. It's Amazing

what can be seen and Accomplished,

the Brightest star

shines when they know their own Capability.

Of Course, it's Always appreciated when someone Bellows

a remark at your Becomings.

But I must be Careful not to let the Compliments

Conflict with my Truth.

I Am worth more than analysis.

My Chocolate color glows without the Assistance

of an applied filter.

Brown eyes burn

softly in the Comfort of

the night. My mind and spirit — my true Assets — Blast

through the Connoisseurs of hate.

I realize that

Anything is possible.

There is no limit Between myself and the sky.

I Cannot Be condensed inside a box

of Conformity. My Beauty becomes

realized.

No filter:

A hashtag

that needs to Be Circulated more often.

If I Were Pregnant With You

ANNA J. WITIUK

*I wrote this poem a while ago. However, I was so influenced by
my mentee Shakeva and her ability to harness and direct the rhythm in her
poetry, that my own piece has gone through many changes since.
This poem is my voice speaking to a faceless "You" but also to Shakeva
as a thank you for her inspiration.*

If I were pregnant with you I would not

take a plane for the whole nine months,

I would not lift

my feet from the ground, just so I'd know

you'd be born that way, bound to cake

-walking, my batch from earth.

If I were pregnant with

you I'd drink honey like gold, bee

bullion down my throat, drip-drying like a mane

around your little skull. If I were pregnant with you

I'd know your breath like a backbeat, listen to it through

a horn, warm brass pressing into your walls

like a murmuring hug of Blues. If I

were pregnant with you I'd be well

-versed in your heartbeat; my love tip

-toeing down the bricks of

my spine like sonnets: iambs

plopping, iambs

whispering: "I am

so in

love with

you lit

-tle moon." If I were pregnant with you, you

would be pregnant with me... the songs I sang wrapped

around you tight to belt you all in, big

with every word I chewed on. You'd swim in psalm,

notes springing up to suspend

you in a spooning middle C, rocking spawn of some

descending progression, which hit me

as hard as a variating minor

for your love.

If I were pregnant with you,

you would be weightless in your impregnation,

but I

would be anchored to your love —

the amount of gravity you pull equivalent to the kisses

I will one day stoop to press to

your little head. If I were pregnant with you.

SHIRLEYKA HECTOR

YEARS AS MENTEE: 2

GRADE: Junior

HIGH SCHOOL:
International High School
at Lafayette

BORN:
Port-au-Prince, Haiti

LIVES: Brooklyn, NY

**PUBLICATIONS
AND RECOGNITIONS:**
Teen Ink Historical Fiction;
Scholastic Art & Writing
Award: Honorable Mention;
International Day of the
Girl Summit 2014 website;
Nuyorican Poets Cafe

Shara and I meet at a Dunkin' Donuts in Union Square on a weekly basis. There we talk and write. Sometimes we write using prompts but when we want to be more creative and go several steps forward, we write in different genres from flash fiction to humorous writing. Shara and I have an amazing relationship. Without her, I do not know where I'd be as both a teenager and a writer. She always gives me great advice when I'm in need. I love her because she's awesome!

SHARA ZAVAL

YEARS AS MENTOR: 1

OCCUPATION:
Editorial Manager,
Teenreads.com/
Kidsreads.com

BORN: Boston, MA

LIVES: Brooklyn, NY

When I asked Shirleyka what she wanted to write about for our upcoming Girls Write Now CHAPTERS Reading Series, she had an answer, immediately. "Last year I wrote about the past," she said. "This year I'm going to write about the future, and everything I want to achieve." There wasn't a hint of doubt, and this unwavering confidence has been a staple throughout our sessions together. Shirleyka knows who she is, what she stands for, and how she can use language to forge her own identity. Her sense of self — and bright smile — inspires me every time I see her.

To One of My Stars Who Departed

SHIRLEYKA HECTOR

*I wrote this piece for my grandmother who always encouraged me
to be myself and to follow my own path. She was very outspoken, so I felt
like the theme "Voice to Voice" was her life's theme.*

Words, truly cannot describe how much you
Meant to me, but I have to say that
I am so glad to have had you as a part of my life.
You were as tiny as an ant,
But your presence was as immense as a lion's.
Your presence was appreciated by everyone
Around you.

Your love was comforting in the most
Profound pain. Your words were sweeter
Than carob in the most unpleasant situation.
Your high-pitched voice remains inside my head,
Reminding me that there is so much
More to life than struggles.
There's so much to enjoy in life
While the time elapses before our eyes.

Everything you've done was done with a special
Purpose and that is carved in our hearts
As we mourn over you. You've proven yourself
By being loving until the very end.
I felt how much you loved all of us. You
Loved me until death took you away from my grasp.
And I will love you until the end of time.
You still reside deep down in my heart.

You were one of my lights. Your bright

Persona influenced my persona. You shined and

You made me shine. Your light penetrated my

Soul and made me a better soul, a better heart,

A better person. As a girl growing up, your light

Illuminated my path. You were one of my stars

And you've departed...

Yet, I can still see before me because you've left your

Perpetual light here to shine on me.

The Puzzle

SHARA ZAVAL

*I've wanted to write about my 90-year-old grandmother's
mental state for a long time, but I couldn't figure out a way to do it justice,
until a recent Girls Write Now Persona Poetry Workshop. The format
helped me empathize with what she goes and went
through on a day-to-day basis, and this poem is dedicated to her.*

I need to know.

It doesn't matter, really.

Monday, Tuesday, Thursday, Sunday.

What is one? What is the other?

I don't know.

But I should know.

And so I need to.

They'll think I'm crazy if I ask.

A roll of the eyes, a chuckle.

It will evolve, the second time, the third,

into a heavy sigh, a snap:

"Nana! It's Sunday."

And then another chuckle. Apologetic, this time.

"It's Sunday, Nana. All day."

Unless it's Monday, of course,
and then they'll say, "Monday,"
same subtle grimace, restrained temper.
Or so I think, anyway.
I don't know.

Puzzle pieces with bits of sky,
blades of grass.
Maybe the logo of a candy bar,
or a scale from a paper dragon.
Each reduced to colorful dots, blots
blurs. When disconnected, they have no meaning.

I see them Monday,
Tuesday, Thursday, Sunday.
Oh, and Thursday, too.
Did I say that, already?

Groceries magically delivered to my fridge.
I open it up and there's sesame chicken in a plastic box.
Shrimp with vegetables.
Potato pancakes.
I didn't buy them.
Who bought them?

Back to the puzzle.
Blue with blue.
Red with red.
It's always hard to find
where they connect.

Tell me — someone tell me.
What day is it?
I don't remember asking
or you answering.
So can't you just pretend,
one time,
that this is the first time?

KIARA JOSEPH

YEARS AS MENTEE: 3

GRADE: Senior

HIGH SCHOOL:
NYC iSchool

BORN: Brooklyn, NY

LIVES: Brooklyn, NY

SCHOLARSHIPS:
University of Alabama Capstone Scholarship; University of Florida Office of Admissions Alumni Scholarship; SUNY Albany Presidential Scholarship; SUNY Buffalo Daniel Acker Scholarship; SUNY Stony Brook Presidential Scholarship

PUBLICATIONS AND RECOGNITIONS:
Scholastic Art and Writing Award: Honorable Mention

As I am writing this, I am sitting in a hole in the wall coffee shop in Chelsea sipping on a hot chocolate with Rachel. This truly captures our relationship. Rachel is more than a mentor or an adult in my life. She is someone that I can relax and be myself around. We typically meet on Friday's to write — the perfect ending to my usually stressful week. Through her voice, I have learned how to effectively channel the stresses from my daily life into a piece of writing.

RACHEL KRANTZ

YEARS AS MENTOR: 3

OCCUPATION:
Senior Features Editor, Bustle

BORN: Oakland, CA

LIVES: Brooklyn, NY

As I walk into the cafe to meet Kiara, I'm struck, once again, by the young woman she's suddenly seemed to become. I've had three years to prepare for her going to college, but I now understand why older folks always used to say to me that it seemed I'd "grown up overnight." Here it is — it's happened. Kiara has transformed into a confident, composed, amazing writer and young woman. I can't wait to see what she does next.

Another Piece, Another Poem

KIARA JOSEPH

*With all the stress of my senior year, I found it hard to write.
This poem highlights the challenge that many writers experience
when trying to channel their inner voice.*

As I sit here writing this,
something else is on my mind.
Another task,
another work,
another piece,
another poem.
These words are simply a byproduct of something all writers are familiar with:
　writers' block.

You haven't truly suffered until you feel that brick wall blocking those tiny little
　synapses in your brain

It eats at you,
It takes a toll on you,
It frustrates you,
it rules you,
and it controls you.
It tears you apart,
It makes you scream.

But then it mocks you,
and stops you from expressing yourself in the only way you know how: through
　your words.

It makes you cry,
and it makes you groan.

But through all of that,

it makes you grow.

It forces you to.

It forces you to think,

to analyze,

to innovate,

to create

in a way that you never deemed possible.

And in the end, you're left with something you're proud of.

Something you want to share with the world.

Something better than you could've ever imagined.

Even if it isn't what you set your heart out to create.

My Backyard

RACHEL KRANTZ

I wrote this to a friend, trying to explain my childhood backyard to him.

the big palm at center, the persimmon tree in the left outfield, the lemon tree under my bedroom,
    stage right.
    i would like to show you the video of me in the backyard with my mom and pedro. it is one of the only live action records i have of us all interacting together. my mom is filling up the kiddie pool, and pedro is filming with his new camcorder. she keeps spraying him with the hose, and you can tell they are very freshly in love, newly committed. he worries she's going to ruin his sandals, but she assures him they are not that material. she knows because she has no doubt bought them for him.
    i run upstairs to change into my swimsuit. i'm four, and just as cute and already myself as you can imagine, only acting more like someone's doll. it seems like maybe the first really hot day in awhile. i always hated being cold, and so, blonde curly hair piled atop my adorable head, i am skeptical, as usual. i will only dip my feet in, ok?
    my mom splashes me, tries to get me to relax into the feeling of cool water. "don't you dare!" i keep squealing in laughter. she sprays me with the hose. "don't you dare,

mommy!" she just laughs, and i am thrilled and offended at once. pedro chuckles that little chuckle of his, no doubt far enough from the stream that his camera is not at risk, dedicatedly documenting. she takes a break from provoking me to splash him on the legs. at some point, his camera pans to our cat benny sunbathing, and you hear our voices, laughing in the background.

when i returned home last december, my mother caught me looking at the backyard. "you know, all this could be yours, rachel. i could live downstairs, or i wouldn't even have to live here if you don't want me to."

"you know, all this could be yours, rachel..."

it is her dream, not mine. and yet, like everything else about her dreams for me, somewhere along the way it became difficult to tell the difference. i know it is a trap, her last way to convince me to come home, short of dying. but oh, the idea of my children playing with my husband in that backyard. it makes me ache.

so far, i've managed to let go of that house in small, painful doses. i visit home and someone i've never met sleeps in my room and plays in my sunroom while i share a bed with my mom downstairs.

it's better than its being gone completely, but it humiliates both of us.

my mother thought the persimmon tree had died when she and pedro broke up, but it began to bear fruit again two years ago. that brings me some comfort.

MARIAM KAMATE

YEARS AS MENTEE: 1

GRADE: Junior

HIGH SCHOOL:
A. Philip Randolph
High School

BORN: New York, NY

LIVES: New York, NY

**PUBLICATIONS
AND RECOGNITIONS:**
Scholastic Art & Writing
Award: Silver Key

*First, I wasn't comfortable sharing my work, mostly my po-
ems. I would think they were stupid. But then, I realized in
time that my mentor is there to help. As a former ESL student,
I make a lot of errors or simple mistakes in my work. I love to
write. I don't think my dream to be a writer would have been
possible without Girls Write Now and my mentor's help.*

ELIZABETH DECKER

YEARS AS MENTOR: 1

OCCUPATION:
Ph.D. Candidate, CUNY
Graduate Center

BORN: Boonton, NJ

LIVES: New York, NY

*Mariam and I have spent a lot of time this year thinking
about her poetry. Mariam is a wonderful poet and we continue to work on finding her own voice as an artist and as a
young woman. In doing so, and in developing her skills and
confidence, Mariam has inspired me to find my own voice as
a writer and woman in this world.*

Here's To All
The Girls Like Me

MARIAM KAMATE

*What inspired me to write this poem was that I wanted
everyone like me (anyone who relates to this poem) to feel comfortable
with who they are, because no one is really perfect.*

You like to wear sweatpants all day
You barely wear skinny jeans
Your feet are big
You like burgers and chocolate
You can't believe anyone doesn't

You aren't afraid to take a fall
You don't have lots of friends
But you aren't lonely
You like "me time"
Your phone is your right hand
Your book is your other right hand

You are often called "ugly "
You sometimes are called "not a girl"
Don't worry you are not a girl
You are a super girl
You are golden
You are the star that shines from the sky

You are not a girl because you
Are stronger than you know
You can't let them change you
Because
Then you become new to yourself and unreal to your friends.

She

ELIZABETH DECKER

My mentee Mariam's poetry has inspired me so much over the last few months, and this piece reflects my nascent attempts at poetry to connect with a lost voice in my own life.

She comes to me in dreams, smiling, laughing, the way we used to be.
Red hair but sometimes shorn — like it was in the end. Cruel beauty.
In the dreams, I can feel her laughter...and it feels like our childhood:
    doll families and dreams of real families,
    plays and dances and secrets and truths,
    stay-up-all-night sleepovers,
    growing and sharing and laughing and laughing and laughing.
A perfect friendship? No, because perfection is fantasy.
A life lost too soon, a smile faded too young, a body too weak to go on.
My heart beats on. And she comes to me in dreams.

KIARA KERINA-RENDINA

YEARS AS MENTEE: 3

GRADE: Senior

HIGH SCHOOL:
Frank Sinatra School
of the Arts

BORN: New York, NY

LIVES: New York, NY

**PUBLICATIONS
AND RECOGNITIONS:**
Scholastic Art & Writing
Awards: Gold Key, Silver
Key, and Honorable Mention

Rory and I have spent a great deal of our time together trying out different voices. We have bounced from poet to novelist and back again, trying out styles similarly to how you would try on choices for your next pair of glasses. For the past three years, she has encouraged me to give the world a piece of my mind (and there are quite a few pieces), and she has showed me, through her own work and experiences, that at the end of the day the best voice I could ever have is my own.

RORY SATRAN

YEARS AS MENTOR: 4

OCCUPATION:
US Editorial Director, i-D

BORN: New York, NY

LIVES: Brooklyn, NY

After working with Kiara for three years, I am already feeling nostalgic for our time together. I know that on Sunday mornings I will feel an itch something like phantom limb syndrome, remembering our provocative and enriching hours spent together. I hope that these years will be the beginning of a lifelong friendship.

Flyaways

KIARA KERINA-RENDINA

*This piece was inspired by the pilgrimage I made with my parents
over the summer to Namibia, where I met most of my maternal grandfather's
side of the family for the very first time. It is a collection of thoughts
and realizations I had before, during, and after my journey.*

I.

We are all beginnings whose faces have been reprinted

decades over.

An essence never fades, despite

exposure to the wind and dirt and sun, despite

all the aches and

pains

of an existence.

I, too, want to keep all of my selves close.

II.

I can see the curve of the earth from here,

I am thousands of feet above everything I have ever known.

It's strange that I will never know

if I am moving in the same direction

in which the world spins.

III.

When I step outside I can feel every vertebra uncurl and realign,

it resembles turning the dial

on a combination lock.

I have always found that

foreign places

have both different air,

and a different air,

and when I step into it

I have to learn how to breathe

all over again.

IV.

The quiet suffering of a people

is very loud here.

V.

To be a separate part

of a whole

and yet so close,

that you are standing

right on top of it

is comforting and uncomfortable.

I want to come back to this place

this whole,

because I want to know

exactly what part I play.

Namibia and Naomi Shihab Nye

RORY SATRAN

*Following my discussion with my mentee, Kiara, about
her decision to write an anthology piece about Namibia, I was
inspired to write a reaction to her piece.*

I'll come clean: I googled Namibia after we spoke. Not because I didn't know what it was, but because I didn't know enough.

Your casual knowledge of your ancestors' country was impressive. And terrifying. Over coffee and soft-boiled eggs in the gentle monopoly of Bleecker Street, you told me about the genocide that wiped out the Herero and the Namaqua people in the early 20th century. A German template for the holocaust that I must have learned about at school and embarrassingly forgot the details of.

It's a frequent cliché that a mentor learns more from her mentee than the other way around. Friends, it is true.

I've always wanted to write about mentoring, but have been afraid of falling down a Tuesdays with Morrie spiral. God save us from "An old man, a young man, and life's greatest lesson." In three years of knowing Kiara, we have confronted every dumb mentoring trope, rejected it, surpassed it, worked through it, and come out on the other side, drinking coffee on a Sunday morning. Ugh, Sundays with Rory.

> "...we have confronted every dumb mentoring trope, rejected it, surpassed it..."

You tell me things, I google them, I know more. I tell you things, you google them, you know more. You show me a picture you drew. I give you a book. We discover Naomi Shihab Nye, on YouTube, together. "I loved that," I say. "Me too," you say.

LULJETA KULLA ZENKA

YEARS AS MENTEE: 3

GRADE: Senior

HIGH SCHOOL:
Susan E. Wagner
High School

BORN: Brooklyn, NY

LIVES: Staten Island, NY

**PUBLICATIONS
AND RECOGNITIONS:**
Scholastic Art & Writing
Award: Gold Key

Lizz was, and still is, one of the few people who actually goes out of her way to help me learn and grow. I still remember one of our first meet-ups. We sat down and just talked about writing new genres. All of a sudden, we were writing poetry, memoirs, and pieces we usually would never write. She was always extremely supportive of me and a great listener, and I will never forget that. She's made the Girls Write Now experience unforgettable for me.

LIZZ CARROLL

YEARS AS MENTOR: 3

OCCUPATION:
Community Content Manager, Foundation Center

BORN: Bogotá, Colombia

LIVES: Montclair, NJ

This year, like previous ones, Luljeta has pushed my creativity and quietly dared me to try something new by leading by example. I was never a poet. In fact, I was scared of poetry. This year's exploration of poetry helped me find a voice for a very personal part of my life. I'm looking forward to digging deeper into that through an upcoming series of poems under one theme. I know for sure that I would never have discovered this without Luljeta's influence.

Never Knew Better

LULJETA KULLA ZENKA

This poem is about someone who feels the need to switch into different personas for different people. These types of people never really take a moment for themselves. The feeling of only living for others and keeping your true feelings in is something I feel everyone can relate to.

My name
is a sigh,
all on its own.

From a labored heartbeat,
to a happy screech.

Tell me
what secrets
my eyes hold, and
I might even share some of them.

I don't find anything
of importance
in the scars on my hands,
where healed skin is cracked with
neglect.
You don't notice them at all.

It's been rough,
getting lost and hurt,
and I can assure you that I'm fine,
I've learned to be fine.
Yet, I still am a supporting character in your story.

I believe,
I think,

I'm sure,

I'm okay with that.

I can stop with self-realization,

and I can squeeze myself into the role

of saint, villain, sister, and selfless friend.

At this point, it's almost natural to.

But, it does get weary,

and I wish my shoulders stopped hurting,

I'd think I'd be okay if the pain stopped,

and I can learn to be okay even if it never does.

"Something wrong?" No. Of course not.

"Are you sure?" Hmm?

"I said, are you sure?" Sorry, yeah, just tired.

I've been tired for years,

and I don't know if it's true anymore

or if it's some lie to make myself and others believe,

that any of my weaknesses come from being tired.

Will you tell me what's wrong with me?

I can wait for your answer, I'm patient.

In the meantime, I'll learn a new role,

for someone else.

I try, sometimes, when the few tears I'm able to spare

are gone,

to take hold of the life I have, that I was gifted.

And at the same time, it falls out of my fingers,

and I fall back into the habit of having too strong a hold on

those feelings, those toxic feelings that are too much.

It's a comfort to not confront myself, and it is my fault,

from the beginning to the end. I take full blame.

So live your life, and don't think too much of the person,

who learns new habits for every person they know,

who knows how to switch their role quickly,

who has learned to live almost like a shadow,
happy and content and not fully there.

My heart breaks for every single person but myself.

she was in the cards

LIZZ CARROLL

This poem is about my adoption and how it affected my transition into womanhood and the formation of my cultural identity. Since the emotions are a bit raw, the words and voice are, too. So I'd like to call this a work-in-progress.

I split the deck.
Dante flipped his tarot cards
and furrowed his brow.

"You have a maternal energy
surrounding you...
she's watching over you..."

My thoughts jump to you, a fluttering in my chest
as I consider
the possibility.
Or the impossibility.

Is it you?
Nearly four decades ago, you gave me away.
Perhaps you no longer walk this earth.
Have you decided, at last,
To guide me, to love me, from beyond?

Maybe you've been there all along.

Are you the force that I feel, the pull?
A gut instinct, impossible to ignore.
Never wrong, can't be explained.

Was that you, leading the way?

Could your memory be in my blood?
Déjá vu doesn't explain what I feel.
Am I seeing things through your eyes?

What have you passed on to me?
The weight of my breasts, the curl in my hair, my pink birthmarks.
My square jaw, my tiny hands, my straight teeth.
The sparkle in my dark eyes.
Are those yours?

Mother
Madre
Desconocida
Stranger

I am my mother.
I am my own mother.
I did what you couldn't do.
What I wished you could do.

I surround myself with beautiful, strong women.
Slowly, I create pieces of you,
filling the void you left.

Yet sometimes the joy of sisterhood
is an incomplete replacement
for a connection

with you.

But how can I feel loss for
Something,
Someone,
I never knew?

Soon a needle will prick my back,
branding me with an ancient symbol of
Motherhood.
Creation.
Bachué.

The blood will flow
and the ink will stay.
I explore
what might have been,
what will be.

Pero me voy con una alma abierta y corazón amoroso
And the salve of strength and beauty will heal
the pain of loss
and ache of the unknown.

KIRBY-ESTAR LAGUERRE

YEARS AS MENTEE: 2

GRADE: Junior

HIGH SCHOOL:
Leon M. Goldstein High
School for the Sciences

BORN: New York, NY

LIVES: Brooklyn, NY

**PUBLICATIONS
AND RECOGNITIONS:**
Performed at the United
Nations for International
Day of the Girl celebration

This year, Avra and I would meet at the Hungry Ghost café — where I happened to find what could very well be the best chocolate chip cookie on planet Earth. Along with this discovery, I had another realization: that I am in fact funny, something I never thought I was before. I know this because Avra has laughed through my pieces on more than one occasion. She has helped me transform my experiences — in endless A.P. classes with immature peers, and at ridiculously extravagant 18th birthday parties — into stories. She has also shown me ways to strengthen my poetry, which is my other favorite genre.

AVRA WING

YEARS AS MENTOR: 2

OCCUPATION:
Writer

BORN: New York, NY

LIVES: Brooklyn, NY

**PUBLICATIONS
AND RECOGNITIONS:**
Finalist for the 2014
Housatonic Book Award:
After Isaac

I am in awe of Kirby's ability to juggle a daunting amount of schoolwork — SAT prep, dance classes, social engagements, and community service — and still get all her assignments in for Girls Write Now. On time, too! It is always a pleasure to meet with her and hear her vivid descriptions of the past week. I think Kirby found her voice in writing this year — a voice that is often humorous, but also filled with sharp observations.

Twisted Meanings

KIRBY-ESTAR LAGUERRE

*Vague. Misleading. These words characterize how imprecisely
we communicate with each other. It's important for me to clarify that
I cannot read minds. No one can. It's a pity so many people are unable,
or unwilling, to clearly state what they mean.*

Why don't people ever say what they mean?

When you text me back

Saying that you're "Fine."

Are you really "Fine"?

Because the mascara streaming down your face,

The broken vases on the floor,

And the tears on your shirt,

Seem to tell me that you're not.

You are anything but "Fine."

You ask me to hang out but do you mean

"Hang out" or "Hang Out ;)"?

Cause when half my closet is on the floor,

And I don't know if I should dress modest or slutty,

It's clear I don't know what you mean by hang out.

He says he "loves" you.

But,

Last time I checked,

Slaps to your face,

Nights spent in another woman's bed,

And feeling like the filthy piece of gum at the bottom of his shoe,

Is not love.

You say

"I don't care anymore, John, do whatever you want."

But,

All the eye-rolling,

3 a.m. crying sessions,

The pangs of jealousy

All scream to me how much you care.

And when I write "I'm over it"

I'm so not over it.

Because the obsessive thoughts,

The tossing and turning in my sleep,

My inability to function,

All say otherwise.

Why don't people ever say what they mean?

Why is it so damn hard?

So hard to admit the pain that burns through us.

I Want to Tell My father

AVRA WING

Women have often been discouraged from speaking up.
Joan Rivers, who was sometimes criticized for being vulgar, was an
important liberating voice. My father was a lovely man, but old-fashioned.
I'm glad this generation of women is freer to speak their minds.

Joan Rivers died,

even though he's been dead for 18 years

and didn't like her dirty language.

Why can't she keep it clean?

he complained after her show at Shorehaven

Beach Club in the Bronx, where the women,

to keep their teased, dyed hair from getting wet,

never took a dip in the salt-water pools

but sat outside playing mahjong; the women
with their girdles from Yetta's Corsetry,
who wore housedresses at home to save their clothes,
put plastic slipcovers on their furniture; the women
with their ironed sheets and Bab-O cleanser.
His kind of women.
Not off-color Joan, the one in front
of the microphone, the one holding the crowd,
the one with the mouth.
She's funny, I told him, testing the waters.
You're 12, he said, a baby. You don't
even know what she's talking about.
I didn't, not really — but I wanted to let him know
I got the joke.

JENNIFER LEE

YEARS AS MENTEE: 2

GRADE: Junior

HIGH SCHOOL:
Hunter College High School

BORN: New Haven, CT

LIVES: Queens, NY

My mentor has challenged me to be brave in my writing by being unconditionally supportive of everything I write. By challenging me to be both honest and critical in my work, she has also taught me to be more compassionate towards myself and my own voice, while also being more aware of the voices of those around me. Although perhaps not as evident in this piece, she challenges me to look at the way politics shape my work, and in turn shape the politics of my work into a meaningful expression of my beliefs and experiences.

ALEX BERG

YEARS AS MENTOR: 5

OCCUPATION:
Producer, HuffPost Live

BORN: Philadelphia, PA

LIVES: Brooklyn, NY

Jennifer graciously invites me into her world during our meetings. She has illuminated the notion that we never have to accept the status quo, whether we're writing or navigating other institutions. She has shown that prose can be political and beautiful, and that we can elevate conversations about race, sexuality, and our personal experiences through creative writing.

Happy

JENNIFER LEE

This piece is important to me because it's the first piece I had ever written expressing my desire to speak to somebody — not just to express anger — but to express compassion as well. Right now, my inability to verbalize certain aspects of my existence seems to be a recurring theme in my work; this piece is where that started.

"Mr. N said it was a cop — out," Alex says, "when I told him that you can never really tell whether or not somebody is happy." It's the fifth day of school, and he's telling me about his English class. "He somehow got to the point where he announced that I'm an example of self-reliance — and then added that it meant that I don't really care about anyone."

I don't understand why Alex is telling me this. I want to know why Mr. N chose to ask specifically, Alex, how you can tell whether or not someone is happy. I remember my conversation with Mr. R from earlier in the day:

"Where's your boyfriend?" Mr. R had asked. "You know, the one who ran away from home." I shook my head, pretending I didn't understand.

"I don't have a boyfriend."

"I can't remember his name, but, you know — the one who ran away from home." Mr. R laughed. I didn't. It's been two years since he ran away, but Mr. R pretends to remember him only by the time he left and not by the fact that he's back, that he's here now, and that he has a name: Alex.

Alex left on a Saturday, the day of my sister's seventh birthday, and the day of my second cousin's wedding. Our global term paper was due the coming Monday, and report cards had come out the day before. It was the penultimate stress-fest, the worst school would get before finals week; I wondered if that was why he ran away. I remember that weekend as fear and anger: fear that Alex wouldn't come back home, that I would fail the term paper, and that Alex was right to leave, that there is nothing in the future beyond school and school and school. I remember that weekend as fear and anger: anger that Alex would leave without at least telling me something when just the week before we'd been sharing sketchy pizza on the 1 train, that he had vanished and that I was lonely and that I still had to write a term paper, and that I could see nothing in the future beyond school and school and school.

Alex came back the next day. Mr. R asked Alex why he hadn't called me. Mr. N tried to convince me to talk to a counselor. I wondered what made it so clear to him that I was unhappy, and I wonder how he would answer the question he asked Alex today, the question of how you can tell whether or not somebody is happy. How could he tell whether or not I was happy?

Mr. R is the only one who ever mentioned Alex running away.

I think about what Alex has just said to me: "You can never really tell whether or not somebody is happy." He's not wrong. But why is he telling me this? Is it his way of covertly sending me a message? And if so, what is the message? Is he telling me that he's unhappy, still unhappy, but that nobody is able to tell? Or is he asking me if I'm unhappy? Because either way, I think I've always just thought of him as being unhappy — although whether it's because I project my own dissatisfaction onto others or because I have no more forgotten about him running away than Mr. R has, I may never know.

I do know, however, that I envy him for having been the first to leave. I wonder if he ever really came back. If he's the sort of unhappy who would leave the house with a backpack, surf the subways for a day, and come back home, then I'm the sort of unhappy who wants to leave

> "I do know, however, that I envy him for having been the first to leave."

and never come back but cannot even force myself out the door because I remember how much it hurt to be the one who was left behind. I wonder if he always intended to come back, or if after he left, he realized it is as terrifying to leave as it is to stay. I think forward to the years of pretending I have before me — of pretending to be happy, to respect people I hate, to care about getting good grades to get into a good college to get a good job.

I want to ask if he is unhappy, but I do not want to further the pretense that I do not know. I want to ask why he is unhappy, but neither of us speaks.

The silence between the two of us scratches at my throat.

Dear Madonna:
Gays and African Americans
Are Women, Too

ALEX BERG

*This piece was originally published in The Huffington Post after
Madonna and Patricia Arquette made sweeping generalizations about the
state of women in America, erasing women of color and LGBTQ
identities. This is my voice calling to the voices of other white feminists
like me, because we must do better.*

There's a seat reserved for Madonna next to Patricia Arquette.

Madge may be the high priestess of pop and an arbiter of pop culture, but the songstress proved no expert in intersectional feminism in an interview with *Out* Magazine about her new album, *Rebel Heart*.

In the story published on Tuesday, Madge opined on the state of women's rights and other social movements. "Gay rights are way more advanced than women's rights. People are a lot more open-minded to the gay community than they are to women, period," she told Christopher Glazek. "It's moved along for the gay community, for the African-American community, but women are still just trading on their ass. To me, the last great frontier is women," she added.

The last great frontier *could* be women — our rights over our bodies, safety and income are under assault around the world and across the United States. Except that LGBTQ people, people of color and women aren't three disparate groups.

Madonna's comments are practically lock-step with Arquette's backstage Oscars call-to-action, where she asked "gay people, and all the people of color that we've all fought for to fight for us now." Arquette's speech was a paradigm of the failings of mainstream feminism boiled down into a single sentence: White woman feminist takes credit for entire movement, erases other identities and entitles herself to the support of the LGBTQ community and people of color.

"...a paradigm of the failings of mainstream feminism boiled down into a single sentence..."

So, here's a quick lesson for Madonna, Patricia and others struggling to understand how these identities interact with each other:

1. Gay people are women, too. We often call ourselves "lesbians" or "bisexuals" or just "LGBTQ."

2. Women are also people of color. Sometimes referred to as WOC for short.

3. Now, let me really blow your mind: There are LGBTQ WOC.

Madonna has long been an ardent supporter of the queer community, at times, a cultural appropriator. Her work has made sex-positivity and feminism accessible to a mainstream audience. She is a trailblazer. But, in the wake of events in Ferguson and Staten Island that have brought national attention to the systematic policing and government sanctioned violence against people of color, bills in state legislatures that are seeking to legalize LGBTQ discrimination on the basis of religious beliefs and the climbing number of murdered transgender women in 2015, comparing how things have "moved along" for one identity over another is willfully ignorant. For those of us who count membership to multiple groups, these challenges to our freedom and equality are amplified and complicated by our intersectional identities.

RUMER LeGENDRE

YEARS AS MENTEE: 3

GRADE: Senior

HIGH SCHOOL:
NYC iSchool

BORN: New York, NY

LIVES: New York, NY

SCHOLARSHIPS:
Run For The Future
scholarship, New York
Road Runners Club

**PUBLICATIONS
AND RECOGNITIONS:**
Project1Voice contest
winner

I have been a part of Girls Write Now for three years, and as a senior, this will be my last. During these three years, my mentor has motivated and supported me through difficult classes, new writing pieces, and the college process. We have bonded over books, Broadway shows, memories from our separate pasts, and, of course, the writing that we do. This may be my final year at Girls Write Now, but it is not the end of my friendship with my amazing mentor.

VIVIAN CONAN

YEARS AS MENTOR: 3

OCCUPATION:
Reference Librarian

BORN: New York, NY

LIVES: New York, NY

**PUBLICATIONS
AND RECOGNITIONS:**
New York Times,
Opinionator/Couch column

A constant theme has been the push-pull between Rumer's desire for caution and her wanting to discover more of the world. She has stepped out of her comfort zone with small steps, one leading to the next, until she's quite far from where she was three years ago. I feel privileged that she lets me see the excitement she feels with each venture; it bubbles just beneath the surface she strives to keep so calm. Yes, the three years are over, but our bond is forever. As Rumer starts college, I look forward to hearing about her new experiences.

Why I Run

RUMER LeGENDRE

*This poem came out of the Girls Write Now Persona Poetry Workshop.
When I looked at the prompt asking me to name someone I found
inspirational, I thought of my running coach from the
summer and imagined what she must feel like as a runner.*

I run.

Why?
That's the question I am asked.

Why?
That's the word from the mouths
of people who don't know me.

Why
do I do what I do?
and do I really enjoy it?

Whenever I am asked that,
I think of this:

My feet hit the pavement
one after another
over and over.
I create my own rhythmic pattern.
The way an artist mixes paint colors.
Everything around me blends together.

I enter a world where the population equals
one.
It equals me.

My eyes focus straight ahead,

my shoulders relax.

I never reach a destination

because I am a runner.

So whenever I'm asked Why?

I give two answers,

One silly and one serious, both true.

The first: I run to eat and eat to run.

The second: I run to exist in my own small world.

Voice To Voicemail

VIVIAN CONAN

Sometimes it takes years for voices to hear voices.
I'm grateful that we had the time.

One day, when I was in my fifties and my mother was in her eighties, as the Jewish holidays were approaching, she said, "On Yom Kippur, before you ask God to forgive you, you're supposed to ask the people you wronged. So I'm asking you, Vivian, do you forgive me for all the bad things I did to you when you were growing up?"

Her question took me by surprise. She had sometimes been short-tempered, and we had an on-again, off-again strained relationship when I was growing up, but nothing earth-shattering. Uncomfortable, I brushed her off with, "Yes, I forgive you."

"That doesn't sound like forgiveness," she said.

I gave her a quick hug and repeated, "Yes, I forgive you."

But over the next several years, forgiveness came by itself. It wasn't so much forgiveness as an understanding of the stresses that had shaped her life. I began to see her not only as my mother, but as someone who was a mixture of competence and insecurity, toughness and vulnerability. Someone who had always longed for love and acceptance and human connection.

I realized that when she mailed me flyers about her current life, like programs from the plays she acted in at the senior center, or notices of the poetry group she attended at the library, she was attempting to bring me into her world. One day, to surprise her, I showed up at her senior center and sat in the audience while she played one of the sisters in The House of Bernarda Alba. Afterward, she took me around to all her friends and proudly introduced me.

When my mother was approaching 90, I began helping her manage her accounts. Once a week, we sat at the table in her Brooklyn apartment and went over her bank statements and telephone bills. I looked forward to the feeling of togetherness I had at those times. My mother felt it, also. "It's love at second sight," she said one day. "I'm so lucky." I felt lucky, too.

When we finished our paperwork, we would go out to eat. She always insisted on paying and on giving me a little extra for myself, saying, "It shouldn't cost you anything to visit your mother."

After the restaurant, when I dropped her off at her house and began my drive back to Manhattan, I would see her getting smaller in my rear-view mirror, waving from the doorway at the top of the stoop. Always, when I got home, there would be a message on my answering machine with the words she couldn't say in person. "Vivian, this is your mother. You just left. I hope you have a safe trip home. I had a wonderful time with you. And Vivian, I love you. I-love-you, I-love-you, I-love-you. Bye, bye, Vivian."

> "Vivian, this is your mother. You just left. I hope you have a safe trip home...."

My mother died peacefully in her sleep a month before her ninety-fifth birthday. Now I was the one waving. Bye, bye, Mom. I love you. I hope you have a safe trip home.

XENA LEYCEA BRUNO

YEARS AS MENTEE: 1

GRADE: Junior

HIGH SCHOOL:
NYC iSchool

BORN: Bronx, NY

LIVES: New York, NY

The women I look up to are my mother and sister. Thanks to Girls Write Now, I have been able to meet my mentor Jeanne who inspires me as well. During our weekly meetings, Jeanne constantly challenges me as a writer by dedicating 10 minutes to free writing. Because my workload at school is heavy, most of what I write are essays. Through these free writes, I am also challenged as an individual with a voice. There have been times when I find my work to be silly, but Jeanne challenges me to find my voice and share my experiences.

JEANNE HODESH

YEARS AS MENTOR: 1

OCCUPATION:
Adjunct Lecturer,
Hunter College

BORN: New York, NY

LIVES: Brooklyn, NY

**PUBLICATIONS
AND RECOGNITIONS:**
Publication in *The Hairpin,*
"Summer of Pie" and
"Ballerina Gets the Ball"

When Xena told me she wanted to apply to an introductory class at the International Center of Photography, I was thrilled. Would I help her with the application? Of course — this is the reason I became a mentor. Two weeks later, she got in! She is learning to develop film, use the dark room, and communicate her ideas visually. Xena's use of imagery shows up in her writing, too. It has been a pleasure watching her connect these two forms of expression. Now, during pair sessions, we often look at books of photography before putting our pens to paper.

Green

XENA LEYCEA BRUNO

*Xena searches the Internet for the name of a color she's
never heard of before, then begins to write.*

A distorted green on the pavement of New York streets
Meant to identify the path for those who journey on two wheels
Why green?
Is it to make up for the towering buildings taking place of the nature
that once thrived here?
Or could it be the city streets wishing commuters luck?
Faded at the boundary line as the white protects the path
Green leading the way home.

Shades of White

JEANNE HODESH

*One day last fall, my mentee Xena told me she was working on a series of
poems inspired by the names of colors. It was such an enticing prompt,
I had to try writing one myself.*

Always a clean slate,
Impossible to keep clean,
Does it fade over time,
White?
Is it the absence of color,

Or all the colors at once?
A blank sheet of paper,
A sweater vest,
A napkin,
A tile,
Molding.

From outside,
The quality of the light
Coming from the fixtures is soft,
The placid orbs welcoming us,
Beaconing,
Come in, have a seat, get warm.
In the darkest days of the year
That stretch right before
The winter solstice,
When it's nighttime
Almost all the time,
When the year is about to end,
And all the mistakes
that happened this year
have happened already.
All the new things,
And the things accomplished
Will soon go into a file,
Be put away.
Quickly now,
They'll grow old.

And white,
Does white ever get old, fade?
Maybe next year
We'll paint a new coat.

MUHUA LI

YEARS AS MENTEE: 1

GRADE: Junior

HIGH SCHOOL:
The Flushing International
High School

BORN: Kaifeng, China

LIVES: Queens, NY

What happens if two writing-lovers meet? They will write together and talk about each other's work. What happens if two eating-lovers meet? I think this is a good chance to improve the Global Per Capita Consumed Animal Rate. Alanna and I are like a perfect pair that mixes both of the two characteristics above. During the year, we try new food together, and write after we eat. I believe food is the best thing that can bring two people together. Maybe you can smell the food when you read our pieces!

ALANNA SCHUBACH

YEARS AS MENTOR: 1

OCCUPATION:
Freelance writer
and teacher

BORN: Oceanside, NY

LIVES: Queens, NY

Muhua and I have an experience in common: we both know what it's like to move to a new country and become immersed in unfamiliar customs and languages. I lived in Japan for several years, and she moved here from Henan, China in 2012. But where I felt timid and self-conscious, Muhua is brave, outgoing, and upbeat. She has a great sense of humor, and deep insight into human behavior. She inspires me to be positive and bold in writing and in life. On top of that, she has introduced me to lots of delicious food in her neighborhood, Flushing, Queens.

You Are My Sunshine

MUHUA LI

Most of the kids have a dream lover when they are young.
That is such a pure and precious feeling. If you say you don't have one,
just read this screenplay. The person who comes to your brain
when you read is the Ron or Yimi of your life.

INT. Classroom, the first day of second grade – DAY

The kids all wear school T-shirts, and are talking and playing around before the first period.

YIMI

(Walks into the classroom, wearing a white dress and an ocean-blue backpack)

CLAUS

(Talks with his friends, sees Yimi accidentally, turns back to his friends and talks. Laughs with his friends.)

(Stands up and walks to Yimi, pretends to take off his invisible hat and salutes like a baron)

Hi, my beautiful girl. You are the new student? I am Claus. May I know your name?

YIMI

My name is Yimi.

(She walks past Claus by his left side, and sits down on an empty seat)

RON

(Has kept his eyes on Yimi since she entered, and looks at Yimi's back when she sits down in front of him)

CLAUS

(Walks back to his seat, sees Ron's emotion on his way back. Stands on Ron's right side, and bends toward Ron)

Hey, wake up!

(Snaps his fingers to wake Ron up)

RON

(Pushes Claus away by his arm)

CLAUS

(Moves to Ron's left side behind him)

> Hey, dude, you know her name? Her name is Yimi! You shouldn't look at her like that!

RON

(Talking in a whisper while he is looking at Yimi's back)

> Oh. Her name is Yimi, that is a pretty name.

CLAUS

(Realizes that Ron didn't pay attention to him at all. Claus holds Ron's shoulder and tries to pull his attention back)

> Hey, look at me, Ron!

RON

(Finally looks at Claus)

CLAUS

> Listen, Ron. I, as your friend, I...

(A teacher walks in and interrupts Claus)

MS. TIFFANY

(Walks into the classroom wearing a black suit and black glasses. The classroom becomes quiet right in that moment.)

> Alright, kittles, time for class. The new semester is starting!

CLAUS

(Whispering)

> Oh my god, why do we have this 'devil wears black' in the beginning of this new semester?!

RON

(Turns his eyes back on Yimi's back)

MS. TIFFANY

> Please go back to your seats, take your books out, and turn to page 1.

(Takes out chalk and starts writing on the black board)

CLAUS

(Rolls his eyes at Ms. Tiffany and glares at Ron)

> Let's talk about this later!

(Goes back to his seat)

INT. Classroom – DAY

Ms. Tiffany is teaching in front of the class. Some kids are sleepy, and some are not paying attention.

RON

(Bends over and talks in a whisper to Yimi)

Hi, Yimi! I am Ron, R-O-N, Ron. Welcome to our class!

YIMI

(Ignores Ron)

RON

This period is boring right? Ms. Tiffany is very strict; she is not as funny as Mr. W.

YIMI

(Ignores Ron again, and Ron continues to talk)

RON

Oh, my bad. You don't know who Mr. W is yet. Never mind, he will teach us today. You will like him.

(Ron thinks about Mr. W. The picture in his head is of Mr. W rapping during class and making everyone laugh. Then Ron laughs out loud, slightly, during class.)

(Ron tries to choke back his laughter, and keeps talking to Yimi)

Trust me, Mr. W will be the most awesome teacher you have ever seen!

YIMI

(Takes a slight breath, turns back to Ron and smiles)

RON

(Shocked, like a statue)

YIMI

(Turns back to the front, and raises her hand)

Ms. Tiffany, Ron keeps talking and talking. He is bothering me!

(Ron's seat is switched by Ms. Tiffany)

VOICEOVER OF RON

Then, my seat was switched by Ms. Tiffany. However, ever since I saw Yimi's smile I started trying all the other ways that can show me that smile once again.

MONTAGE:

INT. Classroom -DAY

Ron gives Yimi a nicely-packed gift; Yimi opens it and sees an ugly bug. Yimi screams.

Ron hits Yimi with a baseball, and laughs and runs away.

Ron draws a grimace on Yimi's notebook while she is doing her homework.

Ron pushes Yimi's head down when she is drinking water, getting Yimi's head wet.

Ron hides Yimi's pencil box and watches Yimi while she is looking for her pencil box.

Yimi realizes that Ron took her pencil case, and she smiles when Ron can see her back. Yimi sits down, hides her head with her arms, and cries deadly.

RON

(Becomes worried about Yimi, and walks toward Yimi with her pencil box)

(Squats down on Yimi's left side)

I am sorry, Yimi. I took your pencil box. I didn't mean to make you cry.

YIMI

(Turns her head to the right side)

RON

(Walks to Yimi's right side behind her and squats down)

I am so sorry, Yimi. I thought you would smile at me again like last time. So I did so many crazy things to you. I apologize.

YIMI

(Head up, looks at Ron with tears)

Really? You just want to see my smile?

RON

(Nods his head slightly)

Yes! My lady.

YIMI

(Smiles at Ron)

RON

(Enthralled)

YIMI

(Turns to a mean face quickly. Uses her bottle to hit Ron's head)

Basil

ALANNA SCHUBACH

Muhua's screenplay is a witty look at childhood romance, which prompted me to remember my own experience with young love. This is a glimpse back at a boy I met in elementary school, with whom I shared a connection I'll always remember.

Among my clearest memories of first grade are the long stretches of time in which teachers would force us to rest our heads on our desks and sit that way silently. I don't know if the children in Lindell Elementary School were more unruly and disobedient than other kids, but the adults' responses to us certainly made it seem as though they were barely keeping a lid on chaos. It felt like they made the class sit that way for hours, with the lights dimmed; for wriggly seven-year-olds, it was torture. I remember a teacher once summoning another adult and telling her in wonder that it was quiet enough to literally hear a pin drop, and then one of them located a pin to test the theory. This, to me, was a surreal exercise — I'd never heard the saying before, and couldn't see what we were meant to learn from this — but then, the motivations of grown-ups were often murky.

First grade wasn't entirely bleak. Part way through the year, a new boy joined our classroom. His family had recently emigrated from the USSR, and his name was Vassily, which his parents had Anglicized, bafflingly, as Basil. Basil had round blue eyes and a soft-spoken manner — probably because he was still learning English — but his gentle, bookish presence was exactly, I thought, what our boisterous group needed.

> "...children don't need so many words — they share something elemental..."

Basil and I hit it off immediately, or rather, I informed him we were going to be friends and he nodded in incomprehension. But I must have persuaded him somehow, because I was the only student invited to his birthday party, where we were served something called pie but which turned out to be savory and alarmingly vegetal — it was made from spinach. On another visit to his home, I found the words "I love Alanna" inscribed in chalk on the side of the apartment building. Basil attributed this to friends who had been teasing him, but I was the only friend of his I knew of.

We lived in a seaside town on Long Island, and sometimes we'd meet up on the beach, scrambling over the lifeguards' mountains of sand, climbing their tall, bright orange chairs, while our parents smiled politely, blinking at each other across the gulf between language and culture. But children don't need so many words — they share something elemental, the implicitly felt struggle of being subject to the inscrutable whims of pin-dropping adults, of having little say in their own lives, save for the other children they allow into them.

TAVANA LIGON

YEARS AS MENTEE: 1

GRADE: Senior

HIGH SCHOOL:
The Urban Assembly
School for Law & Justice

BORN: Brooklyn, NY

LIVES: Brooklyn, NY

COLLEGE:
Medgar Evers College

**PUBLICATIONS
AND RECOGNITIONS:**
Girl Scouts Gold Award

Based on our time working together, I can tell Doreen and I are going to have a great time getting to know each other. We're going to have an interesting time learning each other's styles of writing. So far, she has inspired me to find a love for poetry. I never liked writing poetry or even reading it, but now it's becoming a genre of writing I can't wait to continue working on.

DOREEN ST. FELIX

YEARS AS MENTOR: 1

OCCUPATION:
Freelance writer

BORN: Brooklyn, NY

LIVES: Brooklyn, NY

**PUBLICATIONS
AND RECOGNITIONS:**
Graduated with honors
from Brown University;
n+1, the Guardian, and
Pitchfork

Although Tavana and I met recently, we instantly gravitated towards each other's voices. And they are different voices. Where I enjoy fantasy, Tavana prefers realism; while I'm racking my brain searching for effective language, Tavana trusts her keen and writerly instinct. It's been thrilling to watch elements of our separate styles slip into the others' lexicon. Tavana's empathy, her willingness to make her voice an instrument for self-healing and the healing of others through her poetry — that will inform my own voice for years to come.

A Mother's Pain

TAVANA LIGON

*I was inspired to write this piece because of my mother. I watched
her struggle and deal with stress with such strength. I just wanted to
express what I think she might be feeling deep inside.*

I didn't picture my life was going to be like this

I didn't think I'd be 45 without a man raising two children alone, providing for them alone

No one helps me out but yet you still want money

I bust my ass everyday at work making a living to provide for my children but you can't seem to understand that

You really think me and my children got it easy…Why ?

Because you don't see them complaining about not having something?

That's because I taught my children to be strong just like their mother

Their fathers don't do shit for them, it's only me and you and everyone knows that

Deep down inside it gets to my daughters but they are strong

My oldest is going to college in the fall. Did you know she got accepted to her dream college but I can't afford to send her?

Let me guess, you're going to say "it's because you spend all your money spoiling them" No! Wrong! It goes to all the bills I pay, alone.

My kids work hard for what they get!

Do you know how it feels to tell your daughter you don't have the money she needs to get her hair done or the money she needs to buy new school shirts or that you don't have the money to let her go out for her best friend's birthday or that you don't have the money to buy her dream prom dress knowing that she deserves these things knowing that she worked her butt off in school

> "Do you know how it feels to tell your daughter you don't have the money she needs…"

I remember when I needed to pay my rent and you called me saying you messed up your ankle and you wasn't working

Before you asked for money you didn't even check to see how my day was going or how the kids were doing or if I was even at work or if all of my bills were paid

You didn't even care you just cared about what you could get out of me

The fact that you think I have money to just throw around and give out to the needy and greedy really amazes me

I work all day 9 to 5, most of the time 9 to 8

I take all the overtime I can get just to make sure I have enough money so my kids can eat and the bills can be paid

You think it's easy being a single parent working long hours including weekends?

You think it's easy hearing your children complain that they never see you, that when you're home you're not really home

you're asleep

These are the things I hear when I'm at home

The next time you ask me for money or even anything, think about my life and the things I go through

Take my life into consideration for once

Take my children's lives into consideration for once

Put yourself in my shoes

I bet you'll never ask me for anything ever again

A Sunday Occurrence

DOREEN ST. FELIX

I was intrigued by the mosaics of the artist Chris Ofili, and so this poem came. My mentee Tavana has assumed male personas in her poetry, so I decided to take on the voice of an artist-master watching his work shatter.

Every once in a while, and faintly,
There is a shard of glass on my workroom floor
On which I slip as if it were a banana peel,
Or a rotten mango peel, an exoskeleton bearing no nutrient,
The rind of broken art stabs me in the heel of my foot.

Currently, I am in the glass's moment.

I would rather not recall when the mosaic shattered.
I would rather —
Not green or purple or the color of a baby's new sweat,

All the pieces of glass and porcelain mixed on my workroom floor —
Not recall the face of my neighbor when she heard the face of my scream.

She asked what happened.
I told her what happened.
I told her the face of the woman on my canvas broke,
That an almost real woman broke,
That a world of glass broke,
That that world had been peeled
Into the one thousand glass delicacies that made it,
And one slice of the world had sliced my own rind,
My worked and calloused foot.

JANAE LOWE

YEARS AS MENTEE: 2

GRADE: Sophomore

HIGH SCHOOL:
High School of Economics and Finance

BORN: Bronx, NY

LIVES: Bronx, NY

Channing and I get along extremely well. We connect with each other in so many different ways. Channing helps guide me through difficult situations. She is not my first mentor, but I hope she will be there for me for a long time. Within months we have developed a very strong bond, like close friends.

CHANNING HARGROVE

YEARS AS MENTOR: 1

OCCUPATION:
Freelance Fashion Writer and Blogger,
www.channinginthecity.nyc

BORN: Harrisburg, PA

LIVES: New York, NY

I'm learning so much about myself through Janae. It's a privilege to watch her navigate her teenage angst in a way that the blogger in me wishes I could have. I'm excited to see how she continues to write her journey as she finds her voice and I work to grow confidence in mine.

Write.

JANAE LOWE

*I wrote this so that I could help myself realize why I love to write.
Most of the time I think and am often told that I am not a good writer. When
I read my piece I understand why I love writing.*

I like to write because it is a way to express my feelings. When people read my writing, I want them to feel joy and to know who I really am.

People say that I am a funny, happy person but I don't see it. When people read my writing they always laugh. I don't write often but I write to relax my mind. I am a busy person and a lot goes through my mind. I want people to see the breakthrough I have experienced.

> "It felt good to reflect on my writing with the smell of the ink of the pen and the fresh paper."

Overcoming the death of my grandmother was very hard because it took a lot of energy out of me. After she died, I started writing more. It felt good to reflect on my writing with the smell of the ink of the pen and the fresh paper. Using ink and paper relaxes me — it helps me calm down.

It helps me to be able to write what I wish I could tell her so I feel that I can still communicate with her. It also helps me think about the good things that happened between me and her rather than her death. Writing gives me that wonderful feeling that I am creating something beautiful.

Girls Writing

CHANNING HARGROVE

Every voice is important. In the very beginning of our relationship,
my mentee Janae and I explored what value we thought our voices held.

When Janae and I were paired together at the start of the school year, I had already been unemployed for a month. I wondered what I could add to her life. I know that I don't need a title somewhere to be able to, but I wanted to be good at something for her. I hoped she would still be able to learn from me.

Our first session together, we wrote for 10 minutes about why we write. Her answers were poetic. She loves the way ink smells on fresh pages, the way her fingers sound on the keyboard. Mine were desperate. I write because I have yet to see a story that I can identify with as my own. I want to chronicle my experiences.

We both agreed that we write to express ourselves. The good and the bad.

We were just girls writing.

And that was enough.

WINKIE MA

YEARS AS MENTEE: 1

GRADE: Sophomore

HIGH SCHOOL:
Stuyvesant High School

BORN: Brooklyn, NY

LIVES: Brooklyn, NY

**PUBLICATIONS
AND RECOGNITIONS:**
Scholastic Writing Awards:
Gold Key, Honorable
Mention

I've never been open about my writing. All the techniques I picked up came from school sessions and self-studying. However, I learned more in these few months with my mentor Stephanie than I have in most of my life by myself. It is refreshing to get along with someone who has a similar voice and similar ideas. At the same time, I discover more and more about my voice from her advice and experiences. My voice is always reflected in my writing, and who knows how much more it will develop with Stephanie's guidance.

STEPHANIE GOLDEN

YEARS AS MENTOR: 1

OCCUPATION:
Freelance author

BORN: Brooklyn, NY

LIVES: Brooklyn, NY

In both the monthly workshops and my sessions with Winkie, I've been confronting genres new to me. I started out writing fiction, but then became a nonfiction writer for my entire professional career. And I haven't written poetry since I was in high school. Working with someone who gravitates naturally to fiction and poetry has widened my experience, stretching me as a mentor and perhaps as a writer, too. We'll see!

No Cape

WINKIE MA

*The main male figure in my life — the one who was supposed to
protect me and nurture me — only ended up making me feel worse every
day. In this poem, I finally find the courage and the voice to
create a shield for myself. I finally moved on.*

Daddy found one of my weaknesses
on a black sticky note
tucked deep into my back pocket.
He stitched it on his cape,
fleshing out the wrinkles
for the world to see and laugh at.
He found a flaw
engraved in my mirror
He found an insecurity
dangling beside the bed
and weakness after weakness he found them all,
and sewed them onto his cape.
Daddy draped it over his shoulders,
the collected cloth of power
bolstering him
the collected cloth of power
suffocating me
but he had yet to win.
With the thin thread that remained,
and my strengths — which he had not gained — I wove my own cloak,
His Majesty overthrown.
Daddy didn't wear no cape
and so I made my own.

An exercise in attention

STEPHANIE GOLDEN

This piece came out of a character-description exercise my mentee Winkie and I did together. The idea was to do two descriptions, and in the second one write in each other's voice. But our voices weren't that distinct. My big discovery was something else — the impact of paying attention.

Winkie and I sat on a bench at a mall and picked out a man sitting nearby. For 15 minutes, we each wrote as minutely detailed a description of him as we could, then compared our texts. We chose a woman and repeated the exercise.

Our comparisons weren't that interesting, for we had noted pretty much the same items — clothes, details of face, hair, what the woman was carrying, what we thought each person was feeling — and made similar observations. What did strike me was how interested and involved I became in these two quite unremarkable people.

I had felt resistant to this exercise, perhaps because I associated it with fiction, which I haven't tried to write in a long time, although I've done the same type of description in my nonfiction. But it turned out to be intensely engaging. By the time we finished I was dying to know these people. The man appeared Latino, maybe 60, with a poker face; the woman was black, about 40, very well groomed and dressed. She looked tired.

My change in attitude was due purely to the quality of attention forced on me by the exercise. Because of the set, almost grim expression on the man's face I assumed he was bad-tempered. But I kept watching, because I had to, and saw him smile at the antics of a couple of children; his expression changed completely. Suddenly he seemed quite kindly.

We guessed that the woman was waiting for someone (she looked at her watch), but then I thought: maybe this rest on the bench was a respite — time for herself before she had to go home, cook dinner, take care of other people. The more I watched, the more I felt for her, shouldering these obligations after working all day (all totally my fantasy). No one came, and eventually she hoisted her bags and walked off.

> "The more I watched, the more I felt for her, shouldering these obligations after working all day"

So what generated my involvement? Simply: paying attention. There's a famous story about Louis Agassiz, a nineteenth-century Harvard zoology professor who handed each new student a smelly, hideous preserved fish on a tin platter, with instructions to carefully observe it, then disappeared — for hours. One student, Samuel Scudder, was convinced he had seen everything to be seen in that fish after 10 minutes. But after several hours, desperate, he thought of drawing it, "and now with surprise I began to discover new features in the creature." Agassiz's response: "You have not looked very carefully… look again!" With nothing else to do, Scudder began to see still more in the fish. Still Agassiz only kept repeating, "That is good, but that is not all; go on." The misery continued for "three long days." Only later did Scudder realize "the inestimable value" of this lesson in how to observe.

And here was I, feeling pressured by observing for 15 minutes! Yet even this brief exercise transformed my mental state, bringing forth interest, curiosity, empathy. Supposing I had held out for an hour?

RAYHANA MAAROUF

YEARS AS MENTEE: 3

GRADE: Senior

HIGH SCHOOL: Aviation Career & Technical Education High School

BORN: New York, NY

LIVES: Queens, NY

COLLEGE: LIU Pharmacy School

PUBLICATIONS AND RECOGNITIONS: Scholastic Art & Writing Award: Gold Key; *Of Note* magazine

Working with Nancy has opened a new door for me. Not only did I find a person that can help improve my writing, but I found a friend. She has been there for me when times weren't easy and was able to share her advice and, most importantly, listen to me. She has helped me get comfortable with using my humorous voice, a tone that I am in love with.

NANCY HOOPER

YEARS AS MENTOR: 6

OCCUPATION: Freelance writer and teacher

BORN: Minneapolis, MN

LIVES: New York, NY

PUBLICATIONS AND RECOGNITIONS: Contributor of Chef's Log Blog

At the end of one of our pair sessions, when we both felt we had run out of ideas, Rayhana started telling jokes. I can't remember any of the punch lines, but I was completely surprised by hearing her new comedic voice. We did a little brainstorming for "funny story ideas" and within a week, she was churning out humor writing like a pro. Brava, Rayhana! You make it look so easy.

I Have
A Boy Problem

RAYHANA MAAROUF

*Exploring different writing voices this year — serious and humorous —
has helped me to learn more about my own private
inner voice and the beliefs I hold about the world around me*

I'm not allowed to talk to boys. Let me explain. I'm a 17-year-old Muslim girl who was born and raised in New York. My culture and religion dictate that I can't speak to boys unless it is for a serious matter. For me, that is really difficult to do. I go to Aviation High School where it's 85% boys! Trust me, that's a lot of boys. Interacting with guys is a part of my everyday routine. It's something I find to be natural and part of the culture and society that I've adopted from living in New York. That doesn't stop the guilt from eating me up.

Every day I come back from school feeling bad about what I have done. Not only do I have to answer to my parents, but also to my religion. I have tried my best to distance myself from my male classmates but it is

> "That doesn't stop the guilt from eating me up."

extremely difficult to do. I've tried talking to my parents about how I feel but because they grew up in a strict setting that fostered this belief, they don't understand what I'm going through. It isn't like I don't understand my religion. My religion states that interactions between different sexes ends in sin, a statement that I believe to be true. However, the society that I have grown into promotes healthy relationships between males and females. Even at a young age, in school we were taught to sit in a boy-girl-boy-girl pattern. I can always just be the lonely girl who doesn't talk to anyone, but I want to fit in. I want to have friends and engage in my community. I want the best of both worlds. So how do I do right by my religion — and my parents — and still fit into this society? I just don't know what to do.

What You Can Learn While Making Lasagna

NANCY HOOPER

I teach cooking to kids ages seven through 15 at a progressive school in New York. Writing a blog about the kids' culinary adventures every week is a new experience for me, and has helped me discover my inner comedian!

In honor of Friday the 13th, I posted the word PARASKEVIDEKATRIAPHOBIA at the entrance to the kitchen. A mash-up of Greek words, it refers to a little-known phobia, fear of Friday the 13th. When Thanos asked if we were going to watch the slasher movie and began giggling like Jason, I knew it was time to start the Lasagna lesson.

> "...somewhere between browning Italian sausage and boiling big ribbons of pasta, we began to lose focus."

Everything went smoothly for about five minutes. Then, somewhere between browning Italian sausage and boiling big ribbons of pasta, we began to lose focus. Timo started telling jokes — "Two whales walk into a bar . . . ." Ryan cranked up the volume on the Red Hot Chili Peppers. Ouch! My ears! I begged for The Rolling Stones.

Set Flush Left: Then our powers of concentration really took a dive. Askani wondered whether she might be allergic to lettuce. Alfie got a call from the game Red Crucible — it wanted him back upstairs. Thanos blurted out that Beethoven was deaf! Or dead. Or both!

Our conversation was cooking! What are the dangers of BPAs in plastic? Can fennel seeds freshen breath? What's with Mick Jagger looking so old? I hinted at my age, confessing I'd seen Led Zeppelin perform in the 1970s. Ryan told us a little bit about pretzel-making, which he learned in Bonn, Germany, and said he'd heard Bob Dylan sing in Aspen in 2007. Thanos one-upped us all: his uncle has seen The Grateful Dead hundreds of times! Timo finally brought us back to reality — and to food — by saying he was hungry, and wished he had a bite of his dad's "mean" grilled cheese sandwich, slathered with peanut butter! At that, I think Askani perked up.

In the end, our Italian dish took care of itself. Delicious, I'm told. But who cares? In my book, the rare combination of hearty laughter, good chemistry and engaging chatter wins out over lasagna any day of the week!

SHANILLE MARTIN

YEARS AS MENTEE: 2

GRADE: Junior

HIGH SCHOOL:
Academy for Young Writers

BORN: Kingston, Jamaica

LIVES: Brooklyn, NY

Working with Amanda has been absolutely amazing. This is my second year as a mentee, and not only has she helped me grow as a writer, but also as a person. I used to be afraid about sharing certain things and I was always doubting everything I wrote, but she helped me break out of that. Not only does she help me with my writing, she also helps me deal with whatever I'm going through at the moment. Amanda is not only my mentor — an awesome one at that — she's also my friend. Plus, she's super funny.

AMANDA KRUPMAN

YEARS AS MENTOR: 2

OCCUPATION:
Digital Communications Manager, Colin Powell School, The City College of New York

BORN: Cleveland, OH

LIVES: Brooklyn, NY

PUBLICATIONS AND RECOGNITIONS:
xojane.com

Shanille continues to impress me with her commitment to writing and the sheer volume of creative writing she does on top of her demanding academic responsibilities, her part-time job, and helping out at home. It's delightful to watch her grow in our second year working together — as a writer and a young woman. Every day she seems a bit more settled into herself, a bit more willing to show the world her mischievous sense of humor and adventurous nature. I'm lucky to have her in my life.

Whispers

SHANILLE MARTIN

I wrote this piece as a form of exercise to show how I would feel about a certain situation. I tried to put myself as much as I could in my main character. You get to see how the character reacts to her friends and especially her father.

The whispers aren't whispers anymore. They're songs to my ears. That one annoying song that my brain constantly replays in my head. That song that you hear on the radio and you quickly change it, but it's too late. It's already in your head. The whispers aren't really cruel, not all the time, most are pity whispers. The stares are like swords pressing into me every angle I turn. Then there are my best friends, John and Kathleen, who treat me like a glass doll. Touch me and I'll break.

The kids who don't watch the news would ask: "Why's everyone staring at her?"

Then the kids who know everything even if the situation has nothing to do with them say, "Her dad killed her mom. Now he's going to prison and she's all alone. I mean she lives with her aunt and uncle but they're estranged. It's just so sad."

I don't quite know how to react. I mostly just cried for a while. Everyone hates my dad. I should hate my dad. Yet, I don't. A part of me just knows he didn't do it. Or at least hopes he didn't. He had no reason to.

In the newspapers the headline was:

Domestic violence leads to brutal murder.

Mom and Dad never fought. They had mild arguments but they would make up in minutes. To think of Dad doing that to her is impossible. He loves her more than anything. More than me.

"Bella?" John says.

I shoot the alien prancing towards me.

"Sorry," I mumble.

Kat looks at me. "Don't be. You can fade out whenever you want."

I look around John's basement, which is also his bedroom. There are posters with sport cars, '80s rock bands, and half-naked models. The usual boy things. I actually met John down here. Eight years ago, when Dad was in plumbing. John's dad called for him to fix the pipe. The water was coming out a brownish color. Dad brought along eight-year-old me. John was standing nervously behind his dad. We looked at each other and laughed because we were wearing the same Toy Story T-shirt.

"Why don't you kids go upstairs?" John's dad asked. "This might take a while."

John took me up the stairs and into his old room. It was painted sky blue. A game cube sat in front of the square TV, a Mario cartridge strapped into it. We sat there for the time our dads were downstairs and just played. We talked about Buzz Lightyear and Woody. We laughed at the fact that we had both written Andy beneath our favorite sneakers. As if we were toys with souls and wisdom.

"Bella, your aunt texted me, which is weird because I only spoke to the lady once," Kat says, pulling me away from my thoughts.

"And?" I reply.

She rolls her eyes at me. "She said to tell you to come home whenever you're ready. She's there."

I look at John. "Can I sleep over again?"

He nods. "Any time, Bella."

I was trying to avoid Aunt Lacy and Uncle Mason as much as I could. For two reasons, mostly. One reason being that they've lived in the same state as me but chose never to visit or call. Secondly, because Aunt Lacy looks exactly like my mother. I know they're sisters but they look almost identical. Which can't be because they're not twins and Aunt Lacy is two years older than Mom. I just can't stand looking at her. All I see is Mom. Yet, it isn't her.

She's dead.

Someone killed her.

She's gone.

Never coming back.

Castrata Romano (EXCERPT)

AMANDA KRUPMAN

"Castrata Romano" is a story about escape, redefining oneself against family expectations, and finding one's voice, which are themes that begin to emerge in my mentee Shanille's story, "Whispers."

The Adriatic. A mild though pungent soup, a gleaming section of the Mediterranean. The slithering foam is oily lace. Its green-blue body, a clear, reflective gem: a mystic, soaking and swirling. The sea is mind and body, collected and diffused. It hoists from below, spits in your face, pits brain against stomach. Froth and flounder, high and low, salt in your nose and eyes: the sea.

A vicious, mad-dog sun hit Ren's face and shoulders as he swam up for air and blinked saltwater from his eyes. He felt solitary, unbothered; it felt good, though he was not actually alone. Just 50 feet east sat the Castrata Gitano, a contemporary misfit against its backdrop — a part of the world that to Ren seemed to carry the weight of its history heavily. Cranky spirits of century-old expansions, deceptions, and enslavements clotted the bulk of the dotting islands between the peninsulas — thousands of them, small and large, mostly uninhabited — and were dispersed throughout the fishy air.

These observations were neither romantic nor superstitious. The outlandish youth of their watercraft, the outlandish youth of their ideals: Ren and their group, they were floating graffiti.

They were just two days into their inaugural sail from Koper, the Slovenian coastal town that had been their home during the last part of the building phase. About 10 miles off the coast, they were slow-going — somewhat by design, somewhat by circumstance; they went about three knots an hour when pieces of the raft weren't falling into the slurp. And on the first day they'd been on the water less than an hour before an incredulous Italian coast guard in crisp whites and smart caps stalled them another two with inspection, trying to find a reason to send them back to shore. Eventually they had been made to dock, and as marina boatmen — an Eastern-European mix of robust faces and slender bodies, almost cartoonish in their closely related costumes of striped sweaters and corduroys — laughed their cigarettes out of their mouths at the spectacle of the raft's arrival, Larissa and Otto, backs straight and licenses in hand, followed the officers into town to prove their legitimacy.

They knew that would happen. The raft. Its design could be seen, at once, as tree house, carousel, loading dock, and pop-up book. It was a marvel. And Ren, at a distance, could pause and admire their crafty, thrifty handiwork: the simplicity of the pontoons; mast and boom made with driftwood collected off the beach and other pieces pulled from dumpsters late night in unguarded construction sites; and the engine, a Mercedes five-cylinder diesel, attached to a gassifier that Lynn had designed to make their entire trip run on cooking oil. Now she attended to a leak in the block, so they floated, waiting.

CRYSTAL MARTINEZ

YEARS AS MENTEE: 1

GRADE: Junior

HIGH SCHOOL:
Vanguard High School

BORN:
Pembroke Pines, FL

LIVES: New York, NY

**PUBLICATIONS
AND RECOGNITIONS:**
Scholastic Art & Writing
Award: Silver Key

Our weekly meetings help me grow as a writer because I know that before I share my work with anyone, I have someone to proofread it. My mentor helps me feel confident not only in my writing process and what I write about, but in the way I deliver the message when I read out loud. Thanks to the help of my mentor and the Girls Write Now program, I was given the opportunity to submit several pieces of my poetry to the Scholastic Art & Writing Awards and I was honored to be awarded for all three submissions with the second highest award, the Silver Key.

LYNN LURIE

YEARS AS MENTOR: 3

OCCUPATION:
Writer and Attorney

BORN: New York, NY

LIVES: New York, NY

**PUBLICATIONS
AND RECOGNITIONS:**
Quick Kills

Crystal and I write for similar reasons — to make sense of the world, and to communicate with others. Crystal's dedication to her work and her stoic optimism in the face of adversity are inspirational.

Anonymously

CRYSTAL MARTINEZ

I selected "Anonymously" because it was one of the hardest pieces for me to write. The inspiration behind it hits so close to home that I wanted to share this piece to let others know that these things do happen. I wanted to help others to connect with my work and let them know that they are not alone.

Never shown affection which has led her in the wrong direction
allowing her attacker to openly snatch and corrupt her
growing up wondering what about her was a repellent for all those who should have
    loved her but denied her instead

Thoughts swarm in her head about what she should have done instead
growing up being bruised and constantly abused has broken her down into pieces
wanting to move past it and act like it never happened

And at times wanting to give up on life because she couldn't bring herself to allow
    the words to escape her, her body became an expert at holding things in like
    confessionals consumed sins

She lives in the dark never quite given the opportunity to sprout and emerge from
    all the pain she's endured, at times she feels ashamed because to this day she has
    no one to blame but herself

She must have believed she was untouchable
until a man was crazed enough to believe that her childhood was dispensable

She never spoke of having the fear that the man might have been someone she knew
constantly thinking it through, never feeling safe hiding in such a dark a place

And beginning to believe that maybe she deserved it
never shown love so she wonders if she'll ever even be worth it

Love is a mixture of things she has yet to feel and experience and
till the day she dies she'll wonder if she will ever be able to replace it
that horrid encounter with one of love, affection, and patience

Wanting to be loved and yet scared of finding it in the wrong places

she keeps her mouth shut, eyes wide open

heart zipped up tight locked away in a cage full of fear and rage

Trying day by day to release it on a page and or on a stage and yet never quite being
able to walk away from this pain

But trying so hard to relate to those who have struggled with the same thing

and have remained sane by telling their story without naming names

so she has told her story now anonymously

(Untitled)

LYNN LURIE

*I am working on something that looks as if it will be another novel.
So far it seems to grapple with the desire to turn away from
motherhood and marriage.*

For Halloween we have a Peter Pan and an I Dream of Jeannie at the door. My son the polar bear is covered in cornstarch and appears more like a ghost. My daughter is a Chinese doll dressed in a red silk set with rosy round balls for cheeks. After the screen door slams on my son's face giving him a bloody nose, he says, I hate Halloween.

> "I am sorry I forced you to pretend. But childhood is practicing at pretend."

Me too, I say. I am sorry I forced you to pretend. But childhood is practicing at pretend. It is preparation for adulthood.

They are slumped on the floor in front of the door waiting for the next group. The plastic pumpkin holding their candy is the one I used when I was a kid. It is the only thing I have brought from my childhood.

KARINA MARTINEZ

YEARS AS MENTEE: 2

GRADE: Sophomore

HIGH SCHOOL:
The Bronx High School
of Science

BORN: New York, NY

LIVES: Bronx, NY

**PUBLICATIONS
AND RECOGNITIONS:**
Scholastic Art & Writing
Awards: Silver Key and
Honorable Mention

Danielle helped bring out parts of me that I didn't even know were there. With new prompts every week, the observing of people at Grand Central Terminal, and the occasional Shake Shack burger, I can tell that Danielle and I are going to have a fun and creative year together at Girls Write Now. Hopefully, we'll have more to come.

DANIELLE SCHLANGER

YEARS AS MENTOR: 1

OCCUPATION:
Journalist, New York
Observer

BORN: New York, NY

LIVES: New York, NY

I was immediately impressed with Karina's grace and writing acumen. She wrote about topics that even the most sophisticated writers struggle to articulate well, and did so effortlessly. She is very introspective and creative, which manifests in her work, and I know she has a bright future ahead.

Rush Hour

BY KARINA MARTINEZ

As I stared from high above at the sea of moving people, I couldn't help but notice how beautiful it all was. This poem is a result of a prompt given to me by my mentor Danielle while we were at Grand Central Terminal looking down at the crowd.

The faint smell of cigarette smoke rubs off coats as people brush past one another, not bothering to say a sorry or cast a smile on the person they just shoved. One would think the other people would be offended just having been shoved, but they know what it's like to be in a rush. After all, they're New Yorkers. They've all had to get somewhere quickly, time no longer on their side.

If only they knew how small they looked from above, moving like the well-oiled gears of a brand-new machine. You would think it was planned, that God was looking down at them and smiling at the masterpiece of whipping scarves and clicking heels. He no longer finds pleasure in watching snow fall.

Or maybe he enjoys the fact that the people moving quickly with their heads down and shoulders up all know where they have to be. With no map in hand they travel somewhere familiar or maybe somewhere unknown. Either way they all knew where they are going, and they're okay with where they end up.

It's actions like these that keep God from intervening on life. To Him everything goes quick, like a cartoon moving at the end of turning pages. He wants to know how it all works, how one decision of His resulted in so much, but even His head hurts at the thought of it. So instead of pondering existence, God looks down once more, His eyes admiring the clockwork, thinking how beautiful it would be if everyone in the world were a star.

Around the Turn of April

DANIELLE SCHLANGER

*With spring around the corner, I wrote this poem. It's not only about leaving
this particularly cold, dark winter behind, but also leaving
behind past struggles and more challenging days. Hope springs eternal.*

When the weather drips of April
Flower-boxes overflowing with those daffodils of renewal
(Daffodils speaking foreign dialects, a lighter, unfamiliar song)
The winter we didn't, I didn't, think was survivable
Has melted away.

Tears flow unrestrained
Another season of rebirth says the Hagaddah
Dayenu, it would have been enough to let us escape from Egypt
Free from the shackles of suffering
Of sickness, of hopelessness.

But to be able to enjoy this beautiful city, this beautiful life
Day in and day out for eternity?
It is a fortune brighter
than even the most radiant
spring afternoon.

KAMILAH MAXWELL-BOWDEN

YEARS AS MENTEE: 1

GRADE: Sophomore

HIGH SCHOOL:
Vanguard High School

BORN: New York, NY

LIVES: Brooklyn, NY

**PUBLICATIONS
AND RECOGNITIONS:**
Scholastic Art & Writing
Award: Honorable Mention

This is my first time having a mentor so that alone is a new experience to me. Meeting her made me realize that there are so many people in the world I can connect to or who share my interest. Getting to know her has been fun. It has been great to be able to pitch my ideas to her and have her help with my writing and have her there as a friend. I never thought I could have an adult friend let alone one who is a role model. These past few months have been the best.

ERICA MOROZ

YEARS AS MENTOR: 1

OCCUPATION:
Editor and Doula

BORN: New York, NY

LIVES: Brooklyn, NY

Kamilah leads many different lives inside her novels and poems. She has written in the voices of witches, enchantresses, goddesses, and even creepy brotherhood leaders. She transports her readers to magical worlds, cities, gardens of her own invention. Her fearless storytelling has inspired me to develop my imagination. I feel profoundly lucky to know her, and to be friends and creative comrades.

Caster,
Chapter One Excerpt

KAMILAH MAXWELL-BOWDEN

This is an excerpt from Chapter One of my novel Caster.
*We meet Cordelia and Nora, sisters who are secretly witches in
a society ruled by "The Brothers."*

I sit on my old swing that Father made for me when I was six, hanging from a low
enough limb of the long dead maple tree on the hill that gives a clear view of the
cemetery, the orchards, and the pond. Nora is planting bulbs around the graves, daffodils, lilies, and crocuses. Sweet things for sweet gestures. As the lady of the house
I should make her stop; as her sister I should make her the head gardener — she'd
love that — but instead I just let her do what she wants.
The gardeners know not to mess with her parts of the

> "...she's holding on to
> the gardens
> as a way of holding
> on to Mother."

grounds. She's 12, the youngest girl, and she's holding on
to the gardens as a way of holding on to Mother. In two
months it'll be a year that she's gone, but I don't think
we'll ever stop mourning, ever stop missing her. It's hard
not to miss her, not to look for her, because she's everywhere and yet not here at all.
She is in the gardens pruning her roses, in the kitchen supervising meals, in the parlor
holding teas, in the library reading books. But that's really only her essence, because
really she's in a box in the cemetery, six feet under surrounded by soil.

That's the one place I can't find her though, in the cemetery, because it's hard to
think of her surrounded by so much dead when she should be alive, alive and cheerful
and chasing Caleb around the house, giving us lessons. Both magic and academic,
since we can't go to school. But she's not because she's dead and in the ground, even
though she led us to believe that nothing put in the ground should be dead. That's
why I tried to convince Father to have her cremated but he wanted her buried, and
so did she, she wanted to return to the earth from which she came. The most morbid
yet philosophical thing I've heard from her, even if it was only in words in her "will,"
because how can she have a will if she's not allowed to own anything, another one of
the Brothers' stupid rules.

Sighing, I watch Nora's figure working busily as she hums a silly, made-up song
and start to push myself on the swing, hoping the old thing can last. It has to last. It
was made for me, and I used to push a four-year-old Jess on it as she squealed to go

higher, and then a three-year-old Nora when Mother gave the okay that it was safe and I'd made her promise to hold on tight. It has to last now for Caleb, who might someday be well enough to play outside. It just has to. I don't go that high, don't push that hard, because the thought of pumping my thin legs beneath the heavy skirts now, when I'm 17 and have to keep face — though it's impossible to see inside the grounds over the wall — is just too much. I'd seem silly, even to myself. With that thought in mind I pull my hair clips out and undo the braid. Bright ginger curls, proof I share Father's DNA, spill down my back and over my shoulders. Tilting my head back I stare at the sky and give a gentle push off the ground with my slippered feet so I swing back. This part of the sky is over a tangle of angry dead branches that will never light up with green or brilliant red leaves again. Then there's just blue and a few wispy white clouds as I go forward.

Swinging slowly I start to hum and think about all the things I have to worry about this week because it is Sunday afternoon. Sundays are not the best days, they are fearful ones for witches, especially young ones without a mentor. But we don't use magic in church, and we wouldn't use magic at all if we could help it, but we can't help it because we are witches. Magic is in our blood. This week I'll do the usual four o'clock magic lessons, more practice than lessons though. Tuesday at noon, Jess and I will have a tea with all the respectable girls our age, then on Thursday we'll go to tea at Mrs. Suzuki's. Jess and I will probably have a fight, but we always fight. I am 17, my birthday is six months from now, six months until I have to decide my intentions to marry or join a covenant, doing neither would put me under suspicion, and that would be bad not just for me but for my sisters. But I have six months to decide, six months can be a very long time. I swing, and join Nora in her song about spring.

Ballad of Baba Yaga

ERICA MOROZ

Baba Yaga is a supernatural character from Slavic folklore who is traditionally depicted as wicked and sneaky. I think of her as actually being proud, powerful, and misunderstood, like many of us women.
I'm inspired by my mentee Kamilah's stories about magical women and beings; reading her work is partially what drew me to Baba Yaga.

once I was a small girl
now I am a crone

rummaging round

safe and sound

doling out folklore

once I was a lie-spinner

now I sleep on the floor

children in line

rosy and fine

leaving dimes by my door

once I was an apologist

now I am a stoic

gentlemen appease

on hands and knees

hearts laid on the floor

once I was a joiner

now I am no more

saps of pine

needle and twine

sweeping up's a chore

now I wear this wimple

outside rattlesnakes roar

back and forth

light the torch

palms up, ready for gore

MUSE McCORMACK

YEARS AS MENTEE: 1

GRADE: Junior

HIGH SCHOOL:
Essex Street Academy

BORN: Brooklyn, NY

LIVES: Brooklyn, NY

**PUBLICATIONS
AND RECOGNITIONS:**
Scholastic Art & Writing
Award: Silver Key

When I first met Lia, I knew I liked poetry, but that was it. I had never really read any, and what I had read, I didn't love. I didn't even know why I wrote it, it was just what came most naturally to me. Through Lia, not only have I cultivated my writing skills, but I have also expanded what I like to read. Lia showed me poetry that I love, which wasn't published 200 years ago by old guys. Now I know more about the genre I love, and why I love it, thanks to Lia.

LIA GREENWELL

YEARS AS MENTOR: 1

OCCUPATION:
Manager, Campbell Cheese
& Grocery

BORN: Adrian, MI

LIVES: New York, NY

**PUBLICATIONS
AND RECOGNITIONS:**
*Painted Bride Quarterly;
Poecology; Witness;
Cumberland River Review;
Flyway: Journal of Writing
and Environment; Yew: A
Journal of Innovative Writing & Images by Women*

What has astonished me about Muse from the very beginning is her boldness and authenticity. In her life and in her writing, she is not afraid to speak up and out. Muse loves fantasy and imaginative writing, and she keeps her imagination open and active in her daily life. Where someone might see a dreary subway commute, Muse sees character and intrigue. Keep open to possibility, that is what I've learned from Muse. Her ambition — writing a novel in a month, or an epic poem — has been inspiring for my own commitment to writing.

Silly Girls

MUSE McCORMACK

My memories heavily influence my voice, and while my life is not some evocative painting by Vincent Van Gogh, that is how I like to perceive and remember it. When I write, I like to dip my pen into my brain and see what colors come out onto the page.

As you run through fireworks,

colors whirl around you

like burning coins falling

from the sky

waiting to be caught.

The sounds become almost

tangible.

The laughter

is silk on your skin.

It almost makes you forget the fall wind.

You twirl,

first this way, and then

that.

Hair intertwining with hair

as we leap

like deer in a forest

of flames.

You are blind,

eyes glazed over with purple smoke,

blind to anything

but the sky.

Eyes

becoming pools,

you dip your hand in
to stir the still waters of the stars.
Sparks fall around you.

It's started to rain.
As you go inside,
you can still see yourself:
a shadow dancing on the coals
left in the September grass.
You have forgotten the pain,
despite the small round burns you have
on your hands
to remind you of this night.
You shake your head from the vision of it.

————————

My aunts coo
over my burned hands.
Once I say I'm fine,
they mutter disapprovingly
at my silliness.
My hands heal,
but silver scars remain.
And I trace them
like constellations.
I collect scars now,
each one
a new story,
a new romance,
a new star.

She Speaks

LIA GREENWELL

*All winter I had seen a woman sleeping under scaffolding in my
neighborhood. In the Girls Write Now Persona Poetry Workshop,
I imagined a moment through her eyes.*

The man rounds the corner and steps
on my sleeping bag a little.

I understand how I fade into things,
how the night absorbs me, layered in my coat,
in a sleeping bag, in a black garbage bag
that seals in the heat.

Heat is a memory. The heat of the day leaves me
slowly, as I left my other life. At first,

a drink, a night out from the children,
a new man, a new way to be,
and then the first time I tried it

and lit all my circuits on fire.
A train ride to the city, years,
and years later, and here I am

in January like something untamed
in a torn coat.

I see how you look at me, frightened
as I look back, alive,
still inside.

LAUREN MELENDEZ

YEARS AS MENTEE: 2

GRADE: Junior

HIGH SCHOOL:
Marta Valle High School

BORN: New York, NY

LIVES: Brooklyn, NY

This is my second year at Girls Write Now with a different mentor. Working with my new mentor Terry has been a great experience. Working on "Rewind" with her has been great. I'm learning many things. We meet at a library in Brooklyn, grab something to snack on, something to drink, and it always makes my Monday. She has inspired me to try new things. I love learning new things about her (like our shared love for pizza). Terry has taught me that it is okay to step out of your comfort zone, to write something different, and how to defeat writer's block.

TERRY VANDUYN

YEARS AS MENTOR: 1

OCCUPATION:
Software Product
Manager, Everyday Health

BORN: Cortland, NY

LIVES: Brooklyn, NY

Meeting with Lauren is one of the highlights of my week. At our first meeting, Lauren told me that she wanted to write a science-fiction novel. It's been a lot of fun exploring a new genre and trying new things together. One of my favorite things about Lauren is her sense of humor, which comes across in her writing. We shared a lot of laughs over her "Bagel's Big Adventure" and my "Pizza Sestina." I look forward to more Monday's together and can't wait for our visit to Edgar Allen Poe's home.

Rewind

LAUREN MELENDEZ

This piece is an excerpt from a novel called Rewind *that I have been working on with my mentor. I wanted to write something totally new, something I haven't written before: science fiction.*

As the alarm goes off, Roxane jumps out of bed and throws on her clothes. She runs downstairs to eat breakfast and starts looking in the fridge.

"Where is the milk?" she screams.

Her dad comes downstairs. "Check in the back of fridge."

Roxane looks, but there is no milk. "It's not here. I thought you guys went shopping yesterday," she says.

Her father is walking back and forth. "We did go yesterday. That's weird."

"I'm going to the coffee shop," Roxane says as she walks out the door. She reaches the coffee shop and sees her best friend, Adam.

"I know I left you alone at school yesterday, but I'll make it up to you," Adam says as Roxane sits across from him. "I know you're crazy about the new drink on the menu. Sugar cookie latte?"

Roxane nods.

Adam looks at the menu, but he can't find it. "Hey, I think they stopped making it," Adam says.

"That's impossible, they just added it to the menu," Roxane exclaims.

"Sorry hun, it's not here. There are other things to pick from."

She looks back down at her menu. "A caramel latte sounds fine."

Adam goes up to the counter and orders. They take their lattes to go and start walking to school. On the way, Roxane excitedly tells Adam how amazing the new lockers are.

Adam and Roxane open the front door to the school and Adam looks around the empty hall. "Oh wow!"

Roxane is in a state of shock. "They were here yesterday. Why are the lockers gone?" She grabs Adam's hand and marches down to the Dean's office. With all her strength, she kicks down the door. As small pieces of glass and dust fly around the room, the Dean continues to read his book.

Without looking up, he says, "You're here today early, Ms. Roxane."

She stomps towards his desk shouting, "Where are the lockers, Mr. Lector?"

He looks up at her with a confused look and asks, "Lockers? What lockers?" Roxane's eyes turn blood red.

"Stop trying to make me look crazy!"

"We didn't have enough money in the school budget to get lockers," Mr. Lector says. Adam steps in with a concerned look.

"But just last week you were excited about getting new lockers for the students," Adam says.

Mr. Lector steps away from his desk and looks at both of them. "We don't have the money for new lockers. But you should pray that you have enough money to pay for a new door. That's detention for you, Roxane. Now get out!"

Roxane pulls Adam out of his office. She sees that the new teacher, Rupert, is watching everything that's just happened.

She marches towards him and yells, "What did you do?" He looks down at her.

"All I asked you to do was to follow my commands and to sign the contract. Lessons will be learned." He pats her on the head and walks away. Roxane punches a hole in the wall where the lockers used to be.

―――――

At the end of the day, Roxane walks to detention hall. Rupert is waiting for her outside the door.

"Please, after you," he says as he leads her inside. Once they are seated, Rupert breaks the silence.

"So about our deal, I should explain."

She looks up at him and sits up in her seat while her eyes turn blue. Rupert gets up from the desk and sits next to Roxane.

"You have a chip in your brain that can control the world, you know, kinda like a dictator. I know you're not evil because your parents would never program you that way. But if I get my hands on it, we can dispose of it and everything can be balanced. Then you'll be human again."

"...and everything can be balanced. Then you'll be human again."

Roxane scans Rupert and her analysis says he is lying. She finds something called a bad bone, which is there when a person is more evil than good. "I do admit that being a robot has it perks, but how do I know you won't double cross me?"

He pulls out the contract. "Sign on the dotted line and we have a deal," he says.

She notices he's dodged her question. She asks, "You said there were consequences. What are the consequences?"

He looks her in the eyes. "As time moves forward, things move back, so cherish what you have now. You'll never know when it will disappear."

He gets up, grabs his stuff and leaves the contract with her. "I'm gonna go home, you're free to go. Keep the contract and think about it."

Rupert leaves and Roxane sinks into her seat while her eyes turn a light gray.

The Breakthrough

TERRY VANDUYN

*My mentee Lauren and I have spent hours brainstorming, discussing,
and writing about Roxane. I love Lauren's
story about her and it inspired me to write a prequel.*

Roxane sat on an old dining room chair in the family basement. As a ploy to get her father home for dinner more often, her mother had at some point agreed to convert half of the basement into a laboratory. Roxane could often be found sitting on this chair while her father worked in his laboratory.

Her father stood in front of his stainless steel work bench, its shine dulled from constant use. This problem irked him. He had been working on it for several months, but lacked a breakthrough. This particular Friday afternoon was darkened by the rain and the occasional ominous rumbling of thunder. It was a perfect time to stay in and finally solve the hanging question.

An hour before, her father had a new idea that he thought just might work. He worked intently with a growing excitement, surrounded by electrodes, wires, and tubing. His pace quickened and a quiet whirring began. A small, bright fireball materialized from nowhere while the whirring grew louder, then almost deafening. Before they knew what was happening, the fireball shot across the room and hit Roxane in the chest.

Her father watched in horror as Roxane contorted. Her body moved in a strange, haunting dance. When it was over, she slumped forward in that old dining room chair. Her father ran to her, panic in his eyes, and started to call to her. Roxane's heartbeat was faint, her breathing slow and quiet. He held her for several minutes, silently praying to anyone that would listen.

> "After a seeming eternity, Roxane suddenly gasped and opened her eyes wide."

After a seeming eternity, Roxane suddenly gasped and opened her eyes wide. Her father broke into a deep sob as Roxane came to.

"I thought I lost you," he whispered. Roxane said nothing and looked up at him. He saw her eyes, they were ... different. They had changed from her usual shade of blue to a rainy, dull gray.

He felt an ache deep in his stomach, and realized he had lost at least part of her.

JULIA MERCADO

YEARS AS MENTEE: 2

GRADE: Junior

HIGH SCHOOL:
Manhattan Village Academy

BORN: Brooklyn, NY

LIVES: Queens, NY

Lauren told me we would make a great pair from the beginning. When we sit across from each other in the bakery we've come to love so much, the ideas flow. My voice is never suppressed when we talk and write. With Lauren, I have found out more about myself than I would ever believe. I go home from our meetings smiling because I have gained more of a passion for writing than I had before. I guess that's just our connection, and why my dad deemed Lauren the "Soul Mentor."

LAUREN HESSE

YEARS AS MENTOR: 2

OCCUPATION:
Assistant Manager of
Digital Marketing,
Doubleday

BORN: Albany, NY

LIVES: Brooklyn, NY

One night I approached Rudy's, our favorite bakery in Ridgewood. My mentee was on the phone and giggled, "Yes Dad, I've got to go!" As we settled in to share some cheesecake I asked her what she was laughing about and she explained that her dad asked if she was with her "Soul Mentor." I had to fight back my wild smile. Working with Julia has been an honor; she works hard, is interested in trying new things and loves editing (I call her my dream mentee). I'm so pleased with the risks that Julia has taken and how hard she has worked to develop her voice.

Dear You

JULIA MERCADO

My mom pulled out a former "insecurity sweater" and seeing it brought back some bad memories. Going into myself, I realized I had to talk to the girl who used to wear that sweater. "Dear You" is just my spin on writing in another voice.

Dear You,

You are the one who never washed your hair, wore the same sweater everyday and smiled wide with blue braces. You are the one that bad days are based on. I feel we need to talk and now's the chance.

I know you. I know every detail about you, from your crazy obsessions to your favorite shade of blue. From Julia to Julia, from silent to outspoken.

I never wanted to write to you. I never knew how because it's near impossible to talk to the ghosts that haunt you at night. The ghosts that make me get up out of sleep and write are the ones that affect me the most.

This letter makes me feel like I'm back at my therapist's office and she's having me analyze my life. She asked me to draw my family once.

The mother, the father, and you were drawn. Having no artistic abilities, I was ashamed to show my work to my therapist. I smiled a small smile and she frowned. Immediately, there was something wrong.

"What happened to the ears?" she asked. "Does no one listen to you?"

Not one person on the paper had ears.

I had often told her I had issues trying to get people to listen to me. I didn't think it would affect my drawing. I never think about ears when looking at people. Ears tend to be invisible if I'm not looking at them directly. As a therapist she made me think about it more.

I didn't want to think about it more. I didn't want to have to think about times where I was you. That blue sweater is long gone from my closet but not far off in my memory. It reminds me of times when ears and voices were hard to see and hear.

I remember having nightmares where I couldn't speak to save my life. I could feel myself scream and no sound would come out. I always wondered what that meant to me and it dawned on me; I never speak up.

Throughout my younger years, I stayed quiet and let things play out, but I remember times before you where I didn't do that. My "friends" made fun of a class-mate all the time. I stayed with them to look cool, that way they wouldn't make fun of me. It was the only way to stay safe from humiliation in that class. It wasn't fair that I did this when she was always being humiliated.

They viewed Tiffany as this monster who always had a limp and a school aide with her. It was horrible. Their faces turned red with laughter every time she would walk to throw out her trash with her aide. They pretended to be her and stare into the air with blank faces.

"I think there's something wrong with her brain, She's always staring into space," they would say.

One day, they were laughing so much that spit from their mouths landed all over me; I had to get up to move. I feel like that was the best thing I had ever done in my life.

"I don't want to be over there," were the words that sparked a major turning point in your life. I still remember the look of confusion on her face when I said that. Neither of us knew what effect this moment would have on us.

According to you, the only thing I'm good at is being awkward. Tiffany always sees the opposite in me. She believes in me.

Even when I was you, she was there for me. She saw the beauty past the insecurity and the mute voice. Tiffany knew I was better than you, the one cocooned in awkwardness. I had lost my spunk for a while, but somehow Tiffany knew it would come back. She remembered the girl who did her own thing instead of letting people walk all over her.

> "She saw the beauty past the insecurity and the mute voice."

You are the part of me that is afraid to speak up. You let people say what they wanted to say about you. You believed their rash thoughts about you. I do not want to be you anymore. I still do not speak up and then I realize my day could have been better if I told at least one person how I truly felt.

Believing in yourself is hard because everyone around you is judgmental. Who cares? Only you should care about what YOU do and what YOU say. People want to hear you, so speak loud and clear.

Whenever that past girl haunts you in your dreams, I want you to crack open this letter and read it again: out loud, in your head, or in song, until you absolutely get tired of what is in here and the message has finally gotten through. I would wish you luck in believing yourself, but that's already beginning. You're making yourself be heard in this moment, Little Miss. Keep going.

Yours Truly,

You (with a voice)

Dear Me

LAUREN HESSE

*From a young age, I always wondered what life would be like
in my mid-20s, and I love how my mentee Julia works to find her voice by
writing back to herself. When she decided to write "Dear You,"
I knew I wanted to follow her lead.*

Dear Little One,

I know that right now you want to tell people that you're going to be working at *The New York Times* and living on Fifth Avenue and you'll have a chocolate lab, but I need you to know that none of this will happen by the time you're 25.

You won't study journalism and you'll learn that the New York neighborhoods you saw when you were young house more tourist attractions than homes and I'm pretty sure there isn't an apartment large enough for a Labrador on the island of Manhattan.

I know you worry a lot about the future and that your journals are filled with questions.

You're going to doubt yourself in the coming years. Sometimes when you speak up in class, you'll worry that you're 'out-of-line' or that your opinion isn't validated by expertise or experience or research. Guess what? Sometimes you're going to be really, really wrong. You'll take a seminar in college and will completely miss the point of an assigned reading and the professor will kindly correct you in front of 15 peers. You'll think that your face will never stop burning and you'll feel like the first person to ever speak up and make a mistake.

> "I know you worry a lot about the future and that your journals are filled with questions."

You'll decide you like a book and then you'll realize you don't. You'll vote for Hillary Clinton in the 2008 primary but then take a bus to Pittsburgh to work on Obama's campaign that fall. You'll love a really catchy rap song and then you'll listen to the lyrics and change your mind after your Psychology of Women class.

You'll spend hours flip-flopping with girlfriends: Did that movie speak to you? Do you agree with that restaurant review? Do you even like kale? You'll write papers on identity that you'll look back on it and think "I don't feel like that's who I am." You'll express things quickly and excitedly but as you grow up, your instant voice might feel instantly wrong.

The most important thing to know is this is how you learn. Maybe you'll be "wrong" or you'll change your mind next week, but by saying it or writing it or sharing it, you're starting conversations that will help you. You're going to figure out how you feel by talking and listening and reading and writing.

Also, I don't want to ruin any surprises, but it might comfort you to know that you'll wind up working with books that you love reading and living in a neighborhood that has far better street art than any window display on Fifth Avenue, and you'll have a black cat who drives you crazy and isn't a dog but is really sweet when he wants to be, promise.

Love,

Older One

MARQUISELE MERCEDES

YEARS AS MENTEE: 2

GRADE: Senior

HIGH SCHOOL:
DeWitt Clinton High School

BORN: New York, NY

LIVES: Bronx, NY

COLLEGE:
Hunter College

**PUBLICATIONS
AND RECOGNITIONS:**
Scholastic Art & Writing
Awards: Silver Key and
Honorable Mention; *YC Teen
Student Writer; Teen Ink*

It is almost laughable how comfortable my mentor and I have gotten. There are designated sides of tables and preferred drinks. We have become accustomed to the calm lighting and to the pretty tinkling of ambient background music. Words are second nature and hover around us like the aroma of melting butter we smell while we follow up on the characters in our lives and string stories together like pearls. We do not restrain each other, so there is no hiding. Only real emotion and collaboration at its finest.

JUDITH ROLAND

YEARS AS MENTOR: 3

OCCUPATION:
President, Roland
Communications

BORN: Oceanside, NY

LIVES: New York, NY

Mikey and I know that we can be heard well above the din of the crepe place where we meet. But we don't care. We quickly catch up on the week's events, triumphs and disappointments, and our latest project. We discuss the big stuff — dreams, challenges, successes — and the small, but still important stuff — shoe sales, makeup, and music. Our writing strengthens our bond. Mikey bravely and eloquently shares her experience with me, encouraging me to do the same. We listen intently to each other's voices and marvel at how two people from such vastly different backgrounds can sync and harmonize so beautifully!

Life in Odd Numbers

MARQUISELE MERCEDES

For someone who is never alone, I tend to get caught up in feeling lonely too often. This piece is a reminder of the amazing people I have by my side.

(Three)

The hours on a bus from Albany to the City. It is twenty-one dollars for a ticket, not including the train ride uptown into spray-painted subway signs and late-night service delays. Your sister rolls her black duffle bag through the melted snow on the cracked pavement, ignoring the guys who stand at the corner of Gun Hill Road and Burke Avenue. There is one there who proclaims his love on a regular basis — both directly and indirectly. Yet, she has no time. Franderis moves too fast for his feet and his mind, leaving him to choke on her icy dust. So does she. The cold air constricts her asthmatic airways and makes her wheeze. When she arrives at one in the morning — brown cheeks stained with pink, black hair plastered to her sweaty forehead — she kicks the front door with her boots.

(Five)

The number of twenty dollar bills your mom spares to gift you on your birthday. They are in separate envelopes; the silver and black striped enclosures are embedded with generic phrases like "it's your special day" with too many exclamation points. Her fine, brown fingers cradle the sides of your head and your bashful "thank you" is lost to the sound of her smacking kisses on your

> "...embedded with generic phrases like "it's your special day" with too many exclamation points."

frizzy hair. The custom-made ice cream cake is at the center of the table in front of you, butchered by a hot knife, oozing dulce de leche. It lays beside a present you have yet to open. You wonder in dread how much it cost, but then remember you were born during income tax season. Your stomach stops its churning.

(Seven)

The charms on your bracelet that tinkle like small wind chimes when you move too enthusiastically. You remember how you got each and every single one. The retro sunglasses for the white sand beach of Punta Cana. The crescent moon clip to match the ink behind your ear. The dangling butterfly and heart, both imbued with feelings of "forever." Each one inspires deep, vigorous love — the kind that rushes through you like rapids and threatens to swallow you up when you're lonely. They constantly remind you that you are not — lonely, that is — but you find yourself pushing into the corner of your room, making friends with the loose threads on your stuffed cow. They've come to grips with the fact that it's just who you are.

(Nine)

The grade you slipped on a slope peppered with spikes. You are left with shredded insides and weak legs and a broken mind and it is hard to get back the breath that is knocked out of you. You start to let your mom stroke your hair when the pain is too much and reluctantly admit that you like it when you are left alone and she is at work. At the bottom of the slope is a dark pit and you are in it for three years. At first, you are too broken to try to climb out. You get comfortable on the mold-covered ground, ignore your sour stench, and eat what can stay down. But when you finally hear them calling your name, you start to claw at the walls. Your brain blocks out the climb out, but you suck in the fresh air greedily, hear them cheer despite the fact that everything is different and you are not perfect. And when your feet continue to dangle over the edge of the pit, they do their best to help you not fall in again.

(Eleven)

The hour you were born. Your mom says you and your sister were clean and shiny. Your father is too late to cut your umbilical cord, but that is okay because he doesn't fit in with the rest of the story anyway. Your sister wonders why you are so much lighter than she is, but she still loves you. You can see it in an old, unfocused picture probably taken by Mom. Franderis holds you like she's supposed to and the gap between her two front teeth is brilliant. And in your bones, you know they will stay with you always.

Prince Charming

JUDITH ROLAND

Growing up as a painfully shy kid, I escaped into books and the voices of others, and learned to express my own voice through writing. Fairy tales always enchanted me, so perhaps it's not surprising that I created my own Prince Charming.

When I was 14, my parents sent me to summer camp. I was very awkward and shy. I worried about being the only one in my bunk who didn't have a boyfriend from home who would send me letters. So I invented a boyfriend.

His name was Mitchel. Several months before camp, my friend, Corinne, and I wrote a bunch of letters from Mitchel that she could send me throughout the summer.

Each day that summer, when our mail was delivered there was a flurry of excitement: "Is there anything from Mitchel?" my bunkmates would eagerly ask. As expected, they were impressed every time I got a letter from him. He was cool, sophisticated and I, by association, was awesome, too.

What I did not expect — the magical, mysterious part — was how real my imaginary beau became as I started to fall for him through the letters I had written.

> "He was cool, sophisticated and I, by association, was awesome, too."

BRITTNEY NANTON

YEARS AS MENTEE: 1

GRADE: Sophomore

HIGH SCHOOL:
Landmark High School

BORN: New York, NY

LIVES: New York, NY

Working with Amy has been a really exciting experience. She opened my eyes and helped me branch out in my writing, which is something that I never could have imagined myself doing. She taught me how to be more confident in my writing and how to be more independent and strong as a woman. With her as my mentor, I learned that being abnormal is a good thing and that I should never feel the need to alter who I am in any way to fit in, which was something that I've struggled with for a while.

AMY FLYNTZ

YEARS AS MENTOR: 3

OCCUPATION:
Founder, Amy Flyntz
Copywriting, LLC

BORN: Bridgeport, CT

LIVES: New York, NY

Brittney is one of the most self-posessed and intelligent women I've ever had the pleasure of meeting. As our relationship has grown, I've watched her gain confidence in her writing, in her beliefs, and in herself. She is not afraid to push her own boundaries to become a better writer and her passion for improving her skills is a constant source of inspiration to me. She's reminded me why I love reading, writing, and mentoring so much!

Who Am I?

BRITTNEY NANTON

*The recent events in the news and the innocent people that have lost
their lives due to racism are the main inspiration for this piece.
It was really interesting to write this piece, since I normally don't write
about something that means so much to me.*

If I could express myself in three words, I don't think I would be able to. You see, I don't quite know how to describe myself. Also, I don't feel like it would be right to just label myself in only three words. But if I had to, I think I would chose the words different, introverted, and kind. Though I am many more words than just these three, I think these are the words you would use if you're meeting me for the first time. If so, you are right, but I have more to me than just that. I also like going on the Internet, and staying home. Part of that is because I have no one to hang out with,

and the other part is because I like to be by myself sometimes. Some people think that's a wrong thing though, to be alone. I don't think so. Being alone isn't a bad thing, but, when you actually feel alone, then that's something.

I have a lot of fears. I think I'm mostly scared of everything, or maybe it's just my anxiety that makes me fearful. I don't like bugs, doctor visits, closed-in spaces, the dark, being in groups, and mostly everything else you can think of. I sometimes feel as though having those fears limits me on the certain things that teens my age are doing. While other kids are partying and making memories that they'll keep forever, I'm home alone blogging about random

things. People always tell me that I should be more like an actual teen but mostly, I disagree with them. I don't want to be partying until 7 a.m., and forgetting what happened the night before. I want to do what makes me happy. The terrible

thing about my anxiety is that sometimes I'm uncomfortable in situations.

I am scared. As I have matured from a stubborn little girl into a teen, I've learned about my surroundings. I've lost the young, naive look in my eyes and have replaced it with a sense of anger and anxiousness. So much has changed. So many things have now become a part of my life, it's like I'm finally starting to live. I'm finally starting to observe my surroundings and learn about the world and how harsh it can be. The people that I once thought were the

good guys are actually the ones that are against me. Being a black teenager in a city where so many of us are viewed as nothing more than garbage is tough. I've even started to worry for my black and brown male friends, for they have been targeted as the enemy since the second they've left their mother's womb. They speak differently, dress in clothes that make them look "dangerous" and harmful to others. They, themselves have learned to fear pale skinned men with a blue uniform and badge, because they are the ones that have taken-away their fellow brothers. In school, instead of learning about algebra and historical literature, I'm learning about ways to make myself seem invisible in front of the police. "Be polite," they tell me, "whatever you do, keep your hands where the police can see them." I've thought about how other teenagers in the world don't have to worry about dying while on their way to the store, or getting arrested simply for being a darker skin tone. They don't have a target on their back while melanin boys and girls are born with it stamped on them as if it's some kind of birthmark. The little girl that once viewed the police as my heroes is gone. I now fear that they can take my life without any hesitation. As a young teenage black girl, I am scared. I am so much more than a stereotype. So much more than what you'd expect a girl like me to be. I am stronger than people make me out to be, I have so many goals that I have yet to achieve. I want to knock down the stereotype that has been pinned down on me. I am so much more than the "typical black girl." I am beautiful, I am fearless, and I am strong enough to not let the hatred towards people like me sink me down to the pits where they believe that I belong. I am a human. I am a target. I am not afraid.

> "…I'm learning about ways to make myself seem invisible in front of the police."

I.D. Required

AMY FLYNTZ

I started this piece during the Girls Write Now Persona Poetry Workshop. My mother, who is a constant source of inspiration to me, is the subject of the poem. I found it incredibly challenging to write as if I were her; in fact, working on this piece has sparked meaningful discussions between us!

Who are you, Mom?

It's taken 39 years
But we've arrived

Here

      Between dinner sizzling

      Between dishes clacking

Here

      Between sharing a heartbeat

      Between glossing over details

Here

      Between a shared home

      Between her distant life

Here

      Between the space of longing

      Between the weight of accepting

Oh, I'm fine.

Here

      Between Who

      Between How

I'm amazed at the burden three letters can impose

By the way they mingle with the

"O"

ASHÉ NERVIL

YEARS AS MENTEE: 1

GRADE: Sophomore

HIGH SCHOOL: Democracy Prep Charter High School

BORN: New York, NY

LIVES: New York, NY

When I first met J M, I wasn't used to being around older Caucasian people. Later I discovered that she is not your stereotypical "white haired old lady." She has a youthful spirit. It is through that spirit and wisdom that I got to connect and learn from her. Whenever I present a writing piece to her, she gives me advice that no one else would think of. I am thankful for that — and for her teaching me that not everything is as it seems. I never believed that saying until I started meeting up with J M once a week.

J M STIFLE

YEARS AS MENTOR: 1

OCCUPATION: Writer

BORN: New York, NY

LIVES: New York, NY

Ashé is a bright, deep-thinking, quick-witted, and beautiful girl. I am always learning something from her regarding contemporary culture (Kanye's lyrics were a revelation to me!). She always has a new poem she's written that she shares with me, performing it aloud. A lot of her work focuses on cultural stereotypes, warped images, racism, and that has emboldened me to continue writing about my own "ism" du jour: ageism.

Drowning in Truth

ASHÉ NERVIL

*I believe there is no such thing as the "American Dream." America has a lot
of flaws and through my poem "Drowning in Truth" I express how
I feel about the dream — how hard it is to achieve, and how the achievement
usually involves some type of consequence for someone else.*

After the storm and the water cleared

My momma told me to stay put

The world was too cruel

The world was too heartless

For a little girl to see

For this little girl was driven by curiosity

She was curious about the world beyond the land and the sea

She wanted to lie in a field of lilies and tulips

And dream about how the stars are aligned in the order in which she made it so

Stay put momma said

Don't dream

Do not think

For society will punish you if you think differently

You being different will not bring you luck

Truth is life sucks

So just stay put love

Stay put where it is safe

But this little girl is tired of this suffocating cage

She wants to see the world as it is

No matter the blood and tears

Or if the field I played in was full of dead bodies

Or that our house was built over the pain and grief of our people from slavery

Or the fact that the world is so focused on the fact that #blacklivesmatter

That we don't apologize to the Native Americans for taking their hopes and dreams
and sewing them into European cloth

Then advertise it as our own

We sell this American dream by destroying another's dreams of life, liberty, and
our pursuit of bullshit

Don't sell a product if there is not enough for the consumers to consume

America is doomed

For karma is alive

And soon enough the curse and lies and deceit of our forefathers and American
Dream will all be a mystery

After the storm and the water cleared

My momma told me to stay put

I said no cuz

It is only so much a girl can hold until she explodes

Proud To
Be A C. O. B.

J M STIFLE

*I've been writing what I call a "rant" about my feelings on ageism. When I
heard mentees performing slam poetry, I decided to share what I had written
with my mentee who is very experienced in the genre. When she snapped her
fingers and nodded, I thought I'm on to something.*

Old people are not cute.

Babies are cute. Because they are new. They've just come out of the chute and are
not scarred, shaped, or wizened by experience.

Old people are tough. We are strong. We have to be. Our survival depends on it.

I dare anyone under the age of 30 to spend five minutes in my body. You couldn't. You
wouldn't survive. Because you do not have the stamina of this long-distance runner.

I have been in training for decades. What I lack in physical strength, I have gained
in mental agility, canny observation, rapid analysis and deep understanding. I'll

match wits with the witless and win any day.

Old people aren't cute. We aren't sweet. We are not soft.

We are sour. Salty. Well-seasoned. Hard.

Old people are feisty, tasty, yeasty. Tart. Ripe.

We're not afraid to say what's on our minds. Fuck you. Fuck off. Get the fuck out of my way. I came here to stay. I am here for the duration. What do you have to say? Not much. I thought so.

You, with your soft, supple, unmarked skin. Your unformed minds. Your unstained souls. Your youth is so … uninteresting. I have earned each crease, each line — each white hair on my head is proof of a long life well lived and well learned.

I have no desire to be forever young or 21 or turn back time. I'm not interested in a fountain of youth. You can keep your botox, spackle and filler. Your hair dye. Your vampire blood, your face-lift, and you know where I'd like you to put your scalpel, doctor.

You think I look tired? You bet I'm tired! Tired of the media tirelessly portraying us as desiccated, demented, doddering, discarded, declining, disposable and soon to be deceased.

I want to see old people who are working, not retiring, retreating, giving up, giving out. I want to see them advising, devising, and in advertising that does not involve: Depends, boner pills, incontinence, anxiety, retirement accounts, high blood pressure, plaque, cholesterol — that reduces us to the sum of our ailments real or imagined.

Do NOT dismiss me. I AM NOT dead yet. I will NOT go gently into that good night. I refuse to rot away in a retirement village (what the fuck is that, anyway?) … assisted living (more like "wait until you're dying") … nursing home (whose nurse? whose home?) … long-term care … Florida. I'm gonna die with my boots on or take the long walk off a short pier. Trust me to know when it's time to order the boat and the conflagration.

Don't pass me by.
Look me in the eye and you will see:
I know things.
I am history.
I am your link to the past.
Treasure my wisdom.
Use my knowledge.

And, yes, please do learn from my experience.

It's not about the package.

Go beyond the wrinkles, crinkles, rips and tears.

Untie the knot.

Unwrap me.

Find out what's inside.

BRE'ANN NEWSOME

YEARS AS MENTEE: 4

GRADE: Senior

HIGH SCHOOL:
Bronx Studio School for
Writers and Artists

BORN: Bronx, NY

LIVES: Bronx, NY

COLLEGE:
Lehman College

**PUBLICATIONS
AND RECOGNITIONS:**
Scholastic Art & Writing
Award: Honorable Mention;
Port Magazine website; Po-
et-Linc: Poetry Slam 2014;
Performed at the United
Nations for Internation-
al Day of the Girl; VIDA:
Women in Literary Arts

Kara and I have been working with each other for two years now, and being that this is my final year in Girls Write Now, I couldn't think of anyone else I'd rather go through it with. Having a mentor as supportive and hands-on as Kara has helped me grow both as a poet and person. Being with Girls Write Now for four years has liberated me in my own skin as a young woman of color, and I can I honestly say that I am finally learning to fall in love with the artist that I am becoming.

K.T. BILLEY

YEARS AS MENTOR: 2

OCCUPATION:
Freelance writer and editor

BORN: Red Deer, Canada

LIVES: Brooklyn, NY

**PUBLICATIONS
AND RECOGNITIONS:**
Semi-finalist for the 2015
Parnet River Prize from
YesYes Books; *Cake;*
Palabras Errantes; forthcom-
ing Columbia University Press
anthology; *The New Orleans*
Review; CutBank; Phantom
Limb; Poor Claudia

It has been a privilege to witness Bre'Ann's growth over the past two years. When we met she was still finding her voice, both as a poet/writer, and as an astute, sensitive young woman. Now she uses that voice to express art and opinions that articulate, challenge, and improve the world around her, confident in the validity of her perspective. She is a positive force in several communities, and she inspires me to support others, speak up, and believe in the power of connection.

MAS'SAH

BRE'ANN NEWSOME

"Mas'sah," means "testing trial" in Hebrew. "Mas'sah" incorporates the spirituality, urban politics, and vulnerability surrounding this moment in my life, and my openness in asking for spiritual direction.

I remind myself
that I began as nothing

more than a wisp of dust
scraped from the curbs
of Simpson and Bathgate Avenues,

a solution of saliva, piss, and dirt
that froze into a public
statue, stuck inside every planet

not white or blue-blooded
but red, still green, still black
still life in red, incubated

in the womb of poverty
like my hero, who left
broken teeth in front of the church on Lenox,

uniforms wrinkled and torn
because every other boy's parents
fought for him to be here.

Between the dregs of 163rd and the suppliers
on the northeast corner of Castle Hill

I realize I am a reminder
of every generation's first
problem, Mother's first

force of habit, the first thing

the priest cursed in the morning

and the last thing grandmother prayed for

at night because God knows our parents

needed a blessing, and history

pleaded with him to let their words be one.

My God, believe me when I say

that I am humble, but Lord I am also aware

that I have crossed the streets of new beginnings

I know that I am the answer

to grandma's prayers

a reason for a father's change of heart.

But I need to hear it from you — am I still

a bottle of Hennessey, abandoned in a back room

at a house party — or am I clay

softened by Jamaican rum,

molded by the force of you

on the corner of 37th and 8th, just

off the park at 110th.

Have I made you smile

by making an inmate laugh, or

stroking the wounds of a boy

who knows no tender love?

 Am I not you?

Made in the image

modeled after your finest creation

with the preservation of 1000

words —

I need you to tell me something,

sit down here on the stoop

of 182nd street and look me in the eyes

and God tell me that I am

of value, that I have done something

worth recounting to your angels
even if I am no diamond

I am the best
spit-shined stone
in Grand Concourse station.

Lend me your strength
because Lord I need to kiss
these cuts and bruises too

I'm having trouble reaching
the parts of myself
that are hidden underneath
a public school uniform.

God, if you cannot touch me
to feel me, hold me within
the embrace of your breath.

I need you,
I need you
Lord, have mercy on these streets
because I need you

in the same way prophet
needs faith.

Tell me which cross walk to run
across next, which train to take
in what direction. What scripture

do I need to become the roadmap
to whatever destination
gets me to you.

Never Quick

K.T. BILLEY

*This piece relates to the many discussions with my mentee Bre'Ann and I have
had about the relationships that become more complex as we move into and
through adulthood — especially those between family members. The
challenges of navigating these intimacies are ongoing yet beautiful
in its own way, and my experience with Bre has led me to reflect on the
mentor-like figures in my own life and history.*

How many nights do you spend
on your stomach, comparing birds

carved into baseboards under your bed
before its canopy becomes your in and out, a labyrinth

terminal too sweetly nostalgic, the grenadine
in the Shirley Temple you still can't order.

Years after the estrangement puckers
complete, something like dementia settles

in the perfect recall of food preference, fact
as focal point, fake allergies that must always be

ignored. There's no avoiding her, your hallway
mirror, harrowed sign of home.

Hers is the hand that smoothed hair
at your temples, the fly-a-ways

you suppress but are suspect without—
the younger sisters of put-together women.

ROBERTA NIN FELIZ

YEARS AS MENTEE: 3

GRADE: Junior

HIGH SCHOOL:
Manhattan Center for Science and Mathematics

BORN:
Willemstad, Curacao

LIVES: Bronx, NY

**PUBLICATIONS
AND RECOGNITIONS:**
Newsie Award (high school newspaper competition for New York City student journalists) for best Op/Ed

The countless revisions, drafts, and edits we have done together have revealed Jalylah's brilliance as well as her talent in writing and teaching. Although she has never taken credit for any of my accomplishments, I don't know that they would have been possible without her. Even in the midst of writing her dissertation, she finds time to help me with academics and managing my busy schedule. She has helped me embody the woman I have always aspired to be.

JALYLAH BURRELL

YEARS AS MENTOR: 4

OCCUPATION:
Dissertation Fellow, Yale University

BORN: Seattle, WA

LIVES: New York, NY

**PUBLICATIONS
AND RECOGNITIONS:**
Atwater Fellowship, Yale University

Roberta always has a plan and this year, her junior year of high school, it included applying to more competitive academic enrichment programs, college prep scholarships, and summer institutes than ever. The drafting of essays and short answer responses is no easy task, but I have been taken by Roberta's success at selecting a scientific principle, a scene from a novel or a moment from her childhood to illustrate an element of her identity.

Chercher

ROBERTA NIN FELIZ

*When I turned 16, I felt like I had a clear, solid vision of myself
and my goals. In celebration of finding myself, I wrote this poem
mapping out some of my journey.*

I've been lost the past year and some change

Because I wasn't accustomed

To change

Like spare change in my wallet

16 cents

One for every year I've lived

Under Sweet Gum trees far from

The hair-bleaching sun rays that streaked

My nut brown hair with cinnamon

In my mom's pollo al orno

In the squeaks of my pivoting basketball shoes

I search for me

I'm lost in every curl

zig zag, twist, wave, and coil on my head

Bouncing back

From the limp waves flat-ironing rendered

Wandering the strands of hair that

Still haven't decided whether or not they want to curl completely

And those that curl excruciatingly close to my scalp

Awaiting May

To search in rainbows

Semicircles decorating the sky of my 'hood

Rummaging beneath books and sandy beaches

Jeans, pens, journals, poems

On days where I forget the French words
I flip through my notebook
Failing to find the French words for "I found me"
Vien ici s'il vous plait
Let me be found
Amongst the accent aegis of past participles
Hanging off the cédille of Curaçao
Or balancing on the accent circonflexe of être
Whispering to the clouds
Oui, Oui, "I heard you been looking for me."

Fête de la Crêpe

JALYLAH BURRELL

I was initially excited to learn my mentee Roberta was studying French.
I am a francophile from a family of francophiles but despite decades of study,
including stretches in Paris and Nantes, I have always struggled with fluency.
Taking inspiration from Roberta's French-incorporated poem,
I reflect on moments from my own study.

I remember the chalk Madame Koban threw at Erika, traveling in slow motion. It shed white particles as it revolved on a tilted axis and fractured across the back of my former best friend's black hoodie. That is not how it happened. I remember Erika's partially ponytailed hair, salon-blonde and blown straight. I remember how her shallow chin gave the impression of two and how she cursed her mother for refusing her dessert one of the many times I slept over. I remember fuzzy-braided summer days jet skiing on the lake her family's cabin abutted and the puzzling kleptomania of her well-heeled family friend. I remember our matchless enthusiasm for all things endeavored together and then how she grew to seldom smile and often sat on the floor of our private school's hallways with her knees, peeking through ripped Urban Outfitter jeans, drawn to her chest. I know these memories to be more accurate, still I am reticent to call them facts.

There was no instruction that day in French class. This I can't be sure of but there was a fête and that is all that remains on my palate. Someone brought homemade batter, or actually, we might have made it. Others brought berries and aerosol whip cream; still others, the requisite powdered sugar and lemons. Naturally, Madame Koban provided the Nutella and the crépe makers. They would not resemble the ones I later encountered dans la Rue Mouffetard or on the outskirts of Nantes but they worked. We feasted, all afternoon as I remember, beyond the hour-long constraints of middle school course lengths. It was bright; the blinds might have been drawn, or it might have been the sugar and the wanderlust. By year's end we would all be traipsing the Loire Valley. Most likely this is not true. Some of us had not made the journey. Still others, like Erika, would brood amidst the immaculately tended Chateau gardens unmoved by their distance from the recalcitrant evergreen forests of home. Charmed, I took it as an omen.

I remember buying my mother champignons de la Cave des Roches. Our guide touted the mushrooms as the world's best. A small token of my appreciation for her love, for sending me twice to Europe by the time I turned 14, for always saying yes to what was certain to enrich, I imagined they could represent. "They will not keep," everyone warned. I still stowed them in my suitcase. An hour and half after arriving at Seattle – Tacoma International Airport my luggage lay open on the living room hardwood and I dug the durably packaged champignons from layers of mussed clothes and gifted them to my mother. She smiled, offered great thanks, and carried them into the kitchen where they found rest in the garbage bin. This I know for sure.

ELSHAIMA OMRAN

YEARS AS MENTEE: 2

GRADE: Junior

HIGH SCHOOL: International High School at Lafayette

BORN: Alexandria, Egypt

LIVES: Brooklyn, NY

I would love to thank my beautiful sister, Stacie. I am not bothering to say mentor because it's not true. She is a member of my family now. I trust her with my secrets just like I do with my mom and sisters. She is a cool person that I will want in my life forever. She is easy to understand and funny to talk to. She understands me more than my best friend. My favorite thing about her is that she loves me so much and makes time for me even when she is busy. I will take this opportunity to thank her millions of times for being my sister. We have some odd conversations sometimes, but I really enjoy it so much. Thanks a lot, Stacie, for being an awesome mentor.

STACIE EVANS

YEARS AS MENTOR: 2

OCCUPATION: Policy Writer and Program Developer

BORN: New York, NY

LIVES: Brooklyn, NY

PUBLICATIONS AND RECOGNITIONS: Finalist in the 2014 Flash Fiction Challenge-NYC Midnight; semi-finalist in the 2015 Short Story Contest.

Shaima's confidence with writing has grown so much since last year. Even her texts show a new ease, and seeing those changes inspire me. I think being a part of Shaima's development as a writer pushes me to experiment. When we write together, I always produce work unlike my usual writing. The fun of being Shaima's mentor isn't just about writing. It's about how much I love Shaima. Our conversations are so varied and rich, and she always makes me laugh. She is smart and caring, and being paired with her has been an enormous gift from Girls Write Now.

Freedom of Speech

ELSHAIMA OMRAN

I was inspired by #JeSuisCharlie on the Internet. When I saw it all over the media, I thought, "Why is everyone supporting them and no one thought just for a minute that what they did was absolutely wrong?" Well, I am that person who thinks they are wrong. That is why I wrote my poem.

Freedom of speech
comes from being free.
Expresses a feeling
no one can say,
but think of it?
Is it always fair?
Is it always free?
Is it always what people say?
I don't think so.
Freedom of speech
isn't always what it seems.
Je suis Charlie
Je suis Muslim
Je suis anything
Who cares who you support?
Because I support the right thing.
Freedom isn't about hurting people,
Freedom isn't about talking bad about someone,
Freedom isn't insulting people,
Freedom isn't about being free,
Freedom is about being respectful,
Freedom means being honest,
but when it comes to religion
that's when it stops.

We have freedom of religion, too,

just like speech.

Don't you dare come and say anything about my religion,

and want me to believe you.

Religion is what defines us,

Religion is everything to us.

So, don't you come and insult us.

Freedom of speech

I don't believe in you anymore.

It's not funny

to insult religion

for the freedom to speak.

It's not beautiful

to insult religions,

to insult Muslims,

to use symbols,

to write disrespectfully

on something they care about,

and want me to believe in you.

Freedom of expression

is absolutely okay,

absolutely normal,

absolutely open,

but when it comes to ISLAM

that's where it stops.

The world we live in, is so painful.

That's where freedom of speech should come in.

That is where they should express,

where they should speak out loud.

They can't come to religion and say what they want.

We read about what is going on,

but we never took our time

to know who is right and who is wrong.

Our world was blue,

but in time it became red,

red from all the pain, media caused us to believe,

from disrespecting our people,

from killing each other without reasons.

If each person minds their business

our world will be blue again.

Freedom of speech

I don't believe in you.

Is it always free?

Is it always fair?

It's always what people say.

Now it's not what it seems.

Freedom of speech

I don't believe in you.

Freedom isn't about hurting people

it's about helping them.

Freedom isn't talking bad about someone

it's about helping them understand the right thing.

Freedom isn't about insulting people

it's about treating them equally.

Freedom is being free.

Freedom of speech

I don't believe in you anymore.

#JeNeSuisPasCharlie #JeNePeuxJamaisÊtreCharlie

STACIE EVANS

Shaima and I talked about "Voice to Voice," and she chose "freedom of speech" as our topic, specifically thinking about the responses to the Charlie Hebdo attack. We found we were having some of the same thoughts about those responses, so we freewrote together and our different pieces took shape.

When people talk about free speech, I've noticed that their definition of the term is often narrow. "Free speech" seems to be the right only of people who think the way the speaker thinks, who are saying things the speaker wishes he felt brave enough to say. Freedom of speech … as long as I agree with you. But even in that narrow scope, the freedom the speaker grants is broad, covering every possible expression, excusing all. As long as I agree with you, you can do no wrong. Or something.

After the January 7th attack on the Charlie Hebdo office, it seemed the entire world rose up: marches and protests and government leaders expressing horror and condemnation. And that makes sense. What happened was terrifying and terrible. JeSuisCharlie signs and tweets appeared immediately, as did drawings of a raised fist holding a pencil, illustrating the horror of such a deadly attack on free expression. American celebrities wore JeSuisCharlie pins or carried signs or said the words. We were outraged.

And we should have been. Seventeen people were dead. A city had been terrorized, held hostage for three days.

On January 9th, at least 2,000 residents of Baga, a village in northern Nigeria, were killed by Boko Haram, the same extremists that kidnapped close to 300 girls last year, girls who remain missing and will likely never be rescued. Two thousand people dead. An entire village razed to the ground.

And the news was silent.

The celebrities were silent.

No one marched.

All the lives of every missing schoolgirl in Nigeria matter – the girls from Chibok, the girls from Warabe, the girls taken in the 11 months since those original abductions. All the lives of every villager of Baga matter, but you're angry because I won't wear your Charlie pin?

I am definitely not Charlie. Maybe instead I would use #JeSuisAhmed, the tag for Ahmed Merabet, the Paris police officer, the Muslim man who died defending Charlie Hebdo's assumed right to vilify and mock his religion.

I support freedom of speech, but not as a cloak over prejudice. Not when satire is used to spread hate. Not when "free speech" is expected to absolve the speaker of responsibility for his actions. That's using freedom of speech to get over, to get away with saying and publishing things that actually aren't okay to say and print. #JeSuisCharlie turns the Hebdo staff into heroes and nothing they ever published can be questioned.

Meanwhile, when I say #JeNeSuisPasCharlie, I am told I am on the side of the terrorists, that I am blaming the Hebdo writers for their own murders. As if. I can condemn the Hebdo staff's decisions and the terrorists who murdered them. I condemn the killing … but it annoys me that I am made to feel obligated to state those truths as a way to carve out some permission for me to say the other things I feel.

For it to be real, freedom of speech must be absolute. And I believe in free expression … but not in the freedom to grab that shield because you want to be able to publish hate and not be held accountable. I don't support anyone who stands behind the mask of free speech to excuse racism and religious prejudice. The Hebdo cartoons mocking the Nigerian kidnap victims, the cartoons showing my president and first lady as apes tell me everything I need to know about Charlie Hebdo, thank you. I don't need anyone telling me what the "right" side of that hashtag is.

#JeNeVoudraisJamaisÊtreCharlie

KATHERINE ORTIZ

YEARS AS MENTEE: 3

GRADE: Junior

HIGH SCHOOL:
Metropolitan Expeditionary
Learning School

BORN:
Azua, Dominican Republic

LIVES: Queens, NY

Joy is the wisest, most honest person I've ever had the pleasure to know. She has the most beautiful words of advice and has taught me so much, from religion to my writing to travel. She remembers the smallest details when I fail to do so. She is so patient with my introversion and sympathizes with my problems that seem oh so small but I tend to overreact towards. Joy has managed to become a constant in my life considering I don't often have many constants, and I hope that following my years at Girls Write Now she will continue to advise me, and hopefully I am able to do the same for her.

Y. JOY HARRIS-SMITH

YEARS AS MENTOR: 2

OCCUPATION:
Postdoctoral Teaching
Fellow, Princeton
Theological Seminary

BORN: Bitburg, Germany

LIVES: Queens, NY

**PUBLICATIONS
AND RECOGNITIONS:**
Spiritual Health Identity: Placing black women's lives in the center of analysis; Gender and Diversity Issues in Religious-Based Institutions and Organizations; Postdoctoral Teaching Fellowship at Princeton Theological Seminary; www.joysandtrials.com

I have learned and been reminded through Katherine's voice how pain and honesty can translate into wonderful prose. Her dedication to writing in the midst of a full schedule has inspired me such that I've started my own blog. I admire her commitment to her voice through the written word.

Withering Blossoms

KATHERINE ORTIZ

*I only write when I'm falling in love, or falling apart, and in this case,
it just happened to be both. This piece is from a moment in my life where
everything I felt was raw, and real, and beautiful. Although I was
in pain, I came to the realization that love isn't something easily found,
and shouldn't be something easily given up on.*

She hated a lot of things. She hated her father. She hated him the way she hated misogyny and injustice, all things that he was. She hated him the way she hated peppermint and chemistry: intolerably. She also hated anything complicated, so she immediately disliked boys and math. She hated attention and hated the lack there of. She valued the sound of rain against tin and the way leaves would adorn the urban walkways during the fall. Her father warned her of men and her mother warned her of men like her father. She envisions her future in foreign cities with names she fears to pronounce. She enjoys the simplicity of music and felt everything way too much. She was enamored. She was enamored with a boy whose beauty was endless and whose charm was entwined with every word spoken. His simplistic touch was insanity and his lips were a thought frequent to her. She was frightened. She was frightened of the way she needed him and was frightened of how quickly he could just disappear. She questioned whether she loved him, yet that frightened her, too.

He was everything she could learn to love. He was stubborn beyond repair and his wit caused her chest to erupt with laughter. She adored the raven strands of his hair and the dark marbles that were his eyes. He questioned nearly everything for the purpose of hearing the words said aloud. She adored his vast intelligence and his outspoken ambitions. She loved to remind him of his under-appreciated thoughts and beauty. He was utterly, breathtakingly gorgeous. She would often watch him. She'd watch him as he walked, especially taking notice of his torso, highlighted by his athletic build. She adored the way his hair would curl at the nape of his neck or the way his hands would find hers effortlessly, she continuously found reasons to adore him so. What else? She loved hearing him talk. She adored his voice and longed for the depth of his tone.

Together, they were everything unexpected. Yet, she couldn't help but adore him. She couldn't help but notice the way his lashes would frame his mocha eyes. She thought of the dark depths her mind composed and then thought of the way he'd provide a haven of innocence for her tormented soul to bathe in.

He found himself remembering the day of her birth and the day they declared themselves to one another. He found himself remembering the name of her perfume or the way she would watch *American Horror Story* religiously on Wednesdays. He remembered the digits of her phone number as if they had been engraved on the flesh beneath his eyes. He remembered the way she would feel the need to write as rain poured or the way her eyes would tear as she yawned. He remembered the way she adored the color turquoise and cherry blossom trees.

He remembered because she pointed them out as they bloomed. His hand enveloped hers as she tugged him urgently along, his stubborn personality and teasing words were tugging at the strings of her music-enthralled heart. They trailed the lengths of the walkways along 101 Avenue, their voices echoing against the steady drum of cars. Soon, they find themselves bordering a church. She remembered the way the sun would cast their shadows on the asphalt, the way she would point out how much taller her own shadow was and his coy response of "It's those boots."

That'd been May, somewhere along the memories where she found herself wishing their ending had been different, wishing their ending hadn't come so quickly. Now it was September, and the sight of his careless demeanor brought her to a state of discomfort while she silently suffered inside.

"...somewhere along the memories where she found herself wishing their ending had been different..."

The church remained standing, time not faltering its stance the way it had hers. The cherry blossoms were hinting of a faint brown as the petals hardened to a crisp.

Now, her hands were entwined on her lap, his touch foreign and the thought haunting. She wore those boots frequently, and she'd wear the familiar perfume he would relentlessly comment on.

She didn't recognize the longing emotion, and she didn't recognize the thudding pain. She'd felt pain before, but that was different. That pain didn't remind her of his marble eyes or the thick strands of his raven hair. That pain wasn't caused by the lack of his comforting tone or the simple phrases that would cause my heart to soar and then stop altogether. It was frightening. It is frightening how someone can grasp you and then so easily suffocate you. It's frightening how they can feel so much and express so little.

The idea of his once-sweet words being directed toward another soaring heart pierced the soldiers marching through her chest. The church remained standing. The blossoms of the trees withered away as death loomed over it. The crystalline beads trailed her face reluctantly, selfishly hoping he felt the same.

The Rippling Echo

Y. JOY HARRIS-SMITH

A workshop and this year's theme inspired this poetic offering.
"Voice to Voice" reminds me of those voices that have impacted my life.
I am because they were here and they are because I am still here.

When a pebble is thrown into water there is a ripple effect.
The spot it hits sends communication through waves letting you know there was/is
  contact.

When I speak, they speak...just like that
Voices to voices echoing through time and space
Haunting isn't it?
Voice as presence
Presence as voice

As I take my place amongst humanity so do they — THROUGH me!

Women's names and stories that history refuses to tell
I cannot call them all
But I'll call the ones that ripple, that echo through me
Fannie Mae, Ida B., Crystal and Jaimee
Now part of that great cloud of witnesses
I am because of you

My voice testifies to their voices, to the existence of those who exited life stage left,
  never reaching any kind of fame
Just the ordinary and the mundane
Yet still like a pebble hits the water and sends out a message through waves letting
  you know that there was/is contact...
So their lives and voices ripple through time echoing in me
Can you hear them?

SASHA PARRISH

YEARS AS MENTEE: 1

GRADE: Junior

HIGH SCHOOL:
Essex Street Academy

BORN: New York, NY

LIVES: New York, NY

**PUBLICATIONS
AND RECOGNITIONS:**
Scholastic Art & Writing
Award: Silver Key

Since I met my mentor Amy, I have begun to work on pushing the limits of my writing. I have written in different genres and learned not only to think about the "what" but also the "who," "when," "where," "why" and "how." I've also grown incredibly familiar with the interior of the Barnes & Noble on 82nd Street. Amy taught me not to be so fearful when sharing my writing — which in many ways is sharing myself — because criticism can be kind and helpful. She's helped me believe in myself more as a writer and I am super grateful for that and for her friendship.

AMY KATZEL

YEARS AS MENTOR: 1

OCCUPATION:
Senior Account Supervisor,
Widmeyer Communications

BORN: Baltimore, MD

LIVES: New York, NY

Throughout our time together, Sasha has impressed me not only with her independent and creative persona, but also with her insightful writing — even during on-the-spot journaling and warm-ups — which we like to share with each other. I've been challenging Sasha to reach for the personal in her writing, and she in turn has inspired me to rely more on outward observation. Some weeks, our neighborhood bookstore is so crowded that we write and chat from a spot on the floor between the bookcases. Ironically, this setting has helped us become more spontaneous in our writing together.

Hush Little Baby

SASHA PARRISH

This piece was inspired by a short story in which a marriage is broken up by the loss of an unborn child. It led me to wonder what would happen if the inverse occurred and thus this piece was born.

Eric woke up face down in his pillow at three in the morning and wished for the millionth time that he hadn't woken up at all. It was crying again. Of course it was crying, it was always crying. So selfish always demanding everyone's attention. Taking and taking and taking. Even before it was born it was taking. Taking her strength, taking her food, feeding off of her like a parasite.

Eric turned his head and stared at the cold pillow on the other side of the bed. He hadn't touched it, no one touched it, and he wouldn't let them. He knew it was crazy but he stubbornly held on to the belief that if everything was left exactly the same, then it would be like she was still there. If he tried hard enough he could pretend that Lisa had just left to go to work early, he could pretend that she would be home at five and imagine that seeing all those bottles on the vanity didn't make him feel hollow. Outside his door he could hear his mother padding down the hall to cater to it. A part of him knew that this was supposed to be his job. He was supposed to change the diapers and bathe it and feed it and love it. He just couldn't, he didn't know how. His mother would always praise it, "Oh isn't she beautiful Eric?" or "She looks just like her mother but I see you there, too. Don't you see it, Eric?" Eric would sit in silence and swallow the bile in his throat. Why couldn't she see what it really was? A murderer, the thing that took Lisa away from him, away from everyone. The thing that killed just to live. He still hadn't held it, the doctors had tried to get him to, but he was focused on the dull color of Lisa's eyes and how quickly her brown hands were turning cold in his grasp.

Sometimes he considered getting rid of it. Placing it on the steps of an orphanage — the nearest one was five miles east, he'd Googled it — ringing the doorbell and leaving, going somewhere where no one knew who he was and traces of Lisa weren't everywhere he looked. He couldn't do it, though. He had loved it once or at least believed he had. He had sung to the swell of Lisa's belly and imagined the three of them together, happy and complete. Maybe he had just liked the idea of a new adventure with Lisa more than he loved the idea of being a father. He wasn't sure, he wasn't really sure of anything anymore. He could hear his mother singing the shopping song in the next room and drifted off to sleep. Hush little baby don't say a word, mama's gonna buy you a mockingbird....

————————

Eric was dreaming about it again. He had dreamed it every night for days and it was always the same. *She was dying. Everyone was moving so quickly around him and shouting trying to save her and the baby and at the center of it, she was dying. The light was leaving her eyes even as they widened. Not in the happy surprised way they had when he had presented her with a ring — right next to her eggs and toast — on the morning of her birthday. No, this time they were wide and afraid like a doe stepping into the middle of traffic and realizing the end had come, brown pupils blown and glassy. Her lips were shaking like she wanted to tell him something, but he couldn't hear her. They were all shouting but he couldn't make out the words. Their voices were garbled as though he had heard them underneath the sea. The sheets were red now. The same red was lining the insides of Lisa's mouth.*

She was still trying to tell him something, squeezing his fingers so weakly he wouldn't have noticed if he weren't so attuned to everything she did. He wasn't sure how to label his emotions. Later the doctors would call it shock, panic, fear, grief. He wouldn't call it any of those things. It was more like numbness and confusion rolled into one and topped with uselessness. All he could do was stand and hold her hand and watch. He barely registered the baby's screams in the background, but Lisa did. He saw the panic erase itself from her face and the cor-ners of her mouth pull up as she nodded faintly. Then everything went quiet — just one steady beeping noise. "Time of death 13:43," someone said. He heard a loud sob and it took him a minute to realize it had come from him.

Eric woke up panting, with the taste of salt on his lips. He sighed and rolled out of bed. The damned thing was crying again.

————————

"Mom!"

"Mom it — the baby's crying!"

Eric rose from his place at the dining room table, abandoning his cereal and went to seek out his mother. Instead of finding her, he found a note on the coffee table in the living room that read: *Since I know you weren't listening when I told you, I went across the street to Rhonda's. She has that fabric I asked her for, I'm just picking it up. Be back in 10-15 minutes. Opal's asleep. If she wakes up there's a bottle in the microwave warm and ready to go. xo Mom.*

Eric sighed and walked back into the kitchen to retrieve the bottle. When he returned bottle in hand, he stood at the foot of the swinging bassinet it had been sleeping in. It wasn't that he'd never touched it. He'd placed it in the car seat when he brought it home from the hospital. It had grabbed his finger and stared at him with its huge brown eyes...just like Lisa. The thought of her had been too much and he'd quickly pulled away. Since then his mother did all the cradling and the feeding and the changing and bathing and soothing — the parenting. That didn't mean he didn't know how. Eric had attended all the parenting classes, read all the books, done all the exercises, but he'd done them with Lisa. It had been the two of them together and now he was alone, all because it had forced itself out of her too early and had been too big.

He stared at it. Its face was red and cheeks stained with tears, gums visible and screaming as much and as loud as it could. It was only three weeks old. It had only been three weeks since Lisa had left them, left him. It had grown a lot since then . He'd been confused at how something so small could dismantle all that he had built. It was still small, its brown hands curled into fists as it bellowed its displeasure. He tried to place the bottle in its mouth and it quieted almost immediately. Then just as quickly it had ripped its mouth off the nipple of the bottle and was screaming again. He tried again only to receive the same result and he could feel frustration mingling with the ever-present resentment churning in his core.

"Eric...is everything alright?" He looked up to see his mother looking at the two of them, her face a cross between hope and apprehension.

"It — she won't eat."

"Did you check her diaper?"

"Um...no."

His mother smiled gently at him and went to do just that, picking up the bawling...child and checking its diaper. He should have known that. Lisa would've known to check the diaper. But then again Lisa wasn't around anymore, she never got the option to check diapers. Whose fault was that? His therapist would say it was no one's fault, that life ends and no one knows when and sometimes there is no one to blame. All Eric knows is that one person lived that night because another one died.

"Eric, I'm gonna call the doctor. Her diaper's dry, she's still not feeding, and she feels a little bit warm, plus she's been pretty fussy lately. I'm sure it's not anything big," she's trying to reassure him, he knows but he isn't entirely sure why. Maybe he hasn't fully grasped the potential gravity of the situation yet, or maybe — and this is the part of him that was ugly and bitter and had dominated these last few weeks — he just didn't care. But no, he could feel his face tightening into a frown, his heartbeat quickening and his breaths shortening. This bothered him. Why? He wasn't sure, because this could be his out. The one he'd been too ashamed to fully hope for, but he believed he needed. He sat on the couch and ran his hands over his face, fingers skimming over the permanent bags beneath his eyes. He could hear his mother's voice in the kitchen rattling off symptoms on the phone. She quieted and he heard her walk into the living room.

"Maybe he hasn't fully grasped the potential gravity of the situation yet, or maybe — and this is the part of him that was ugly and bitter and had dominated these last few weeks — he just didn't care."

"Eric, the doctor said she may have a fever. I'm gonna head out to the pharmacy and pick up some children's Tylenol. He said if that doesn't work then we'll take her to the doctor. Keep an eye on her and call me if anything changes. "

"Ok."

Eric's mother had given it the medicine 15 minutes ago and the fever still had not gone down. He could feel a bubble of panic building in his chest and wondered when it had gotten there and above all else why he felt it in the first place. The problem was that he knew the answers to both questions and wasn't sure he could face them yet. However, at this point, he didn't think he could avoid it anymore. He had never moved from his spot on the couch. His mother had long since gone upstairs to take a nap since she'd been up with it all night. *Up with her all night. It's a person. It's your daughter and a baby at that,* the better part of his mind said. It was funny how its voice sounded like Lisa's. He looked down at it — her — where she was sound asleep sucking lightly on her pacifier, a slight frown on her face. Lisa had said he slept with a frown too, like he was trying to solve a huge equation in his dreams. Lisa had also said she was so happy they were going to be a family. *Lisa wouldn't want this. And you know it.*

Eric felt a burning behind his eyes and a lump rising in his chest, he missed her so much all the time. He didn't know how to live, how to breathe, without her and he was always so angry. Angry at this child for taking her away from him and angry for being all he had left of her. Wiping his eyes, he slowly reached out to the bassinet then stopped, hesitated, and continued. Gently, ever so gently so as not to wake her he lifted her up — hands cradling her neck just like they taught him in all the classes — and brought her to his chest for the first time. She was so small, so fragile, and so breakable, he wondered how he ever thought she could ever do something as heinous as kill. Nothing with hands that small and a heart that beat that quickly could ever hurt anyone. The tears were flowing freely now, as he realized she could be taken away from him, too. And it would be too late to apologize, or to make it right, and every part of Lisa would be gone forever before he could — *Oh!* She was awake, staring at him with Lisa's eyes and he knew then and there he had to make it right.

"Okay," he whispered, "You and me are gonna start over, okay? I think I'm ready now, and I'm sorry I made you wait so long. But I think we can do this together. First, you have to get better and if you can do that, well, I promise to be there when you do, and every day after that, too." She had wrapped her tiny fingers around his larger ones and was waving them around. The resentment wasn't gone but for the first time it showed signs of leaving. He could do this, for her and for Lisa he could do this. He could love his daughter. He could be a father. He took a deep breath and began to rock her gently.

"Hush little baby, don't say a word, Papa's gonna buy you a mockingbird ..."

Melissa walked into the living room to find her son fast asleep on the couch, her granddaughter lying on his chest. The sight of it brought a small smile to her face as she walked over and checked the baby's temperature with the ear thermometer she had brought down with her. Her fever had broken. She walked over to the kitchen careful to be quiet, so as not to wake them. In the doorway she turned to get one last look before sending a prayer up to God and her daughter-in-law and went to make lunch.

The first time
I sang in public

AMY KATZEL

My mentee Sasha and I experimented with a poetry prompt asking us to write about a "first time" — the first time driving a car, the first time home alone, etc. Sasha's acute and seemingly effortless descriptions in her writing inspired me to rely more on detailed observations of my own.

Jamie and me in the instrument closet,
a wall of trumpets and clarinets quiet
in their cases, "Don't look at me!"
"I'm not!" — our backs turned, the heavy
plastic-like rocks of a cliffside staring
at my open mouth. Oh, to finger the valves,
that slight, soft spring and big breath
and then the silence just before the horn's
croon, full and surprising —

VALERIE PEREYRA

YEARS AS MENTEE: 1

GRADE: Junior

HIGH SCHOOL:
The Beacon School

BORN: Queens, NY

LIVES: Brooklyn, NY

**PUBLICATIONS
AND RECOGNITIONS:**
Scholastic Art & Writing
Award: Honorable Mention

While our meetings have covered the basics of character development to hardcore editing and meeting deadlines (that's me), I also found safety in talking to her about my life and hers. She is such a strong mentor and woman who has guided me to improve as a writer and person.

KELLY SWARTZ

YEARS AS MENTOR: 1

OCCUPATION:
Ph.D. Candidate, The
Graduate Center, CUNY

BORN:
Mexico City, México

LIVES: Jersey City, NJ

Valerie reminds me of myself at her age: a big voice in a shy, self-conscious, teenage body. She has made me rediscover the voice I shut out because it was too loud or not loud enough or there was no one there to hear it. Valerie's powerful and empathic voice speaks for/ to my inner teenager.

The Case of the Ugly, Black Shoes

BY VALERIE PEREYRA

My piece is an abridged version of a work inspired by my parents and their struggle to gain residency. While writing this, many moments came to light. It was interesting to see how things were so different from my memories.

There is a children's song my mother used to sing on nights she came home early. My sister on the top bunk and I on the lower, we'd listen to "los pollitos dicen." This is a rough translation:

The little chicks say
Pio, pio, pio
When they're hungry
And when they're cold
The mother hen looks for
Corn and wheat
She feeds them and
Covers them with warmth
Under her two wings

Whenever I heard it, I drifted off into complete serenity to a place where all was safe and warm. I felt at ease because I could feel the weight of my parents' presence at the end of my bed, their voices guiding me into dreamland. I was *bajo sus alas.*

This was the song I heard the night before their court case. At six years old I had no idea what was happening nor did I know I would have to leave their protective wings in order to help them.

It was a February morning, bitter cold as it usually was in New York City at this time. I rubbed my eyes disturbed by the dim lighting in this strange room with long rows of benches.

At the front there was an elevated, large desk. Behind it sat a woman in a billowing, black robe with dark, watchful eyes. She oozed a presence of strong authority and terrified me.

Thankfully, I was burrowed between my mama and my dad. His leg moved up and down as the lady lawyer we had met in the lobby talked on and on. I peeked over at my older sister who was listening intently like she was going to speak. I turned my attention once again to the lady lawyer after my mom squeezed my shoulder leaving a moist imprint.

"Your honor, this case urges special consideration for their daughter requires medical treatment. She has been wearing orthopedic shoes for over a year due to a walking disability…"

I looked down at the horrible, ugly shoes that graced my feet swinging slightly above the floor: my sworn enemy.

"Would you care to explain how this disability was detected…"

Boy, would I.

It had been a busy day, rushing to keep up with my mom. I had fallen behind when I couldn't hold onto the stroller of the kid she babysat anymore when she called my name, *"Valerie, ¡apúrate!"*

She finally had to stop because I was a good five feet behind her, she looked at me funny. *"¿Por qué estás caminando así?"*

Walking like what?

"¡Como un pato! Stop it." I continued to walk making sure I was at her side, but she kept giving me a sideways glance, *"Hmm. Ay, no."*

Did I do something wrong?

"A year ago the doctor at the clinic reported that her right foot was turning inwards when she walked, therefore orthopedic shoes were required."

"I see, how has this affected her besides the physical aspects?"

Silence.

The judge's intense eyes turned to me, *"Valerie, will you walk for me please?"*

I shakily got up, wincing as I heard the steel-toed shoes make that dreadful metallic sound every step I took. I kept my head down as I made my way back.

"Sweetie, what do you feel like when you wear those shoes?"

I felt strange, I hated wearing them in school because I was scared everyone was staring since they were so ugly and weird. I tried everything to get out of wearing them but my mother was relentless when it came to my well-being.

"I shakily got up, wincing as I heard the steel-toed shoes make that dreadful metallic sound every step I took."

"I don't like how they look. I think the other kids will make fun of me. But I have to wear them because my mom says it will make me better. I won't walk like a duck."

The judge smiled and nodded, understanding.

My parents snuggled me between them once again, giving me small smiles. They knew how hard speaking to the judge was for their little chick.

"After hearing your case, I've come to the decision …"

I don't remember the verdict, the big words were beyond my six-year-old mind. The one thing I can never forget was my dad bursting out in tears. I had never seen my dad cry.

That was how it was for my parents for over 10 years. They provided their little chicks with food, shelter and warmth in a country where they were stuck in a perpetual state of fear of losing everything. But we were so lucky: my parents had been granted residency.

I was lucky to have my hen and rooster to block me from this fear with the power of their strong wings. While I didn't know it at the time, walking with those shoes I greatly detested was my way to reciprocate the protection they had shown me. In the end, the case of the ugly shoes was won and they relinquished their fear. From then on, I knew I would never "chicken out" when it came to helping my family.

The moments reflected

KELLY A.K.

Every morning you are a different person. I see myself in my mentee.
I see myself in my memories. We try to recognize
the mirrored image of the moments that changed it all.

There are a few moments in a woman's life when everything changes: waking up and not running, but strutting to the mirror. Looking. Gazing at oneself. Something is different. Something must be different.

You gaze and scrutinize your face, looking at the eyes that stare back. The mouth is as half smiley as it has always been. There are a few freckles you have acquired with age. Maybe even a few lines.

There may be a hair or two out of place. You might reach for the tweezers, forgetting, for a moment, why you are there, so close to the mirror.

You may tweeze, or the moment you have the tweezers in your hand you remember. You step back, trying to regain perspective. You tread back in.

You look at your lashes and close one eye, then the other. You try to stare at yourself within yourself.

Something has changed. You are looking for that on your face. It must show.

You just got your period.

You are a woman now, whatever the hell that means. Even though you have felt like a woman for a very long time; even if the term woman makes you feel uncomfortable. This thing that happened to you, which you were waiting for or maybe caught you by surprise, this thing that makes you feel empowered and utterly vulnerable and very uncomfortable. This massive colossal happening between your legs should be showing on your face, no?

You continue staring. The reflection gazes back, undented, unbothered.

You walked fast to the bathroom. You wanted the privacy. You forgot to pee first. The mirror is so much more relevant at this moment. You stare.

Is the fact that your hymen is no longer intact showing? If you walk down the hallways will somebody be able to tell that you know what it is to have somebody inside you?

Your eyes look tired but also have a glint. It happened. The big V you had carried along is no longer on your shoulders, or rather, between your legs.

Is it in your smile? Is it on your cheeks? Is it written across your face the way you feel it inscribed across your whole body…?

The mirror is quiet. Quieter than you even suspected.

You woke up with the urgency of the bathroom. You know. You knew the night before and even when you doubted. You just knew. And then you peed on a stick and it was a miracle and scary and oh boy, everything will change now.

You feel relieved but know you will be turning to your friend, the toilet, much more often. In the mean time you stare. You look at yourself. You stare at this new image of you. You have metamorphosed for yourself. You are now a science experiment, a being within a being.

You glare and scrutinize. Can you tell? Is your face any different now that you are carrying a living thing inside you?

Is it obvious?

You are certain that within your face inhabits the reflection of the vital moments happening within your body.

Is your menstruation? Your first sexual encounter? Your upcoming motherhood? Are any of those pivotal moments showing on your face?

Would you want them to? Or are you just searching because this morning you woke up feeling like a leaf has turned, like you are another version of yourself.

TIFFANI REN

YEARS AS MENTEE: 2

GRADE: Senior

HIGH SCHOOL:
Stuyvesant High School

BORN: Queens, NY

LIVES: Queens, NY

**PUBLICATIONS
AND RECOGNITIONS:**
Scholastic Art & Writing
Award: Silver Key

We don't write during our pair sessions; we edit, edit, edit. Our pair sessions have become a lovely interplay between our two voices, both on paper and off. Stacy is my go-to editor, my first reader, and the best mentor I could ask for. In giving me guidance on everything from relationships to my parents to schoolwork, she is motherly and frank and supportive. And her ultimate challenge to me is to be kinder to myself and confident in everything I do.

STACY CHINA

YEARS AS MENTOR: 2

OCCUPATION:
Copy Editor,
The New York Times

BORN: Brooklyn, NY

LIVES: Hillside, NJ

As I've said to Tiffani several times this year, this is the first time in her life she gets to make adult decisions. I have been urging her to make them, despite fear. In doing so, I have been reminded that the process does not end, really; many years into adulthood, we still struggle with living the life we envision as opposed to the one envisioned for us by others. As she gains her footing and learns how to assert herself, I have been refining my own process and applying more grace to my own assertions.

par-TI-si-PA-sion

TIFFANI REN

I loved the style of writing in Mrs. Dalloway *(really everything about it), and used it to try to capture the struggles I've had with participation. This piece draws inspiration not only from* Mrs. Dalloway, *but also from my experience in reading the novel.*

Eloise runs a finger over the spine of *Mrs. Dalloway* and, as she watches her feet, stepping mechanically upward, she flips through the book, catching her finger on one of the pages.

She reads under her breath: And as if to prove it (scientifically) wherever he looked at the houses, at the railings, at the antelopes stretching over the palings, beauty sprang instantly. (She laughs to herself; realizing railing and palings sound out a rhyme; that poetic surprise in a work of prose.)

To watch a leaf quivering in the rush of air was an exquisite joy. (Eloise sighs happily as she stands in front of the English classroom, a shudder running down her shoulder in utter delight; the combinations of words so beautiful as quivering, quiver-ing, and rush, and exquisite, ex-quizite, x-qui-zite!).

"How are you, Eloise?"

The sudden voice jolts her a little bit and she looks up into the face of Mr. Good-man, who's wearing his classic blue-checkered collared shirt and dark jeans.

She talks to Mr. Goodman haltingly, with hand gestures that don't quite fit with her words. He asks how *Dalloway*'s going and she breaks into a smile, as she lays down the cadences deliberately, drawing out the words lovingly.

"You should say that in class!"

She feels the bile rising. She steps into the classroom.

"So, what's up with Septimus's suicide?"

Mr. Goodman smiles. "Take a minute, in your notebook."

Eloise's heart starts to droop and Mr. Goodman catches her eye like a penny for a quick second, and smiles knowingly.

And so it begins.

Eloise has her thumb on page 185.

Somehow it was her disaster — her disgrace. It was her punishment to see sink and disappear (Eloise mentally extends her hand and dips it for emphasis, like a conductor decked in black) here a man, there a woman, in this profound darkness, (she finishes contemptuously) and she is forced to stand here in her evening dress.

(Eloise tries to swallow) This heartbreaking passage — oh, how she wants to reach through the dead pages and fish through the profound darkness and pull out all the people drowning there, (Her left knee starts shaking in anxiety, quivering, qui-ver-ing like a leaf in that rush of wind) how despicable, how constraining, is that formality, is that white evening gown!

Mr. Goodman brings the passage up only to say: "You know, reading *Mrs. Dalloway* time and time again makes me think that this is heroic."

She feels like silently screaming into the void, I do not understand why this is so heroic! — someone else, ask the dreaded question, why putting on masks is he-ro-ic — (Eloise, unable to quell the quivering of her knee, angrily looks down at her paper, at the scribbled quotes and infinite questions) — H-h-ow IS this he-ro-ic —

If only she could have a script sometimes! — she could not understand how everyone else did it; without prompt; with such ease: how responses and answers flowed out of their mouths like silver silken water, while her words tumbled out dirty golden coins, tripping over each other.

"Yet! What feelings beating in her chest that rebel against her insecurity..."

Yet! What feelings beating in her chest that rebel against her insecurity (yet she is the resentful dictator, putting down rebellion) — because it is a fight (Her words rise like bile up her scorched throat); and she has only herself to blame, herself: the enemy, herself: the villain, never the victor, even when she is only fighting herself.

But she must wonder if everyone else can see her, too, Clarissa; standing there, the expensive, airy detail on the edge of the train of her pure ball gown trailing behind her.

If they can feel the tension in her heart; if they know what it is like — keeping a face while everything is shattering around you — what it feels like, being someone no one else ever hears —

The cruel, drawn-out bell sounds again.

Everyone shoves their binders into their backpacks, shrugging their shoulder bags on, actors perfectly on cue.

Eloise sits in her chair, rooted, as if by freezing, she could stop everyone else in this infinite play; as if by muddling up the act, someone would notice.

Nobody notices and, forced by the ever-constant rotation of the Earth and the hand of Time, which refused to stop for her, she moved to go to the next class: walking out of the classroom slowly breathing, brea-THing, br-ea-th-ing, in and out; clutching her copy of *Mrs. Dalloway* and her searing, perpetual, per-PE-tual insecurities beating just underneath her heart.

defining touch

STACY CHINA

This poem is about a visceral reaction to a verbal experience.

you never touched me

I am sure this is one of your defenses

it was never real

nothing happened

it wasn't true

because you never touched me

humph.

there was a day in the middle of fall

it was already cold and the sun was already half-lit

you talked to me about your trip

and your dreams

and your wishes

none of which was particularly out of the ordinary, really

but then came the book

a large, coffee-table sized book

you wanted me to see the work you admired

the mastery you were searching for in yourself

and I looked

and I listened

and as the pages turned, something happened

you forgot about the other people standing around

you forgot about the spectres of your other women,

 always hovering, even if rarely mentioned

the pages turned

and midway through the book

there was only the book

me

and you

everything else fell away

what I remember most

is the sunlight

and the warmth

there was an already-cold November wind blowing

and for the first time since late summer

I wasn't cold

the spell broke, of course

I don't remember how

but you went back to work

and I went back to class

and slowly, my sweater came back in handy

before it did, though

you touched me

unmistakably

on purpose

with intent

so when you say nothing happened

that may be true

at least for you

but don't ever say

you never touched me

JADE RODRIGUEZ

YEARS AS MENTEE: 2

GRADE: Junior

HIGH SCHOOL: Bronx Studio School for Artists and Writers

BORN: New York, NY

LIVES: Bronx, NY

PUBLICATIONS AND RECOGNITIONS: Scholastic Art & Writing Award: Silver Key

Both Linda and I don't have the best relationships with our parents and I immediately connected with her over that. She has helped me work through my anger with them and stay on track to live a better life. She has helped me find a voice to write about my father, which was something that was extremely hard to do at first. I am glad I did it, and without Linda I probably never would have. I am grateful that I have this relationship with Linda, and I can't wait to see what the future has in store for us.

LINDA CORMAN

YEARS AS MENTOR: 5

OCCUPATION: Freelance editor and writer

BORN: Newton, MA

LIVES: New York, NY

On the surface, Jade and I have very different lives, but we share fundamental experiences that have shaped who we are. Both of us feel that our mothers have shortchanged us, and we both have reacted to that hurt by being furious. In our writing and talking, I am constantly reminded of the destructiveness of fury, and what's a more helpful response.

Fight

JADE RODRIGUEZ

This piece is extremely close to me. It's about a dad who cares for his daughter, which is something I've been deprived of. This is the first time I have ever based a story on my father. My mentor Linda helped me find the voice to finally talk about him.

Liam. That sense of danger and never knowing what will happen. That's what I liked about him. I wish it were still like that. When he took me to the water tower, a forbidden area in our town, on our first date, I never felt so alive. That was also where I got my first kiss. When I got home, however, with multiple hickeys on my neck, my dad was up waiting for me. The grandfather clock said 2:15; curfew was at 11:30.

"Samantha Luna Barnes, where have you been?"

"Dad, I'm sorry. We went to see a movie. We lost track of time." I tightened the thick wool mustard scarf.

"Take off your scarf, Samantha!"

"Um...I'm kinda tired, Dad. I'm just about to go to bed."

As I headed toward the stairs, I felt a tug and when I turned around my scarf was in my dad's hands.

"Samantha, you have hickeys on your neck. Were you with Liam Jennings?"

"Yeah, why?"

"He's bad news, Sammy. Please stay away. He's been in juvie and lives on the wrong side of town. He made you a fucking leopard with all those hickeys. You are never seeing that boy ever again."

"I'd like to see you try and stop me!"

––––––––––

"Samantha, where are you going?"

"To Jenny's, Dad, for a movie night."

"I am trusting you'll be back at 12:30."

"Alright."

After I walked out of my house, I unzipped my baggy gym sweater to reveal a crop top and I pulled down my Adidas sweatpants to show skin-tight black skinny jeans. Liam was coming up the street to pick me up. I ran to his car, threw my cover clothes in the back and wrapped my arms around Liam.

"Can't wait for this party, Sam. I need to let off some steam."

"Me, too. Dad has been on my case a lot. I don't know how to get him to lighten up."

"Just be like me — don't give a fuck."

When we arrived at the party, my friend Amber — well, more like a frenemy — gave us both drinks.

I looked down at my drink and saw two little blue pills. I glanced over at Liam. His drink had blue pills too.

"Liam, what are those?"

"Ecstasy, I think."

"Have you ever tried drugs?"

"No, I hate that feeling of being out of control. You?"

"Never."

"Why don't we try it together to see if we like it?"

"You sure, Sam?"

"Yeah, what's the worst that can happen?"

"We overdose and die."

"That's not going to happen."

We both took our drinks. After about 10 minutes it kicked in. After around 10:30, I didn't remember anything really, just having fun and dancing with Liam.

I woke up in a room. A familiar room. Liam's.

He was staring down at me.

"Liam, that was an amazing night."

"Yeah, it was pretty intense," he said, shaking his head.

"Did you enjoy the ex?" I said with a smile.

"No, actually I didn't. Sure, I had fun while I was on it, but I didn't like how I wasn't in complete control."

"Really? It was amazing for me."

"No, it's not good."

"You sure that you don't want to try it again?"

"No, Sam."

"I think you're right. I won't do ex anymore."

———————

The money is gone and my body is crying for the ex. I walked into my parents' bedroom; my father was downstairs watching the game. I took the blue egg with gold designs and swiped it into my pocket. The white-gold one next.

> "The money is gone and my body is crying ..."

"Samantha Luna Barnes! What on earth are you doing?"

He grabbed the egg from my hand. Then he went into my pockets and withdrew the blue one too.

"WHAT THE FUCK IS THE MATTER WITH YOU?! Those were your grandmother's! Is this why things in this house are going missing? Is Liam making you do this?"

"LIAM IS NOT MAKING ME DO ANYTHING, LEAVE ME ALONE. KEEP THE GODDAMN EGGS. FUCK YOU, BYE!"

I ran out of the house. When I pulled out my phone, I felt something in my pocket. This should hold me till I find a way to buy more. I put the pill into my mouth and let heaven come.

————————

Goddamn it, Sam! I always did what I wanted and protected the ones I loved, somehow managing to stay in control. This is the first time I couldn't do anything. ANSWER THE PHONE! I slammed my phone on my dashboard and started the car. I knocked on the door and Sam's dad answered. He looked older than he did the last time I saw him. Looks like I'm not the only one Sam is stressing out.

"Hello, Mr. Barnes. Is Sam here?"

"I thought she was with you, you low-life criminal."

"I know you don't like me, but I love your daughter and I'm worried about her."

"I SHOULD BE THE ONE WORRYING! YOU TURNED HER INTO A THIEF!"

"I didn't. She's doing that all on her own. I think she has a problem."

"Yeah, that problem is you!"

"A DRUG PROBLEM!"

"I knew something was off. We have to find her."

"I think, I might know where she is."

"No, I would feel better if the police got involved."

"Mr. Barnes."

He turned toward me.

"Trust me, I know it's hard to do, but please trust me."

"Okay, let's go."

I Can't Come With You

LINDA CORMAN

My mentee Jade and I were talking about our fathers and their shortcomings. After we wrote about what we didn't like about them, we thought it would be interesting to write about what our ideal fathers would be like. I ended up writing about my father and his father, to explore why I think my father was the way he was.

Harry'd been riveted by the radio broadcast that morning. Charles Lindbergh was about to make his second try at crossing the Atlantic, this time in the Spirit of St. Louis. Harry was supposed to meet with the rabbi for his bar mitzvah preparation class at 10 a.m., but Lindbergh was still talking about the improvements he'd made on his plane at 9:55 a.m.

"Come on, I go now," his father had said, getting on his good dark wool coat and felt hat that he wore to temple. That had been 10 minutes ago.

"Wait," Harry had said from the kitchen table, where he sat with his ear inches from their boxy old Crosley 51.

"Now," his father had said. "Turn the radio off!"

Harry was pretty sure his father didn't have anything against flying. Flying was miraculous. Imagine zooming up into the sky, better than being a baseball, diving in and out of the clouds, tilting your wings, peering down at the tiny people, buildings, roads and cars below.

The problem was Lindbergh. Lindbergh's ranting against the Jews turned Harry's stomach too. But what could he do? His parents had escaped the pogroms when they were teenagers, leaving their parents behind. They'd made it to America. Who did it help to close your life in because there were Jew haters everywhere? Better to enjoy their great good fortune in being here, and the incredible future they were lucky enough to have a chance to be a part of — the age of flight, some were calling it.

He really didn't want to make his father mad. He actually wished they could go flying together. He thought his father would love it, if he'd only let himself. But it seemed like his father had to disapprove of just about anything he wanted.

> "He thought his father would love it, if he'd only let himself."

"And, today, you stay for Torah study. None of this bezball."

Harry didn't say anything. If his own father hadn't stayed in the old country, spending his life reading and parsing sacred texts, why should he do it in this new one? He knew it was his father's way of trying to feel like he still had parents, to do something for them. But he wasn't doing it.

As soon as the Hebrew class was over, Harry bolted home to change his clothes and be one of the first at the Franklin Field diamond. His father, his bald head shining, watched expressionless from the temple steps.

As Harry zig-zagged between people on the sidewalk making their way home after shul, he wondered if this was how his father had felt when he stole off in the middle of the night without telling his parents, hitching rides on wagons headed for Odessa, and spending his last shekels to get passage on a ship to America.

On Monday, after classes were over, Harry had agreed to meet his parents to translate for them at his younger sister's parent-teacher conference. But when he arrived in the school's lobby, where he was to meet them, his elder sister Anne was standing with his parents.

"Anne's going with us. Your help, we can do without," his father said, as the three of them turned away and walked toward the school office.

CATHIOSKA RODRIGUEZ

YEARS AS MENTEE: 1

GRADE: Sophomore

HIGH SCHOOL:
The Bronx School for Law, Government, and Justice

BORN: New York, NY

LIVES: Bronx, NY

PUBLICATIONS AND RECOGNITIONS:
Scholastic Art & Writing Award: Silver Key

Nicole is more than just my mentor. To me, she's like my older cousin who would invite me for a sleepover, take me to dinner if my mom would let me, and be the one to ask me how I'm doing inside and outside of school. I am not hesitant to tell her anything. I enjoy meeting with Nicole once a week. This relationship began with Nicole writing quotes in my journal and me talking about everything and anything. It's crazy how we have similar backgrounds but different experiences, which is what makes us click. It sounds like a cliché, but it was 'fate'. It was fate because she made me step out of my comfort zone and think outside the box. Nicole is one of the funniest, coolest, open-minded, nice, outgoing, and patient adults I've ever met outside of school.

NICOLE GERVASIO

YEARS AS MENTOR: 1

OCCUPATION:
Graduate student in English Ph.D. Program, Columbia University

BORN: Trenton, NJ

LIVES: New York, NY

Maybe it sounds like an exaggeration to say that Cathioska has been a lifesaver for me, but it's true. Getting to write with Cathioska and talk about her own trials and achievements has been the highlight of every week. Her courage and resilience as a young writer remind me that facing adversity with elegance is a strength we share. While her conscientiousness and creativity bring to mind my younger self from time to time, what I'm really looking forward to is supporting Cathioska in her own future as she figures out what the horizon has to offer her.

Different

CATHIOSKA RODRIGUEZ

*The Girls Write Now Persona Poetry Workshop inspired me
to write a poem about a very close friend of mine.*

Elementary School

The unknown is known

when the stars are bright

"It's better said than done"
   is what she said

"Listen here, young one. The sky is blue so
   God loves U"

She giggled and laughed among the rest

her pigtails bouncing in the school playground

a symbol and sign of purity and confusion

Middle School

She spoke about her love,

but never wondered how

"It's better said than done"
   is what she said

"Listen here, young one. The sky is blue so
   God loves U"

Never exposed to others, only

what's inside the circle of basic

play

never out

Early High School

Nowhere to hide

with no corners

"It's better said than done"

is what she said

"Listen here, young one. The sky is blue so

changing

    God loves U"

Adaptation is a way to learn how

to change due to the

environment

"U don't know God"

She thought it was for the better

to not believe in Him

'real world' was now in her vocabulary

Early to Mid High School

    She wanted to write

about anybody but herself

When asked why

    she never knew why

She would hesitate and stutter

    Silence would rise and

    "I don't know" would

break it

Present

Life's necessities and

love would make her

Forget and not know

    how to respond to

the repeated

statements

But then silence would rise as

    hesitation came into

as if the mouth was

the stage

Future

alive and not dead

    is how she'll be

"Go with the flow"

    she told herself

She felt neutral about
changing
It took decades to change
but no feelings were felt

Blood Ties

NICOLE GERVASIO

*When my mentee Cathioska started writing her poem, I decided
the best way for me to be inspired by it would be to pick up one of her
lines and put a story to it in my own words.*

"The sky is blue." These were her first words upon waking in her hospital bed. There was a poster of wheat fields lit up by a blue sky across from her. On the opposite wall hung a cross-stitch of the Serenity Prayer. *God, grant me wisdom to know the difference.* What is a difference, she thought? What is wheat? What is thread?

Her sister was the first to hear her declare the only thing she knew. "The sky is blue." Claire had suffered a stroke, and her memory was a limp, yellow thing. She noticed the magazine open on her sister's lap; in a flit of consciousness she recalled having read an article about strokes in women skyrocketing past age 85. But how old was she? 20? 30? She couldn't remember, and she began to crunch the starchy hospital sheets in her fists, and her dry heels began to knead the base of her waiflike mattress. She looked up at the wheat but the word wouldn't come to mind. Instead a number of associations surfaced: poison, sickness, guts, donuts, pain. She realized she was very hungry, that her stomach was yawning with hunger, and that the thought of donuts made her nauseous. Is this what irony feels like, she thought?

> "…she began to crunch the starchy hospital sheets in her fists, and her dry heels began to knead the base of her waiflike mattress."

"Claire," her sister called her attention in a too calm voice. "Calm down. You had a stroke." What is a stroke? Claire asked herself. Memories butted up against a crumbling wall in her brain. A stroke of genius. A stroke of luck. The back of a hand stroking her thigh. Whose hand had that been?

Her sister saw fear the color of jet shimmering in her eyes like hot oil. She pushed aside the magazine and held down each of her sister's wrists just as she began to tear at the tubes. "Claire," she spoke her sister's name for the second time in two weeks. She cleared her throat. "Claire." She said her name more sternly, more like she would to a child, and Claire, the older sister before this, snapped her head in the right direction.

"The sky is blue," she said a third time, with infinite conviction. And it was not Claire but her sister who suddenly began to cry, whose tears tumbled in big warm drops onto Claire's kept hands and her hospital gown. Her sister relaxed her grip. Claire instinctively held her close while she whimpered. "Is this what a problem looks like?" Claire asked no one in particular. "Not at all," her sister sniffled. "You woke up like I knew you would."

LUNA ROJAS

YEARS AS MENTEE: 1

GRADE: Sophomore

HIGH SCHOOL:
Cobble Hill School of
American Studies

BORN: New York, NY

LIVES: Brooklyn, NY

**PUBLICATIONS
AND RECOGNITIONS:**
Scholastic Art & Writing
Award: Honorable Mention

Entrepreneur Jim Rohn once said, "You are the average of the five people you spend the most time with." This year I was introduced to a new experience, being accepted into a community where I could freely express myself, be creative and be proud of my identity as a young woman. Girls Write Now, incredibly, is all of this and more. It also introduced me to my mentor and confidante, Julia Sanches, who is a vibrant, interesting woman. She quotes Lydia Davis and downloads The New Yorker fiction podcasts on my iPhone. I never imagined reading the variety of authors she's given me. Julia not only has expanded my literary tastes but questions me to think more deeply. With Julia there is always something to learn. If I am the average of the five people I spend the most time with, I'm proud to say my Girls Write Now mentor Julia Sanches is one of them.

JULIA SANCHES

YEARS AS MENTOR: 1

OCCUPATION:
Assistant Literary Agent,
The Wylie Agency

BORN: São Paulo, Brazil

LIVES: Brooklyn, NY

Working with Luna has been a pleasure. It has given structure and substance to my Sunday mornings and has punctuated my week. Every weekend we meet at a cafe called Sit & Wonder, where Luna buys a chocolate chip cookie and encourages me to share it with her. We talk about what we're reading and about language, about our families and friends. Every week, it makes me so happy to see that Luna is writing — poetry, fragments of stories, thoughts — and that she sits down every day to do so; it encourages me to do the same. She is sweet, generous, and enthusiastic, and I'm very happy we were paired together by Girls Write Now.

House

LUNA ROJAS

The persona poem "House" signifies two individuals who are confronted with an awful situation. They are unsure of how to cope, and so in secret they share the burden of the situation. When things begin to fall out of place, they rejoice because they are exposing this burden, and without the secrecy it doesn't carry as much weight. It is the transition from the dark to a lively moment.

I had a house like that once
White picket fence and all
With a backyard tended by a gardener
And a back patio where the deck stood

I had a house like that once
Like the kind on TV
All American
With a porch and driveway

I had a house like that once
Yet the house never really felt quite ours
Hung in the closet were coats
That didn't belong to us
In the drying machine a lone sock was left
But it was not yours
Or mine

They say caged birds sing
Yet the cage we reside in is so tainted
That chirping is agony
They say caged birds will sing
But our song ended long ago

I had a house like that once

And then the roof caved in
Our gardener was gone
And the picket fence turned black

When the house finally fell
It rained from our eyes
And we splashed
And rejoiced
In puddles of happiness

Biometric

JULIA SANCHES

I wrote this poem shortly after a visit to the U.S. immigration offices, so that they could take my fingerprints and I could renew my green card. I kept trying to make the immigration officer laugh because I was so nervous — what if there was something wrong with my fingerprints and they wouldn't let me renew my residency? — but I kept failing. My voice, and hers, got lost in that quagmiric bureaucracy.

Her chubby fingers
signal for me to drop
my purse. Drop my
coat. Turn. Face her.
Give her my hands.

She armors herself with silence like shark-
scales: if rubbed wrong, it is razor-like and the
skin grazes off. I try to break it with small

talk that tip-
toes toward her
with the tiny
feet of chitchat.

The room has

unfolded around me in the glare of disgruntled
faces in fluorescent light that keeps night
on stand-by. Her rough hands force my fingers

onto a screen
that shows
my prints like
a weather map
tracking storms

on repeat. My younger immigration
days were of ink and paper and I drew
biometrics with finger-paints. She squashes

my fingers on
the screen like
soft rolling pins
kneading the
hard glass

dough. "I remember," I say, "when we did this
with ink," fingers soft on the soft moss of ink-pads
leaving tracks on paper like handstands in sand.

It's as if I'm five
years old and hold
a caterpillar cupped
in my palms like
a new island.

"You must get this all the time," I say.
Her mouth is a permanent wrinkle. She turns
it toward me. It hesitates. Grunts. The park

bully, mouth wide
like the ocean, finding
it all unamusing, slaps
my cupped palms with
the blow of a wave.

NAJAYA ROYAL

YEARS AS MENTEE: 4

GRADE: Senior

HIGH SCHOOL:
Benjamin Banneker
Academy

BORN: Brooklyn, NY

LIVES: Brooklyn, NY

COLLEGE:
The University
of New Haven

**PUBLICATIONS
AND RECOGNITIONS:**
Poems set to opera;
co-wrote the lyrics to the
music video "Ode to Mala-
la" which was performed
at the United Nations
and the 35th City Council
District Swearing in Cer-
emony for Laurie Angela
Cumbo; Peter Jay Sharp
Youth Award

Working with Anuja has been one of the best journeys I've ever had, but this is only the beginning. She has become family and will always be my big sister. I know I can sometimes be a little difficult, but she is always here for me and I love that about our relationship. Anuja was honestly a dream come true and even though I will be graduating in a couple of months, I hope to keep her in my life after this chapter ends.

ANUJA MADAR

YEARS AS MENTOR: 8

OCCUPATION:
Content Strategist,
Marriott International

BORN: Binghamton, NY

LIVES: New York, NY

**PUBLICATIONS
AND RECOGNITIONS:**
Updated Harlem chapter for
Fodor's New York City 2016

During our last year together at Girls Write Now, I've seen my teenage self in Najaya more than ever. Whether she's expressing fears about going away to college or dealing with typical mother-daughter issues, I've been able to help her by sharing my own experiences. A recurring joke between us is that I lament that "I'm old," to which she replies "You're not!" Jokes aside, our dynamic together has helped me find my own voice as an "older" woman, and no matter how old we both get, I'll always have that to share with her.

Lost

NAJAYA ROYAL

*This poem is inspired by a couple of people I've come across in
my teenage years who have lost their way, or even lost themselves, after
being hurt by someone. I wrote from their perspective.*

I rise from what I no longer am

Oblivious

Have you ever seen a love so thick?

Trickle down the other cheek that's been turned over constantly

Overseasoned with forgiveness

Watered down agony

I no longer feel pity

Going against the grain

These burns only made me colder

I fall far from my purpose

Passing out in a fog that offers a dose of amnesia

I need this

The same way I thought I needed another being to be beside me

Falling so deep into myself

I begin to lose sight of the light I was in pursuit of

Maybe it's for the best

I become my own deep dark secret

Falling past my identity

Lost in a flood of black

I'm not sure if I can be saved

When my savior is as lost as I am

A victim of hurt

At least I'm not lost alone

A Voice Is Born

ANUJA MADAR

*Finding your voice is a turning point in becoming a woman
and something that we struggle with at various points in our lives.
I've used that as inspiration for my piece*

My voice isn't simply overshadowed by yours — it's swallowed whole. Consumed only to be spit out. Spit at.

Your words punctuate the dead air. Punch at me metaphorically. My silence speaks at a volume that's deafening to my ears.

Words develop into phrases yet remain unborn, afraid to leave the warmth of my womb.

They exist quietly, joined by brothers and sisters. Band together, expand together. Soon I'm bursting at the seams.

They plot their escape, yet fear I'll stifle them into silence. At times they're invaded by others who slip in from your mouth to mine.

There comes a point when the fullness is unbearable, pulling me down constantly. It's at this point I decide that to live a full life, I'll have to give birth to a new one.

And so I speak.

FAREENA SAMAD

YEARS AS MENTEE: 1

GRADE: Junior

HIGH SCHOOL: Hillside Arts and Letters Academy

BORN: Queens, NY

LIVES: Queens, NY

PUBLICATIONS AND RECOGNITIONS: Scholastic Art & Writing Award: Honorable Mention

Growing up I haven't had a lot of opportunities to openly discuss and express my views on the world. My mentor Nan has become my trusted confidant and helped me become more confident both as a writer and as a person. Her voice has made me question how I see the world and how I see myself. I am learning from Nan how to see from all perspectives in life and that sometimes it's better to think small than to go big. She is helping me become the writer I hope to be.

NAN BAUER-MAGLIN

YEARS AS MENTOR: 1

OCCUPATION: Professor and Academic Director, CUNY (retired)

BORN: New York, NY

LIVES: New York, NY

PUBLICATIONS AND RECOGNITIONS: Co-editor of *Final Acts: Death, Dying, and the Choices We Make; Women Confronting Retirement* and three other books

From the start, Fareena and I have debated whether one should write about what one knows or to venture away from that. We have challenged each other to think out of the box. We have learned from each other's voice as we have also incorporated the voices of many writers into our discussions as well. I am impressed with Fareena's dedication to the hard work of writing and her risk-taking with her writing. She is fearless; she lets her imagination fly high.

Bedroom Voices

FAREENA SAMAD

*This piece was originally written as a freewrite during a
Girls Write Now Workshop that eventually turned into something bigger. It
describes the many voices in my head that consume me.
Those same voices help me as a writer.*

It is quiet. When I'm alone in that room I finally get some time for myself. Whenever I feel crowded by the rest of the world or I am fed up with everyone, I escape into my bedroom. Every single time I do so, I try to hide from whomever or whatever is making me feel like this. But it's what happens next that I hate. Once I'm alone with myself I can hear my thoughts. My thoughts always want to be heard. My thoughts are always screaming, banging into each other and making so much noise. My thoughts never stop talking; they are just unspoken. My thoughts are the ones that don't need to speak to be heard. These are the thoughts that I fear the most. My thoughts always get the best of me.

I enter my bedroom, put on the nightlight, shut the door behind me and sit down. I take a long, sweeping look ataround my room and sigh. The bland walls and boring setting of the room don't scream "children's room!" but rather meekly mutters "guest room." But I've never had a problem with it because a room's a room and no matter how humdrum the setting is, I have grown to love my bedroom.

I try to tune the noise out. It starts out as a loud howl echoing inside my skull. I hum a little tune to myself; I try to read a book; I think about balancing chemical equations; I sing along to heavy orchestra music; I talk about my day to my teddy bears and pretend they talk back in response. Nothing works.

> "I try to tune the noise out. It starts out as a loud howl echoing inside my skull."

I bang my fists hard into my head thinking it will stop all the voices. I grow angry at my bedroom because while a war is being fought in my head, my bedroom stays quiet. The shots being fired, the screams that follow, the last cries of life, the sounds of dying, the crying, the yelling, the blood, the murder — my bedroom does nothing. It is unaffected by all the turmoil going on in my mind. It plays dumb; it acts as if nothing is happening, as if nobody is suffering. Only I can hear the battle, only I can hear the voices that resonate through my head. And no one seems to notice what is going on. Nobody hears anything.

A few minutes pass and it turns into a low whisper. I close my eyes and breathe in and out. I concentrate hard enough and it is a gentle hum. Suddenly, I hear a news reporter talking about breaking news from the kitchen television. I hear my parents talking. My father's voice booming as if he's over a loud microphone, my mother's voice competing with the news reporter. My sister runs through the halls, her feet beating a drum on the floorboards; my parrot squawks in the living room, his barks now ringing a bell in my ear. My eyes flutter open and I grit my teeth in frustration. My sister turns the doorknob to try to get into our room but she can't — it's locked. She stops and runs back into the living room to reunite with our parrot. My chest rises high as I sigh deeply. I can never be alone.

I hold my tears back as I get up to leave the room. No one seems to notice me as I slip away from my bedroom and into the bathroom. I walk in, flip the light on and sit on the mat. The white light shines brightly from the light bulb, the fan blares a loud noise. I bring my knees up to my chest and rest my head on them. The noisy fan blocks everything out — the television, my parents, my sister, my parrot, the thoughts, the whispers, the howls, the yelling, the screaming — I hear nothing. The fan hums a roaring lullaby that eventually puts me to sleep. As I hang between consciousness and sleep, reality and fantasy, life and death, I relish the brief moment of silence I have. My chest rises and falls with every breath I take. My eyes are closed and all I see is darkness. Except for the fan, there is a complete absence of sound. All the voices start to fade away until I hear nothing at all. And it is the same quietude that rocks my body to sleep.

Mentor / Mentee Dialogue

NAN BAUER-MAGLIN

At our fall meetings, my mentee Fareena and I brainstormed several lists: facts about ourselves, our family, our fears and hopes, what we have lost and found. We shared these lists in order to get to know each other and to identify our similarities and differences. This dialogue is drawn from the lists.

FAREENA: I am 15 going on 16.

NAN: I am way over 50.

F: My parents came to America from Guyana in the 1990s.

N: My great (maybe great great) grandparents emigrated from Germany in the late 1880s.

F: I am Muslim.

N: I am a nonbelieving Jew.

N: I like that my family is very diverse in ethnicities and religions and that it is quite big — maybe too big.

F: I like that my mother cooks tacos for me and that my father is a great talker.

F: I like to talk to bugs and spiders I encounter in my home.

N: I do not really converse with insects.

N: I like kale salad.

F: What is kale salad?

F: I am a creature of the night.

N: I like to walk in the city, both day and night.

F: I play the trombone.

N: I wished I had been given music lessons.

F: I lost a pair of really great headphones. Update: I found them under my bed.

N: I lost my daughter when she was a teenager. I found her when she turned 20.

N: I fear getting old.

F: I fear that I won't be accepted into any college.

F: I hope that I can get into college.

N: I teach college.

F: I have been a loyal fan of *The Vampire Diaries* for five years.

N: Hmmmm...I do not get this vampire craze.

F: Well, do we have anything in common?

N: Yes, do we have anything in common?

F: I am an avid reader.

N: So am I!

N: I have edited five books.

F: I hope to be a writer.

Ah, reading/writing — perfect for a GWN partnership.

GENESIS SEVERINO

YEARS AS MENTEE: 1
GRADE: Sophomore
HIGH SCHOOL:
Pelham Lab High School
BORN: Bronx, NY
LIVES: Bronx, NY

Working with Arianna has greatly impacted my life. I love how much of a strong individual she is helping me become. I know that this journey as writers is not over, but I would like to thank her for opening my eyes to a genre beyond my own and helping me explore a new perspective on life.

ARIANNA DAVIS

YEARS AS MENTOR: 1
OCCUPATION:
Associate Editor, O, The
Oprah Magazine
BORN: St. Louis, MO
LIVES: New York, NY

My mentee Genesis is outspoken, hilarious, and opinionated. Her mature and honest outlook on life has inspired me to look at how I view my own life — and also my creative writing and poetry. After reading her work, I've found myself motivated to write a response or write something similar that we can share together. I'm looking forward to the years ahead as we continue to get to know one another — as women and writers!

No, It's Not a Nightmare, It's a Life

GENESIS SEVERINO

*Since I was born, I have wondered what the point of everything is —
school, jobs, and overall hardships — if death is inevitable.
This poem shows my basic understanding of what I do and don't have,
and why I disagree with all the hard work we put into things.*

A lot of us never
asked to be born
yet here we are
with our hopes up
and our hearts torn.

See, unless you were
born into fame
you will always have
to work really hard
because you're part of the game.

Unless you already
have all the money
and don't really need to work
you're basically a slave
isn't that funny?

So here I am,
working really hard,
but afraid to swipe
because I fear being in debt
with my own credit card

So my question is why,
no, seriously — why?

we are born into this life
to work really hard
get our nirvana, and die.

No I'm not a communist
but I believe in equality
because every human being
deserves comfort in life
to me, that is the key.

The Destination

ARIANNA DAVIS

*This is a response to the poem "No, It's Not a Nightmare, It's a Life" by
my mentee Genesis. Her work — which I largely agreed with —
inspired me to create my own piece to show her that even
though the journey is long, it's worth it when you get to the destination.*

Work hard, play hard
That's what I was told
So that's on my to-do list
Until I get old

Sometimes the 9 to 5
Weighs heavy on my mind
But when I dream, I see light
At the end of the grind

It's a jungle out there
A rat race, they say
And it's not always worth
The price that we pay

Long days, long nights
All passion, no money

Long bills, long cries
All bitter, no honey

Tears and frustration
Behind the bright lights
But I'll keep pushing
Keep reading new heights

See, this is a journey
And the ride isn't perfect
But they'll remember my name
And it will be worth it.

MEEK THOMAS

YEARS AS MENTEE: 1

GRADE: Sophomore

HIGH SCHOOL:
Uncommon Charter
High School

BORN: Brooklyn, NY

LIVES: Brooklyn, NY

For the past six months, exploring horizons with my mentor Carlene has taught me that stepping out of my shell is an everyday process. By motivating me to take leaps — although I rarely listen — she persuades me to be a better me. In a way, this is also a challenge I believe we are both overcoming. Also, with her obsession to travel the world and try new things, she pushes me to pursue my wildest dreams involving writing and other personal goals. For this reason, she has inspired me and become a daily encouragement.

CARLENE OLSEN

YEARS AS MENTOR: 1

OCCUPATION:
Administrative Assistant,
Banco Popular

BORN: New Haven, CT

LIVES: Brooklyn, NY

**PUBLICATIONS
AND RECOGNITIONS:**
Will attend Columbia
University School of
Journalism

The first day I met my mentee, Meek, she told me about her goal to live abroad and learn about different cultures. I knew in an instant we'd be a great match! Meek pushes me to think abstractly every time we meet. Through our writing, we've explored ways of stepping into someone else's shoes and trying on new, often unfamiliar, voices. So far this year, we've written from the perspective of teen boys, street-cart vendors, and students struggling with a serious illness. Also, Meek and I also are hopeless romantics, which explains our "Voice to Voice" submissions!

Hurt

MEEK THOMAS

Inspired by my first heartbreak, this poem poured out during a Girls Write Now Workshop on a cold Saturday. It is a revelation to others and myself that it's fine to be hurt once in a while. Although the feeling may suck, you can get through it. I know I did with the help of my notebook and my pen.

I broke your heart?

You broke my heart.

That seems like a personal problem
I was bored and you were an easy target.
Like a wolf I like my prey vulnerable,
Fluffy-tailed and wide-eyed

I shouldn't have been so easy. So open.
Like a newborn baby, trusting a mother she's never seen,
I shouldn't have let him in

She asked me "so everything was a lie?"
Dumb question.

I asked him "was everything a lie?"
From the empty promises to graveyard dreams
"I'll never hurt you," "You're all I need"
They were all lies.

We were never really "we"
I will always remain me
and you were searching for you,
Another personal problem

There was no us, no we
a bit naïve, I was still searching for me,
lost in what I thought was love

I don't feel bad that I hurt her.
She should've seen it coming

I hit her where it hurts, pointed out all her insecurities
"I love you" she cried, another personal problem.

He broke me and he knows it
Punched me right where it hurts
I've fallen.
"I love you," I wept. I still do. And for now

Goodbye

CARLENE OLSEN

*Writing this piece was a challenge for me. I revisited the memory of a final
goodbye and reflected on the voice of someone I once knew well.
Sharing such an intimate moment stretches beyond my comfort zone,
but my mentee Meek inspired me to go for it!*

the time we didn't say it
that's when I knew
I knew standing on the subway platform
staring at my shoes
this time
      this time
           this time
goodbye was long past due
the word we took for granted
stripped of meaning
overused

"I'll see you before I leave," he said
but I read his face and —
saw it wasn't true
"when?" I asked, shouted
over the screaming silence
that was ours
as trains zoomed through and through
"before I leave" he said, again

que in shades of blue

I felt empty
not in a bad way
just in a way that
makes you feel
you know
not full
he looked defeated, worn
aware
there was nothing else to do

"next time I'll make salmon"
I held tight to our routine
he smiled, arms open
holding tight to me
"perfect, I'll bring wine"
wine we'd never see

then he walked away
we walked away
I made me walk away
at 7:30 am
wednesday
we boarded separate trains

the time we didn't say it
that's when I knew
I knew standing on the subway platform
staring at my shoes
this time
      this time
           this time
goodbye was long past due
the word we took for granted
stripped of meaning
overused
suddenly goodbye
felt heavy, real —

for the first time
it felt true

CHARLENE VASQUEZ

YEARS AS MENTEE: 1

GRADE: Sophomore

HIGH SCHOOL:
Bronx Career & College
Preparatory High School

BORN: New York, NY

LIVES: Bronx, NY

**PUBLICATIONS
AND RECOGNITIONS:**
117 Wade Academies
Junior High School
Creative Writing Award

Caitlin is great at giving insight on different parts of my work, which to me shows that she thinks outside the box. This helps me write much more clearly and comfortably. She makes me feel like my writing is worth sharing, which is a struggle I think that most women writers feel. My personal essay is my most beautiful piece to me, and I thank her for that. It makes writing a rose that's blooming into something extravagant.

CAITLIN RIMSHNICK

YEARS AS MENTOR: 1

OCCUPATION:
Writing Instructor and
Graduate Student,
Columbia University

BORN: Denver, CO

LIVES: New York, NY

Charlene's voice as a writer and a person is thoughtful, unique, and bold. In our first pair session, as an exercise we both wrote down five things we loved. I listed: my husband, my nieces, etc. — all the normal stuff. Charlene wrote that she loved the complexity of humans. I thought, whoa, I need to up my game. From that point on, Charlene has inspired me to push myself to think and write in a way that is truer to my individual voice rather than settle for the first, perhaps more generic, response that comes to mind. What a gift!

Autism Is...

CHARLENE VASQUEZ

*Being diagnosed with autism is challenging, but not bad. My voice is
my advocate for autism. This voice that I own is one that needs to be heard
more often, and I am happy to possess this voice.*

Autism. This word can mean anything to anyone. It's such a varied term; those who
have it can't express what it is either. It is not something you can feel — or touch.
Autism? Oh no, it is much more than that. Autism is color; it is complexity. It is day
and night, happy and sad. It's not one thing only and it is not rare. Although this is
my own opinion that I speak, autism can be anything. There is no definite answer as
to what it is or what it is not. Merely, autism is.

It never occurred to me that autism affected my
whole life — oh, but I was wrong. I was diagnosed at
birth, and it startled my mother. Was I sick? It was such
a foreign... conception. I was the first child to be diagnosed in my family of three siblings, and so she cried.
Tears were shed. It was heartbreaking. My mother,
a warrior who ambled on burning coal since her teenage years, had no idea what
autism was or if her second daughter would be... "mentally ill." With the help of a psychologist, she sought and got help, and she learned along the way that autism can't
be "cured." She continued, biting back tears and frustration, to get me to be the very
best I could be. It was working, and I, at the age of two, finally learned how to speak.
"Mama! Papa!" and it was a mother's miracle. All I could say, she said, were those two
words... until I stopped altogether by five years old. When I couldn't speak anymore,
it raised concern. Most of my family members were alerted. Surely it was a mystery.

> "My mother, a warrior
> who ambled on
> burning coal since her
> teenage years..."

My mom brought me to the psychologist again for answers to this dilemma and
the answer was given — I really did have autism. Imagine this: a friend comes up to
you and tells you to get something for them, but you have no idea why they need it
but you do it anyway. My mom felt this way about my autism, but she never gave up
on trying to get me the right support. Support, huh? I didn't know what that was until
I turned 10, and even then I didn't pay any mind to it. My comprehension matched
the level of my general age group or higher — so why should I have paid any mind?
It wasn't until my mother explained her journey to keep me stable that I was aware

of such a word; but that was only the exposure. I still couldn't actually comprehend what that incredibly complex thing was.

Coming of age, that's when I started to open my mind a little more. I fell into a depression at the age of 15 out of the yearning to not fail in school. Keep in mind that I had support — had. There was a battle between my preference of not wanting to travel to my appointments and the necessity for the appointments, so this caused my mom to shut down my support for about two years. This was happening around the same time that I was transitioning from the private schooling system to public, so my mom had to put a lot of thought into these decisions, which raised questions, too. Was it a mistake to remove my support? Was it a mistake to put me into mainstream after nine years of attending one private school? I was finally placed in public school, with a delicate yet intelligent mind at 13. I prospered like it was a dream that I could vividly see in my sleep. And yet this transition raised another dilemma for me. They put me in sixth grade to begin middle school and once my school guidance teacher noticed something was off, it was eighth grade for me in one year. What a transition!

Now let's fast forward to now. One year in middle school and now I'm in ninth grade. It's not a rare case to skip grades, of course, so I don't have the heart to say it's something I can brag about. Now I roam high school premises wondering who I am and why I do what I do. Bingo, I fell into a pit of darkness and anxiety. Of course I know everyone gets depressed or anxious, for they would be inhuman if that wasn't the case, but because of this great fall, I realized how capable I am for someone diagnosed with autism and struggling. It surely is evident in my school work, and my principal came up to my mom herself and brought up how remarkable my effort is. Now I wonder, how did I accomplish this? Although, without a doubt, I am capable.

With this capability that I possess, I do notice why I went through what I did. It wasn't easy to distinguish my intelligence and my mental state. Even to my current days, if I am to tell someone that I have this disability, they wouldn't believe me. I don't blame them. It is stereotyped that autistic kids are "incapable." Even I, myself, forget. It's something to focus on, but to not fuss over. So once it leaves your mind, then what? People forget autism, then they forget that autism is a world of differences — no two are the same and we can only acknowledge similarities. Sounds familiar, right? It should sound like the human population; something so diverse that if an alien asks about who and what we are, we would all have different answers. Science has that answer, maybe? But no, humans are not just one thing: we are many things and that applies to autistic children as well. Generalization is easy, but not right. Autism isn't one thing; it's many things and it's beautiful, so that should never bring anyone down to hear, "your child has autism." Autism simply... Is.

A Boston Winter

CAITLIN RIMSHNICK

*My mentee Charlene challenged me to write something experimental in one
of our sessions. Primarily a prose writer, I took a crack at a poem about the
many blizzards in Boston this past winter. The never-ending snow
had a quality of magical realism I found intriguing and wanted to capture.*

It started innocently enough:
a few puffs fell from the sky,
slowly.

Plop, plop.
The flecks stuck to the sidewalk,
like cute little lint balls.

But then there were more,
so many more.

The snow fell for days.

After each mad flurry,
people looked at each other
and said: "That must have been the last one,
the last blizzard of the season."
But it wasn't.

Soon the fluffy stuff was piled high.

It was so high,
if you hoisted yourself on top of it,
you could jump onto your roof.

It was impossible to walk anywhere,
too much snow.

So people got creative.

They pulled their kids in sleds,
just to go to the store.

Sometimes they gave up
on the errand they were running
and flung themselves onto a snow bank
just to float for a while.

JAELA VAUGHN

YEARS AS MENTEE: 1

GRADE: Sophomore

HIGH SCHOOL:
Richard R. Green High
School of Teaching

BORN: Bronx, NY

LIVES: Bronx, NY

**PUBLICATIONS
AND RECOGNITIONS:**
Scholastic Art & Writing
Award: Honorable Mention

My relationship with my mentor Laura is borne from common interests and a passion for writing. With a fine love for sarcasm and culture, I thank Girls Write Now for giving me the chance to meet her.

LAURA BUCHWALD

YEARS AS MENTOR: 1

OCCUPATION:
Writer and Editor

BORN: New York, NY

LIVES: New York, NY

My work with Jaela is fun and challenging. She continues to impress me with both her writing and her knowledge of English culture, LGBT issues, and all things Benedict Cumberbatch. That a 15-year-old from the Bronx has become an avid Anglophile is one of the brilliant side effects of reading and writing with an open mind.

Coming Home

JAELA VAUGHN

My piece takes place in England during the Thatcher tyranny (1980s).
I was inspired to write about this after hearing the stories and music of that
time, as well as seeing the movie Pride, *which depicts the Lesbians and*
Gays Supports the Miners (LGSM) strike.

He raised his fist to the decorated mahogany door. He couldn't quite make contact with the wood. He knew what lay behind the door. It was his parents, whom he closely associated with every evil parent in the fairytales he taught himself to read. They were the two people who hadn't spoken to him since they'd heard the news of his dating Tristan. What would they know about happiness anyway? They'd never met until the day of their wedding, which was arranged by their families.

He took a deep breath, closed his eyes, and listened to the rhythmic tapping of his knocking.

His mother sat in silence and stared at him with a solemn expression. She didn't seem to mind her husband throwing his favorite whiskey glass at the nearest wall.

"What do you mean you're 'engaged'?"

Simon's voice was robotic. He shouldn't have come.

"It means that I'm going to get married."

His mom bit her bottom lip; her eyes got teary.

"I swear if you say that...poof, Tristan!"

Simon's eyes snapped up at his father.

"Who else would it be? God knows he's the only one who cares!"

His father held his finger up.

"Your mother and I do care!"

"You cared enough to throw me out on the street because I had a drug problem?"

The parents were silent.

"But Simon," his mother began. Her lilting French accent romanticized her words and made them sound more kind-hearted than condescending. "This relationship you are pursuing, you don't really want it. You're being rebellious."

"Excuse me? This is the happiest I've ever been. Of course I want it!"

"No you don't," his father interrupted. His accent was posh — he came from a rich upbringing — and slightly harsh, his baritone voice emitting some words harder than others. "You know that this is just a phase. You don't love Tristan! He's a man — you can't be happy with another man."

Simon was crying now. How dare they talk about his relationship so heartlessly.

"Says the man who doesn't love his own wife!"

He did it. He pissed his father off. And in no time, he was being held by the shirt, and he could smell his father's alcohol-ridden breath. It made him sick to his stomach. His father hadn't sobered up after all of these years.

"You don't get to say that. You don't get to compare your...unnatural relationship with mine. Two men don't belong together."

Simon was silent and listened to his father's low grumblings.

"Now I'm going to tell you what you're going to do. You're going to piss off, like the filth that you are, and I don't want to see your face back here until you finally come to your senses and leave him. Do you understand?"

Simon remained motionless; he was trying hard to keep his composure. He was already crying, what more did they want from him? Not saying a word, he pushed his father's large and powerful hands off the collar of his shirt and stormed to the door. Along the way, he saw his mother seated on the couch, staring at the empty fireplace, pretending that there was fire in it, that she hadn't witnessed her husband about to beat their child for the simple fact that he was engaged to another man. Simon had tried loving her, and that's as far as he got. Now there was no love for either parent in his heart.

"When had they ever showed him the appreciation and love that is expected of parents, especially those with only one child?"

He should have expected it, honestly. When had they ever showed signs of change? When had they ever showed him the appreciation and love that is expected of parents, especially those with only one child? Never, they never so much as glanced his way after he left for university, they barely gave him enough money to survive. Were they surprised that he turned to drugs?

He slammed the door and hoped that he broke something on the way out. Of course, they let him run out. Why had he even come? Did he expect them to change? The answer, he found all those years ago was no. All the times his dad stormed into his room to let him know that he was a disgrace and that he would ruin the family name. All of the times his mother would watch him come home from school, beaten and broken, and flash him a small smile and little else. He'd wished for a family like Tristan's. They knew what it meant to be parents and to love unconditionally. Simon would sometimes wonder about his upbringing if he were born into another family. He would be happier; he wouldn't have tried to kill himself with drugs. He probably wouldn't have met Tristan. Simon's self-hatred grew with an intensity as he walked back to his home. The home that he built with Tristan during their years together. The bookstore that has become all but famous in their town. The flat that they bought with their hard-earned money, and the marriage that was to come. Tristan is his home.

When I was Fifteen

LAURA BUCHWALD

Jaela is interested in the Victorian Era in London, as well as the 1980s.
Since I can't speak for the first of these eras, I have compiled a short list of
my life in the second — the 1980s, when I was the age that she is now.

When I was fifteen,

I had long, late conversations with my best friend on the yellow rotary wall phone in our kitchen. While we'd talk I'd untangle the cord, only to have it coil back up as soon as we hung up. The notion of having my own phone — and one that I could carry in my pocket — was science fiction.

I didn't know how to type, though I'd practiced a bit on the light blue Smith and Corona my mother kept in her office; no one I knew had a computer.

My favorite band was Duran Duran, and I had all of their albums and a few cassette tapes, because those were portable. We learned about new music through MTV.

We were the last people in our neighborhood to get cable TV; the first movie I watched, on HBO, was Zeffirelli's Romeo and Juliet. Cable TV had dozens of channels — the options were boundless.

> "I wrote letters. On paper.
> By hand."

We were late in getting an answering machine; if someone told us they'd called, we had to take them at their word. And calling was how we most often communicated. I wrote letters. On paper. By hand.

AIDS was just becoming a household word; it would be five or so years until Magic Johnson would become the heterosexual celebrity face of the epidemic.

Ronald Reagan was president. Again.

The Challenger blew up. It was a snow day and I watched it happen, live, on the tiny black and white Sony TV by my mother's bed.

The Twin Towers were the tallest buildings in Manhattan; I'd first visited them in the '70s, shortly after they were constructed, on a second grade class trip.

The foreign threat we feared most was that the Russians would attack us with nuclear bombs. We'd seen The Day After — we knew what it would look like.

Ed Koch, Mayor of New York City, signed the city's first Gay Rights Bill.

The subway cost one dollar.

Girls Write Now did not yet exist, and there was as much a need for it then as there is today.

SEANNA VIECHWEG

YEARS AS MENTEE: 1

GRADE: Senior

HIGH SCHOOL:
The Young Women's
Leadership School of
East Harlem

BORN: Brooklyn, NY

LIVES: Bronx, NY

**PUBLICATIONS
AND RECOGNITIONS:**
Scholastic Art & Writing
Award: Honorable Mention

My mentor Katie may be small, but she has a big personality. As a person, I consider myself reserved, as I cannot always find the courage to speak up. Katie, experienced and daring as she is, could be considered the opposite of me. Despite our similarities (we're both bookworms!), I am grateful for this difference, as her voice has inspired me to raise my own. Whether it is in workshops where she articulates her ideas beautifully, or sharing at our weekly sessions, seeing her helps me know that I should voice my opinions in whatever challenge I face — because if Katie can do it, I can too.

KATIE GEMMILL

YEARS AS MENTOR: 1

OCCUPATION:
PhD Student

BORN: Ottawa, Canada

LIVES: Brooklyn, NY

**PUBLICATIONS
AND RECOGNITIONS:**
"Must We Have Lives?"
An essay published in
Public Books

I remember my first impression of Seanna: striking, with great style and an earnest, sweet disposition. Though she can be soft-spoken, I quickly learned that this is a young woman who knows her mind. She loves dystopian fiction and Disney movies. She wants to change how women are represented in the media. She dreams of going to a great college, and is going after it with a work ethic that leaves me in awe. Seanna's optimism makes me feel like anything is possible; and her quiet determination has taught me that you don't have to be the loudest voice in the room to float above the rest.

Sidechick #6

SEANNA VIECHWEG

*Because of the way "sidechicks" are mocked on social networks, I wrote this
piece from the perspective of a girl who finds herself in that position. I hope
to shed light on her circumstances and give voice to her feelings.
Not only do "sidechicks" face the challenge of being considered second-
class by the boys they like, but also by fellow girls around them.*

Before you judge me
Before you laugh with your friends
Over a screenshot of our conversation
A conversation between me and him
That I thought was special
Just try to understand.
You didn't see him the way I did
You weren't there
You weren't there for all the nights
We spent talking
past midnight when we both should have
Been sleeping
You didn't see the way he looked at me when
we were together
The way every girl wants to be looked at
Studied unaware, when even she
isn't looking.

I didn't intend to be his sidechick —
Anyone's sidechick for that matter
It just happened
Who doesn't know what that's like?
if you don't, I'll understand

It's always been women

Against women

pointing fingers

at the wrong person

I don't want to do that with you.

But you haven't even considered

what I was thinking.

That I was thinking

I would be the one

our love would be the one

to make him realize

relationships are a real thing

Worth trying

And that one-stands are a thing of the past

Because staying in for the morning

Is just as good as banging.

Women have made my battle worse

Not only am I fighting for his attention

But for my "sisters" not to shame me

Treat me like I am worthless

As if love is an object

I am not deserving of.

Because if I lose

I lose everything

Everything he and I were

Building

Even the way

He began to see me —

The real me

The one no one is ashamed

Of showing.

Feline Address

KATIE GEMMILL

My poem about catcalling features some of the voices in our culture that I don't
want to hear, and makes an attempt to answer them in my own words. The
piece was inspired by my mentee Seanna, who questions gender inequality in
much of her poetry, especially the popular language that perpetuates it.

He says —

        hey infant how you doin

        damn, you're piled high

as I walk by,

        i bet you're an unclean female dog

he shouts

you've got such a murderous rump

i'm gonna drive you

and arrive

all over it

I just want to do my day, but

        i wanna apply pressure to your mammary glands

he says

        with my hands

just wanna ingest that kitten

hammer and hit

that cat

he leers, but

"just joking," seriously

hey, chill out

        i know you want to give me some cranium

imma show you my inflexible rooster

make you apply much suction

really?

his words only used to be fresh
now they're dead weight
dark comedy of animals
and flesh

What about my language?
Dig deep and translate
he says
hey
i'm here
as I walk by
just, wait —
i feel alone
your shame
and your fear
            make me feel less
my own

GNESIS VILLAR

YEARS AS MENTEE: 1

GRADE: Senior

HIGH SCHOOL: Institute For Collaborative Education

BORN: New York, NY

LIVES: Brooklyn, NY

PUBLICATIONS AND RECOGNITIONS: Scholastic Art & Writing Award: Gold Key for Writing Portfolio

My mentor Alice is young enough to humor my questions but wise enough to answer them. When we first met, I was surprised by how young she was. Unconsciously, I was expecting an older mentor, but after working together I'm glad how things turned out. I feel comfortable asking her for advice.

ALICE HINES

YEARS AS MENTOR: 1

OCCUPATION: Freelance Journalist

BORN: Austin, TX

LIVES: Brooklyn, NY

PUBLICATIONS AND RECOGNITIONS: i-D; Smithsonian; The Awl; Gawker; Talking Points Memo; New York Magazine

The first time I met my mentee Gnesis, she asked, "What's it like to be an adult?" I've continued to think about this throughout our year together, as Gnesis prepares to move from high school to college. Both of our writing has dealt with growth and personal identity, and while neither of us have come up with definitive answers, we've had some great conversations along the way. If anything, I've realized being an adult means being able to give a brilliant 18-year-old answers to some (if never all!) of her questions.

FRACTURE

GNESIS VILLAR

*This piece was not inspired by anything. Most of the time when
I write poetry I just see a line I like and write something to go with it.*

Most nights my mind and my body
refuse to be in the same room once
sunset folds itself into evening's shadows.
My mind is off picking its way through
the Milky Way, shaking
buildings to rubble in Indonesia
or forming cracks in Californian sidewalks
that look like the razor line of a smile.
My body is left behind, smothered by
the sheets in my room that lacks ventilation.

Later I try to link hands with my thoughts,
like we're children learning how to cross
streets all over again, and I'm showing
the way home like we're not both lost.
We stumble back in when dawn
is filtering through my cheap blinds
— limbs clashing,
feet aching —
and head off to bed. In the space
between wakefulness and sleep,
I couldn't feel colder.

Why I Talk To Men
Who Catcall Me

ALICE HINES

Working with my mentee Gnesis prompted me to reflect on my own memories of being a teenager. This piece, excerpted from a personal essay I previously published, is about a gap year I spent in Paris before college.

I learned French in bars getting hit on by weird men. Also: in subway cars and public parks, in Internet cafes looking for apartments, and shopping for cheap kitchenware at outdoor flea markets. At first, I didn't understand anything they were saying to me, but eventually, I picked up patterns. Ça va? ("What's up?") was innocuous — usually fine to ask the person for directions or even a metro ticket. Vous êtes charmante ("You're charming") was best ignored. Anything resembling "tu suces" (not to be confused with marché aux puces, a landmark near my apartment) meant I should walk away as fast as possible.

When I moved to Paris, I had a hunch that not knowing anyone would force me into the kinds of awkward situations where I would naturally pick up the language. I was right. My first day in the city, I actually spent 10 hours straight walking around different neighborhoods, with two suitcases and only the vaguest of plans. The next few months were similar. Until I could build the components of a private life — job, friends, an apartment — I spent a huge portion of my existence in public, and consequently, getting hit on by men in a language I could barely understand.

> "...and consequently, getting hit on by men in a language I could barely understand."

These interactions started, for the most part, as standard street harassment fare: sexual invitations couched in various degrees of creativity and politeness. Sometimes, they were worse — insults, verbal abuse, and once, a groping. But, occasionally, they also turned out to be interesting. Two men who introduced themselves with a Vous êtes charmante showed me how to play a didgeridoo months later. I learned about the only store in Paris that sold peanut butter (a sorely missed item) from a dude who insisted on badgering me about my bread and cheese lunch as I ate on a park bench. None of these interactions turned into lasting friendships, but that doesn't mean they weren't useful or thought-provoking.

Eight years later, now living in New York City, I still talk to men on the street, and I still find the experience interesting. When one of them says "hey," I often say "hey" back, before I've determined whether or not the greeting has a sexual undercurrent. That doesn't mean I'm nice to everyone, or that I never respond with silence, a "fuck off," or a police report when I feel they're fitting. It does mean that I'll occasionally find myself talking on the subway with a guy sitting next to me while a female friend watches on uncomfortably. Or, when a construction worker asks me how my day is going, answer and ask him the same question, because I want to know. In Paris, I talked to strange men because it was the only way to break out of linguistic and social isolation. Now, I do it because I'm curious. I'm not going to learn a new language, but I might get a window into another person's thoughts. If they're not good thoughts, I can walk away.

AMBER WADE

YEARS AS MENTEE: 1

GRADE: Junior

HIGH SCHOOL:
The Urban Assembly
Institute of Math and
Science for Young Women

BORN: Brooklyn, NY

LIVES: Brooklyn, NY

It's only been my first year at Girls Write Now, yet I have experienced wonderful things. It's like entering a world of writing. Kate is one of the coolest mentors a girl could have, and she's always there to make sure I have spaces after my periods. Kate and I come up with weird but fascinating stories, whether it's from a trip to the Brooklyn Museum or just a meeting at Starbucks. Even when I'm not with Kate, I tend to find my hands itching, to continue building my sci-fi collection of stories.

KATE PETTY

YEARS AS MENTOR: 1

OCCUPATION:
Writer

BORN: Cheverly, MD

LIVES: Brooklyn, NY

This year has flown by so fast. My mentee Amber brings incredibly creative ideas to our meetings and a sly sense of humor to everything she writes. She challenges me to keep up, and to bring new and better ideas for writing prompts to our meetings. Working together as both of our voices grow — and as our science fiction ideas get crazier — has been such fun.

Excerpt from "Milk"

AMBER WADE

This piece started at a pair-session with my mentor, grew over several weeks and turned out great. The following is just an excerpt. Justin, whose only friend is his robot, discovers his expiration date and only wants one thing — to leave a legacy for Mr. Klipspringer, the guy who gave him confidence.

Justin headed to Mr. K's office and saw John and his father, Mr. Giovanni, there.

"Where's Mr. K?" asked Justin, curiously.

"He's dead," answered Giovanni, bluntly.

"Why'd you kill him, he was everything to me, he helped me defeat my self-esteem issues and made me feel worth something. And guess what, you want to know who caused it? You. John. You're the one who bullied me every day, made me feel less than nothing and made my life, in a way, miserable," Justin stated in a strong voice.

"Oh, I'm so sorry for ruining your little life of nothingness," John said sarcastically. He was about to utter something else but looked at his father with sadness in his eyes. "Dad, you ruined my life and caused me to have self-esteem issues. You abused me and tormented me throughout my whole life. I believe that's why I want to make Justin here feel like nothing. Not because I'm some bully but because you made me into one. Uncle K always helped me with my issues and made me feel better. Now he's dead and you're the killer," said John.

John pulled out his LOGICGun and shot his father right in the heart. Where he deserved to be shot. He didn't have one to begin with.

Looking towards Justin he said: "I'm deeply sorry for how I made you feel. I hope you don't end up like me, and my father. Mr. Klipspringer was a very good person and he didn't deserve to die at the hands of his own brother," John said quietly.

John did the unthinkable and shot himself.

Justin just stood there in disbelief and awe, he was shocked that John would feel that bad and take his own life.

Justin didn't even take his LOGICar back home, he just slowly walked.

With his head down.

Justin was left with no one now. Except Mobot.

————

Justin arrived home with nearly 15 hours left.

Mobot was there waiting for him of course with his favorite meal already made: rice pilaf and grilled salmon. Justin plopped down on the couch and stared aimlessly. He still was in total shock. He didn't process that he had witnessed two killings.

Mobot kept asking him "Are you alright?" "Was my observation correct?" "How much time is left?"

Justin was zoned out. He ate his dinner and went back to just staring. Not because he had literally 12 hours left of his life. But because he had just witnessed the worst thing a Sunnan can ever imagine. Justin decided on accepting his death but wanted to leave behind something that anyone can benefit from.

> "Justin was zoned out. He ate his dinner and went back to just staring."

"Hey, Bot can I inform you on something?" Justin asked.

"Yeah, sure, Justin, what's going on?" Bot asked worriedly.

"My professor, Mr. Giovanni taught me and the class that it's proven that a Sonarian like you can turn into a Sunnan. But there's a catch, you have to drink milk and so do I. But it's okay Mobot, I'm dying in fewer than 11 hours, and my only dream is for you to become Mr. Klipspringer. He was my mentor, my friend, and the only person that made me feel like I am worth anything. He taught me how to overcome my self-esteem issues. Mobot I'll teach you everything you'll ever need to know in these 11 hours I have left. Just, please, Mobot, do this for me, for Mr. Klipspringer, and for all the people out there with problems like mine," Justin said, pleading.

"Okay, Justin, if that's what makes you happy and if that's what will make you peaceful even when you're not here anymore, than sure I will," Mobot reassured him.

Hours and hours passed and Justin taught Mobot everything he needed to know. They laughed and talked and had the best time ever. They ate all the salmon, rice pilaf, and sundaes they wanted. But the whole time Mobot thought about what he would do without Justin.

Justin had 10 minutes left after he finished mentoring Mobot.

Mobot took some milk from his drain port.

"Here goes nothing," said Mobot, about to drink it.

"Wait. Bot, I just want you to know, you've been the best buddy any Sunnan can have. I think you'll be the perfect mentor and I love you Bot," Justin said.

"Thanks, Justin. I love you too buddy," Bot said sadly.

They held hands and drank the milk simultaneously.

Bot looked and Justin wasn't there anymore. His buddy and owner was gone.

Two months later, Mobot, now Mr. Monsu, was walking down the street, posting his self-esteem class sign-ups for teens. Walking away from the community board, he spotted this young man walking with his head held low.

He knew it was a sign.

He knew it was Justin.

Star-Crossed

KATE PETTY

Amber's interest in science fiction has given me a totally fresh perspective on the genre. This fake movie review (in the style of The New Yorker*) is my best attempt at keeping up with her creativity.*

How did the astronauts get over the seven-year itch? There should be a joke somewhere in this premise, but Whitney Albom's new film takes itself as seriously as a moon landing conspiracy theorist. Astronauts John Maslow and Amy Hendricks (Greg Win and Alicia Mitchell), a husband-and-wife team, sign up for one last mission: A long jaunt through space to fix a broken Mars satellite and a bruised marriage. The third leg of the love triangle is Hutch Gideon (Blake Sellers), who's ostensibly the ship's mechanic, but who seems to apply most of the elbow grease to his biceps. The movie veers unintentionally into slapstick comedy (an early scene of Hendricks and Gideon avoiding contact while bumping through a narrow, no-gravity control room is memorable), and the introduction of cannibal space pirate aliens is flat out ridiculousness. The invaders capture Hendricks; Gideon goes mad with terror; Maslow is left to choose between a cozy escape pod and a suicide mission to save his wife. So how did the astronauts save their marriage? Turns out it was easy: You just have to not let the other one die. With Tom Waits as the cannibal space pirate aliens' sexy mechanic. In wide release.

MYA WATKINS

YEARS AS MENTEE: 2

GRADE: Junior

HIGH SCHOOL:
Brooklyn Technical
High School

BORN: Queens, NY

LIVES: Queens, NY

**PUBLICATIONS
AND RECOGNITIONS:**
Scholastic Art & Writing
Award: Silver Key

It has been a wonderful experience to be a part of Girls Write Now My mentor, Ines, has helped push my writing to new levels. I have loved working with her. She has helped me develop my writing in ways I never thought of.

INES PUJOS

YEARS AS MENTOR: 1

OCCUPATION:
Coeditor, Print
Oriented Bastards

BORN: Lyon, France

LIVES: Brooklyn, NY

**PUBLICATIONS
AND RECOGNITIONS:**
*Print Oriented Bastards;
Day One; Bone Bouquet;
Gulfcoast; Hayden's Ferry;
Phantom Limb; Cimarron
Review; Puerto del Sol*

I've had the pleasure of working with my mentee Mya this past school year. It has been awesome to try new writing prompts, and writing in different genres and styles. This year we spent a lot of time with poetry. Mya has grown so much within these last months and her images are incredibly lush, her work brilliant and heartbreaking. Working with her has also allowed me to spend more time with my writing and trying different forms and styles. One thing that we both enjoy is writing through different narratives — often we do poems based off the prompt, "Self-portrait as..." This allows us to write from various masks and explore new voices.

What Moths Are Drawn To

MYA WATKINS

*A prompt my mentor Ines gave me sparked the idea for
this poem. Writing it was a lot of fun, and it was interesting to talk about
the feelings I have of the perfect version of me.*

I'm flooded with sights of a girl

with skin as gold as sun.

Her face,

some rejected Native-American goddess,

too sensual to be holy,

her body as soft as clay,

but never as pliable.

And when she opens her mouth

how the mountains move!

But here, where spider webs

seem more abundant than clouds,

I wonder if I even know what beautiful is.

What gives her that flame

moths are drawn to?

I would like

for once,

To be seen in that way,

where I could create a tsunami

with a flip of my hair.

The Swallows

INES PUJOS

I wrote this piece in response to the violence targeted towards women in Juarez, Mexico. I wanted the piece to have a strange smallness to it — and the attention to the dog only echoes the mistreatment of women and maternal figures in our society. Let it be a haunting image.

The cathedral's coffin-carved
doors remain parted. Our Lady
— with hands cupped upward —welcomes the masses, knee
to marble, arms heavy with Mary
& sorrow to a chalk Christ.
I light the waxed wicks.
Along the Jaurez Border,
Hundreds of pink crucifixes gather.
A pregnant Chihuahua drags
its tits across the pavement
her little intestines moving

DIONDI WILLIAMS

YEARS AS MENTEE: 1

GRADE: Freshman

HIGH SCHOOL:
Academy for Young Writers

BORN: Brooklyn, NY

LIVES: Brooklyn, NY

Spending time with Nicole has really helped me. Through the program at Girls Write Now, I have someone to guide me through the rough patches and help me fix the mistakes I've been making. Nicole is a great influence on me — she is like a big sister. Nicole has a great personality and accepts who I really am. I couldn't have asked for a better mentor from Girls Write Now.

NICOLE COUNTS

YEARS AS MENTOR: 1

OCCUPATION:
Marketing Coordinator,
PublicAffairs and
Nation Books

BORN: Plainsboro, NJ

LIVES: Brooklyn, NY

In many ways I came into this relationship thinking I'd help inspire Diondi. I hoped to help open her eyes to the authors that raised me, the words I found comfort in, and the tools that helped me dig into the deepest corners of my life. However, not only has Diondi reminded me of the power writing has, she has reminded me of my own power, my own strength, and my own beauty. I am in awe of her courage and of her willingness to understand. My only hope is for both of us to be able to heal through our writing.

The Death of Hospitals

DIONDI WILLIAMS

"The Death of Hospitals" is about staying in a hospital for a week and feeling like it's your second home. The worst part is having doctors wake you up in the middle of the night — while dreams are dancing in your head. Oh, and the odor and the medicine...

My hands are shaking, my feet are throbbing, I hated being in the hospitals. The stinky smell, the medicine the awaking nurses give you. I couldn't handle it, I didn't want to close my eyes and have my dreams haunt and taunt me, but I had no choice. The liquid from the IV entered my arm, I can picture my blood fighting with the medicine. I can smell the leftovers from the bathroom... Ehh... Ew. This is why I hate hospitals. I missed my friends! I missed my bed! I missed school, I missed home. My feet would combine with the floor as I walked, then cold air traveled up my pants to my stomach, I felt it turn, I was so hungry. I walked out to find a way to escape but there were too many nurses. I walked passed one who said "good night" to me. She sounded like she was from India. I walked pass the front desk to the boys' side, in one of the rooms it had a wonderful view of the ocean and the lights. That was when I definitely wanted to go home. I watched as the cars raced each other down the highway, honking their horns. Yellow car, white, black, silver and all different types of colors. A tear from my eye fell onto my gown. I felt lonely with no one to talk to. I didn't want to talk to the nurses, because I felt like they didn't understand me. The nurse came walking into the room telling me it's time to take my medicine. I really didn't want to but I had no choice. Once again my feet combined with the floor as the beeper rolled behind me. I can't get the memory out of my head when the nurses sticked me so many times with the needle that my arm was almost swollen to death! I return to the room and lay on the bed, she puts the liquid through the IV and I feel the medicine run into my body. My eyes close as I fall into a deep sleep. Everything is pitch black and I can't see a thing. I force myself to open my eyes but my brain tells me to do another thing. I feel a hard tap on my leg, I quickly woke up, I couldn't see who it was it was so blurry. Everything got clear and it was a patient across the room from me; she couldn't sleep. I didn't know what I was supposed to say. She asked me can she sleep on my side, so I told her go to ahead! She walked to the chair like an elderly woman and laid in the chair and went to sleep.

A Reminder

NICOLE COUNTS

I asked my mentee Diondi once, "What do you look for in a friend?"
Her response: faith. This piece is dedicated to women who harvest, believe,
support, love and raise other women. Here's to faith in friendship, faith in
change, faith in better days to come, faith that they are already here.

I saw you on the train this morning.

You sat across from me with legs crossed. You sat beside me lightly brushing against my shoulder. You were a few rows over nodding your head to music. Yes, you stood holding the silver pole dusted with a thousand fingerprints. You towered over me as I looked up at your armpit while you held on above me.

You were behind plastic glass, yes I'm sure, you were behind glass streaked with rain and urine, sprinkled with dirt. You tapped the window and my eyes followed. You looked at me with eyes lined in thick black liquid. You looked like a cat. Neat springs fell onto your forehead. They were the color of your eyes — beautifully dark against your pale skin. Your lips were plum. Your eyes spoke intently and mine listened. You did not look away and you never did say goodbye. Twenty secondsminuteshours later you dissolved into the train.

But it was you, speaking gently to me,

saying faintly

to be.

AMY ZHANG

YEARS AS MENTEE: 1

GRADE: Sophomore

HIGH SCHOOL:
Frank Sinatra School
of the Arts

BORN: New York, NY

LIVES: Queens, NY

I come from a family of three kids and I'm the oldest. Everything I did while growing up was self-taught. I couldn't rely on my parents because they didn't speak English and were busy working. Before I joined Girls Write Now, I hadn't worked closely with an adult. Working with my mentor Leslie has given me a tremendous amount of knowledge in writing. She has inspired me to write outside of my comfort zone. But probably the most important thing she helped me with is pinpointing my voice.

LESLIE NIPKOW

YEARS AS MENTOR: 1

OCCUPATION:
Writer

BORN: Westminster, MD

LIVES: New York, NY

**PUBLICATIONS
AND RECOGNITIONS:**
Participant in A Fresh
Chapter's trip to India, one
of 10 cancer survivors cho-
sen to volunteer with local
NGOs and cancer support
organizations

Before our weekly pair sessions, I worry. What if today Amy discovers she is the real teacher? She speaks in clear, full sentences; I rely on faces, made-up words, and mime to make my point. I panic. What if I run out of things to teach her? Then Amy walks in, and I take a breath and simply listen. Who is this endlessly fascinating, accomplished young woman? How can I help her translate that funny, endearing, one-of-a-kind voice to the page? I listen for the truth, which, in turn, makes me a better writer. Amy is totally my teacher.

Conversations

AMY ZHANG

*This piece captures the thoughts I have at night. All those minutes
at night spent reflecting over memories and deep in introspective thought.
Although there are many more topics that run through my head
during the nocturnal hours, here is one of them.*

I am shy. I don't seem like the shy type with my friends because I'm the loud one. But when I talk to someone who doesn't know how I tick, I act like I'm listening while I am melting inside. What if they think I'm boring? What if they're just being polite? Do I look bored? Am I coming off like a crappy person? Am I blinking weird? Should I make eye contact? Wait, how much eye contact? Oh man, they think I'm insane. I unsuccessfully try to hold in the slippery dangerous words. Did that make sense? Why did I even say that? Wow, I don't love myself. This silence is so awkward. I feel it. It's my fault. What is wrong with me? How do I get out of this? That's when I start uncontrollably blushing.

> "That's when I start
> uncontrollably
> blushing."

In my mind, I think that I can contribute without turning into Clifford. A red face is a pain in the butt. Oh, you think it's cute, but it's not at all, especially when you're talking about the Holocaust or the meaning behind Frankenstein's creature.

I don't even have the guts to just say "Hi" to my crush in the hallway. When I see him in my periphery, I get super interactive with the person I'm talking to or the stuff in my locker or I fastwalk to my next class lickety split. I am easier to read than a Dr. Seuss book. He'll know by one look. He'll know from something I said that was just too nice. He'll know from my pink cheeks and how I can't keep eye contact.

I remember everything he's ever said to me. Especially that time I ended up taking the subway home with him alone. It was nerve-wracking and exciting at the same time.

Me: This is so awkward.

Wait, did I just say that to him aloud? Wow, what a great start.

Him: Give me something to work with.

Football.

Me: Did you see the last game on Sunday? That call on Vick was crap. He didn't even do anything. "Bad Sportsmanship" more like "Blind Refs."

Him: No, I didn't watch the game.

Michael. Achievement Hunter.

Me: So who's your favorite Achievement Hunter?

Oh god, I can feel the blood rushing to my face. Who called Clifford? Great, the train is coming. At least the conversation is going and he's talking about Minecraft now. He's such a nerd. I like it.

Him: Obviously, Ray and then Michael. Ryan or Jack. Geoff and Gavin are the worst.

Me: But Jack is only good at Trial games.

The train is too loud. Oh my gosh, he bent over just to listen to what I have to say. He cares about what I have to say. How many stops until his? Is he going to sit down on those empty seats? He can get off here and catch an express train.

Me: Hey, don't you get off here?

Him: Yeah, but I can take this to the last stop.

He stayed! He's too nice. Wow, what do I talk to him about next?

Me: Words are hard.

Gah!

Him: (Laughs)

Yes! I got him to laugh. Am I blinking weird? Am I smiling too much? Am I blushing already?

Me: I don't think anyone should waste time with stuff that won't matter.

Him: I love wasting time. (laughs) Sometimes at 12 a.m. I get up to do push ups.

Me: Weren't you late to class one day because you were out jogging?

Him: Let's not talk about that. (laughs) So what are your favorite football games you have watched?

He wants to know things. About me.

Me: I don't have favorites. I just want a good game to watch.

Him: Me, too.

Me: Your Jets are doing pretty bad this season.

Him: Yeah, but I'll keep rooting for them.

That smile.

Me: This is my stop.

Him: See you, Amy.

Me: Bye!

I'll definitely see you tomorrow.

I cannot do conversations. But practice makes perfect, right?

Future Tense

LESLIE NIPKOW

*My mentee Amy has taught me the joy of watching someone discover
their own voice. She inspired me to travel halfway around the
world to teach English to young people from India's slums. Voice to voice
to voice, in an endless chain, we help one another grow.*

As I enter the bare classroom at the NGO Magic Bus in Jasola, New Delhi, 15 young men and women shoot out of their chairs with an eager chorus of "Good morning, ma'am!" I turn to the teacher for introduction, but he has vanished. Youthful faces beam in my direction, awaiting today's conversational English lesson. I have no idea what to do, but I can't disappoint these carefully dressed, open-faced kids from Delhi's slums, here to better their lives. I will be here two weeks. I have to try to leave them with something that will last.

I set only one rule. Mistakes will be made, but silence is not an option. In solidarity, I demonstrate my Rosetta Stone Hindi with my most impressive phrase: "six white eggs." My earnest ineptitude inspires hearty laughter. We are underway.

> "Mistakes will be made, but silence is not an option."

I ask each student to stand and, using full sentences, tell me their name and where they imagine themselves five years from now. The class is visibly confounded. My heart aches as it dawns on me: these young people have no experience with dreams. They can't make a sentence that begins "I will be." Who knew imagination was a luxury?

I desperately want to teach them to speak the future.

Two weeks later, I ask the class to close their eyes. Most do; only Vikesh, proud but shy, keeps his wide open. I suspect he hasn't understood the instruction. "Picture yourself in 2020. Where are you? What's your job? How does it feel?"

In the rare Delhi quiet, the energy in the room shifts. I watch the unguarded faces, suffused with yearning. I don't want to bring them out of their dreams, but our time together is limited.

I ask each student to share (in full sentences, of course) where their desire took them. There is a long, reluctant pause, as a battle rages between what-I-want and what-if-it-never-comes-true, but slowly, one by one, the students speak. Julie wants to be a famous TV reporter. "In Hindi," she stresses. Rajneet, a spindly teen who likes to take things apart, wants to be a mechanical engineer. Earlier, while working on resumes, he'd omitted his self-taught mechanical skills in favor of "my good strength." (Translation: he can lift heavy objects.) Rajneet dreamt of inventing new modes of transportation, but could not imagine a possibility beyond loading trucks. There are businessmen, civil engineers, hackers, musicians, a political professor, and the future world's best cricketer. Finally, there is only Vikesh. He stutters painfully through the phrase "I will be," then presses his hands to his chest as if to pluck out his desire to show me. I know he loves children, so I gamble on one of my favorite Hindi words: shikshak. Teacher. As soon as I say it, Vikesh tears up, replying in a mishmash of Hinglish. His friends translate with obvious affection. "Vikesh wants to be a teacher at the Magic Bus." Choking back tears, I ask him to repeat after me, using full sentences.

RACHEL ZHAO

YEARS AS MENTEE: 3

GRADE: Senior

HIGH SCHOOL:
Millennium High School

BORN: Brooklyn, NY

LIVES: Brooklyn, NY

**PUBLICATIONS
AND RECOGNITIONS:**
Scholastic Art & Writing
Award: Honorable Mention

This is my last year at Girls Write Now, which is quite a milestone in my writing and in my relationship with my mentor Nina. At our tiny table in the midst of noisy Tuesday afternoons at the Brooklyn Library, we have explored the difficulty of dialogue through playwriting and monologue, as well as the nuances of body language. In that hour, we challenge the boundaries of our writing and explore the complexities of our stories, even in the form of college admissions essays. Nina has helped me craft a story that I am proud to submit, after months of work, regardless of any response I receive.

NINA AGRAWAL

YEARS AS MENTOR: 3

OCCUPATION:
Graduate Student,
Columbia University

BORN: Los Angeles, CA

LIVES: Brooklyn, NY

After three years of being writing partners, I am going to miss my mentee Rachel when she goes off to college. She has shown a true fearlessness in her writing, gamely trying out new genres and storytelling structures. She has also developed a strong voice that is rich in wit and humor. Together, we have explored using different voices in different situations, whether we are imagining how a character's mood shifts when he describes a building, or imitating Kurt Vonnegut in writing a quotidian scene. I am so proud of how much Rachel has grown, and I am thankful I had the opportunity to grow with her.

The Dinner Party

RACHEL ZHAO

This year's theme is "Voice to Voice." I decided to write about a conversation in which only one voice dominated, creating quite a conundrum for all the other silent voices in the room. A conversation revealed the internal problems that were left unspoken as well as the state of the relationship between family members.

Uncle Mike wiped his mouth and stood up after finishing off the lobster. He held his wine glass delicately between his fingers as he tapped the glass with a fork. The chatter trickled down to silence as everyone turned their attention towards him.

"I just want to acknowledge the wonderful effort that the women in this family have given to prepare this dinner. It was truly delicious and I think I speak for all of us when I say that maybe it isn't just grey hair that I'll be gaining this year." He chuckled, patting his gut. There were murmurs of laughter around the table and everyone began to turn back to their dinner.

"And," he continued, as Father sighed and put his utensils down, "Isn't it great how the family is together tonight? We're here to celebrate the New Year." He cleared his throat and took a sip from his glass. "I just want to take this moment to thank my wonderful family. Luck has been hard to come by this year, but having my wonderful wife and beautiful daughter is all the luck I need." He adjusted his tie. "First of all, my beautiful, resilient wife, Carol." He gestured his wine glass in Aunt Carol's direction. Her lips thinned as he continued to speak. "We've been through so much. In fact, our 30-year wedding anniversary is coming up. We expect great gifts," he chortled, nudging at Father. Uncle moved to refill his glass and took another sip of wine. "Anyway, it's a new year and I just want to thank you for being so understanding and patient with me and 30 years have made us and the store as strong as ever." Aunt Carol's face tightened as she speared a pea on her plate. Uncle Mike downed the rest of his glass again and coughed, his face turning bright red.

"...but having my wonderful wife and beautiful daughter is all the luck I need."

"And my child, my only daughter. You've made us so proud this past year. I remember when you were born. You were so small. You know, I originally wanted a boy to carry on the family name but you've grown to prove that you are just as capable as any male progeny." Marcia bit her lip and shifted her eyes away from her father, turning red. "And you still graduated this year despite any struggles you've faced. Your mother and I are still so proud of you!" He swayed slightly at this point and began to open his mouth to say more, but Aunt Carol quickly got up, cutting him off.

"Is it time for some dessert?" She smiled thinly as she went to take the cake from the oven.

They held their silence until they reached the bridge. It was as if their polite facade could only be contained within the boundaries of the city. The moment they crossed into Brooklyn, exclamations and questions erupted from everyone in the car.

"Did you see how he — "

"And the way he adjusted his tie — "

"Carol looked so uncomfortable — "

"I think it was quite clear," Father said, his voice rising above the rest, "that Uncle is not faring very well financially. He was sweating bullets tonight and he nearly downed the entire bottle of wine."

"He's having marriage troubles," Mother declared. "Carol did look rather angry tonight. She wouldn't stop fidgeting and she couldn't even look at him as he talked. She just kept on staring at her food! I don't think she smiled once the entire dinner. And 30 years is a long time, maybe they're getting tired of each other. They're probably fighting." Mother sat up, her voice growing higher as she jumped to her final conclusion, "Maybe-maybe he cheated on her!"

"You don't know that for sure," Father sighed.

"A woman knows the look of a jilter," Mother snapped, sending a sharp glare towards her husband. "Or maybe they're getting a divorce. Either way, their marriage is on the rocks."

"No way Mike would let that happen," Father said firmly, "Mom would kill him if he ever got a divorce and besides, they never signed a prenup."

"Nah, I think there's something wrong with Marcia," Jan piped from the backseat. "She was on her phone all night. She wouldn't even look at me when I talked to her. When I asked her what her plans were for college — she ignored me!" She huffed. "There's something she's not telling me. Maybe she didn't even get into college! Oh well, it serves her right for only applying to the Ivy Leagues!"

"Not that either," Father sighed. "Mike would sell his house and bribe an official to send her to college."

There was silence as they drove down streets that had become foreign in the night. Then from the very back of the car, Bobby, the youngest, emitted a small gasp as his palms pressed against the window.

"Isn't that Uncle's business?" his small voice questioned. All the heads in the car whipped around to look at the large sign perched in the front yard with the damning word, "Foreclosed."

Story Excerpt: Untitled

NINA AGRAWAL

Since I joined Girls Write Now, I have been wanting to write a short story about my parents' experiences as newlyweds and recent immigrants to America. Their voices and stories filled my childhood, and now they have become a part of my own voice. The Short Story Workshop this year inspired me to finally give the story a try.

Sangeeta hung up the phone in exasperation. How many more times would she have to call the program director before he agreed to hire her?

She took a breath and set her lips in a firm line. Oh, well. I'll just have to call again next Monday.

Since passing her Medical Boards, Sangeeta was itching to start working again. It had been almost three years since she saw a patient. And there was only so much cooking and cleaning to be done.

> "...there was no point turning over the what-ifs in her mind."

If I had stayed in India, I would have been a ward director at my hospital by now. Sangeeta shook her head, banishing the thought. She had chosen to marry someone who lived in America and to start over here, so there was no point turning over the what-ifs in her mind.

She picked up the phone again and dialed her friend Kiran. "Hi, Kiran, how are you? Want to go to the movies? I need to get out of the house."

Thank goodness for Kiran. They had met at a party at the company where both their husbands worked as engineers. Kiran was applying for jobs as a biochemist, but she hadn't had any luck so far. In the meantime, Sangeeta and Kiran had taken ballet lessons, played tennis at the YMCA, and learned how to swim. If it weren't for her, Sangeeta was sure she would have died of loneliness after coming to America.

TIANA ZUNIGA

YEARS AS MENTEE: 1

GRADE: Sophomore

HIGH SCHOOL:
Bronx Center for Science
and Mathematics

BORN: New York, NY

LIVES: Bronx, NY

Being in Girls Write Now has meant that I'm constantly juggling my writing along with my Advanced Placement essays so that I can start taking college-level classes next year. But if you really knew me, you would know that I always get the job done. Jan really inspired me to write about what's on my mind and express my emotions. The time we've spent together has not only made me a more mature writer but has allowed me to be myself.

JAN ALEXANDER

YEARS AS MENTOR: 1

OCCUPATION:
Senior Editor, Strategy;
Creative writer

BORN: Chicago, IL

LIVES: New York, NY

**PUBLICATIONS
AND RECOGNITIONS:**
Editor-at-large for The
Neworld Review (www.
neworldreview.com)

Right from the start I was awed by the way Tiana understood the power she had as a girl with a talent for writing stories that probe what it means to be human. In our weekly meetings, she's explored how women feel but also how men feel, and what it's like to live in a world dramatically different from her own. It took me years of traveling and writing about other cultures to learn the life lessons that inform Tiana's writing: that you can separate people by ethnicity, gender, age, etc. but beneath the surface everyone has a universal story.

Raw Beauty

TIANA ZUNIGA

*My piece is about how society favors certain people because of
their looks. At the same time, definitions of beauty change, and that puts
pressure on people to constantly change the way they look.*

I think of beauty as something that should be unique, that defines each person differently. But most people seem to think there's only one definition of beauty. For example, my family's view of beauty is that it means having straight, soft hair. I've been relaxing my hair since I was in fifth grade and over the years my hair has been suffering from all the chemicals I apply to it. This caused chunks of my hair to fall out.

There was a time that I wanted to control my own hair and leave out the chemicals. I didn't mind that it would mean my hair wouldn't be straight and soft anymore. But my family, especially my aunt, hated nappy hair and always wanted me to perm it. It hurt me and made me think that my family doesn't want me to be the real me. My natural hair is a part of me.

At school, my friends have specific ideas about what's beautiful as well. There's this girl named Lilly in my school who has natural hair that's short and uncombed. People make fun of her constantly. One Friday, a friend of mine drew a picture of a tree and told me that the head of the tree looks like Lilly's hair. This pretty much hurt me because if my friends are that harsh about Lilly's hair in its natural state, what might they say about me? There were times that my hair was the center of my friends' focus. They would ask me, "Tiana why doesn't your hair grow as fast as that girl's?" Don't they know that there are genetic factors behind how fast your hair grows? Hair is every girl's burden. The same goes for looks in general. So I decided to write about the way I look.

The thing I hate the most about my hair is its slow growth rate. This year I've decided to give it a break from all the constricted ponytails and killer chemicals. I even feed it. When I say feed it, I mean I literally serve it breakfast, which includes egg and coffee. I take a small bowl and mix an egg and coffee together in it. Then when I get into the shower, I pour the yolk all over my hair. It's icy cold. Sadly, I still get zero results.

Still, my hair is my own and it's part of what makes me uniquely me. The thing I love most about my hair is its thickness. I love how I can walk my fingers along what feels like sidewalks running across my scalp. It feels like a pillow that has never been touched, and the volume is bigger than the Empire State Building. Most people want thicker hair, but I already have it. Yet I'd rather have people love me for me instead of my thick head of hair.

When I think of other features, there are things I hate about my legs, but also things I love. I don't like their shape. I feel like a bell when I walk. Then when someone interacts with me, I jingle. But what I love most about my legs is how cold they feel. I know this sounds weird, but I love cool skin. I love rubbing my feet and I love to bend my legs. Most of all, I love walking with them. Not everyone can walk. I have strong legs that can carry me places.

> "Most of all, I love walking with them. Not everyone can walk. I have strong legs that can carry me places.."

I love to laugh, but I don't like how big my smile can get when I'm laughing. I look like one of those clowns who haunt you at night. I try to be more of a mime who has no emotion and no smile. But that doesn't work so well. So instead, I try to cover my mouth every time I laugh. It looks as if I have just said a curse word. In other words, I laugh so much that I drown in my own laughter. One time I was even punished for laughing in my seventh grade science class because I was laughing at a SpongeBob episode. I ended up having to stand up and face the wall in front of the class. But the whole time I was thinking it's good to laugh, and I wasn't sorry.

And besides, even if my smile is big, it's perfect. I used to have braces and I'm not going to lie; they were extremely uncomfortable at times. However, the braces did their job of straightening my teeth and allowing me to smile at things I think are great. Plus, smiles just make you a more positive, more attractive person. Maybe the bigger your smile is, the better.

The Power of My Crooked Smile

JAN ALEXANDER

My mentee Tiana and I started talking about beauty and the power it gives you, especially in high school. I've never forgotten my own teenage insecurities, but I've learned that real beauty has little to do with perfect features.

Let's talk about beauty, feature by feature. This time I'll take the mouth. I had a non-existent mouth in high school; that is, I was invisible beside my friend Dana, who was beautiful, and mute beside my friend Sandie, who was cute and witty. Dana had

pouty pink lips. Sandy had a wide mouth. "See, I can fit a golf ball in it," she'd say —
then demonstrate — and boys fell in love with her because she made them laugh. My
mouth seemed designed for making silent vows, like "someday I'm going to live in
New York and be glamorous."

It wasn't until I was in college that I learned I had a funny mouth. "You have a
lopsided smile," my college boyfriend told me. He said my smile tilted to the right,
and it made me look like an old-time English comic named Stan Laurel. I took it as an
insult; my college boyfriend was into insult humor. But a few years later, in my twen-
ties, another male friend said, "You look like Stan Laurel when you smile that way."
By then, I'd kind of figured out what it took to look a little glamorous, but I wanted
to be more than attractive — commanding and entertaining, for starters. Sometimes
when people told me I was pretty, I'd say, "Actually, I look like Stan Laurel." Then I'd
show them the face. It would open up the conversation to so much more than looks.

> "...my mouth feels beautiful to me when I'm laughing, or plotting how to save the world, or tasting something delicious..."

Something I've learned: my mouth feels beautiful
to me when I'm laughing, or plotting how to save the
world, or tasting something delicious, or yawning luxu-
riously at the end of a busy day. Women who get lip jobs
are missing the point. What gives a mouth power is what
you can do with it.

Something I wish: that instead of spending all those hours envying my high
school girlfriends, I'd learned to play the flute. Some great flutists play out of one side
of their mouths.

Ready, Set, Write!

PROMPTS AND WRITING EXERCISES
FOR INDIVIDUALS AND GROUPS

The theme of this year's anthology "Voice to Voice" represents the power behind our ever-evolving and interconnected narratives.

The mentoring relationships and friendships we developed over the year encouraged us to express and celebrate our diverse voices. Separately, in pairs, and in groups, we articulated our experiences and thoughts, shaping our voices, investigating our identities. With the theme "Voice to Voice" as a guide, we explored different genres such as fiction, memoir, poetry, screenwriting, and more.

Try the exercises below to explore your voice and the lens through which you perceive the world. Your unique voice will resonate in the writing you do in this book and beyond.

— **AARTI MONTEIRO,** Senior Program Coordinator
CHRISTINA DRILL, Senior Program Coordinator

GETTING STARTED: VOICE TO VOICE

To help discover your voice, start by answering the following prompts.

When I feel misunderstood:
I speak...

_____

I wish...

_____

I think...

_____

I can...

_____

When I feel like I am being heard:
I speak...

_____

I wish...

_____

I think...

_____

I can...

_____

When I witness injustice:
I speak...

_____

I wish...

_____

I think...

_____

I can...

_____

When I read the news:
I speak...

_____

I wish...

_____

I think...

_____

I can...

_____

RECOMMENDED READING

See Lulejeta Kulla Zenka's "Never Knew Better" for an example
of a piece with a strong voice throughout (p. 100).
Bad Feminist, Roxane Gay
Water by the Spoonful, Quiara Alegria Hudes
Station Eleven, Emily St. John Mandel
Land of Love and Drowning, Tiphanie Yanique

FICTION: SHORT STORIES

In these exercises, you'll work on creating characters
and conflict to write a compelling short story.

OPENING LINES: Think of a person you saw outside your immediate circle of friends who intrigues you. Use this person as inspiration to build a character for your story. With your imagination, fill in the parts you don't know. You can add, invent, or manipulate any part of their physical or personality traits.

Describe the character in physical terms. What does she look like, sound like, smell like? How does she walk, dress, talk? Any particular mannerisms?

_____

_____

_____

_____

_____

Describe the world of this character. What time and place does she live in? Does she have a family and a job? Does she have friends, and if so, who are they?

_____

_____

_____

_____

_____

What is your character's desire in life? What does she want more than anything? What drives her?

_____

_____

_____

_____

_____

What is standing in the way of your character getting what she wants? It could be an internal conflict, where she is standing in her own way, or an external conflict, where someone or something is standing in her way.

_____

_____

_____

_____

_____

FREEWRITE: Now that you have given your character a conflict, write a story in which she must deal with it.

_____
_____
_____
_____
_____
_____
_____
_____
_____
_____
_____
_____
_____
_____
_____
_____
_____
_____
_____
_____
_____

Bonus: Write a scene about your character from a different point of view. For example, if you wrote the story in third person, try writing in first person to get to know your character better.

RECOMMENDED READING
See Shanille Martin's piece "Whispers" for an example of an imaginative story (p. 142).
Krik? Krak!, Edwidge Danticat
Drown, Junot Diaz
Magic for Beginners, Kelly Link
Birds of America, Lorrie Moore
Drinking Coffee Elsewhere, ZZ Packer

MEMOIR: WHEN PLACE IS A CHARACTER

*In these exercises, you will use place as a way
into your memory to help you write a vivid memoir.*

OPENING LINES: PART I. For each of the prompts below, indicate a place where you have felt the given emotion. Feel free to write down more than one place if you want. For now, don't worry about writing the actual memory or what that place looked like.

A place where I have felt joyful is...

_____

_____

_____

_____

_____

A place where I have felt safe is...

_____

_____

_____

_____

_____

A place where I have felt brave is...

_____

_____

_____

_____

_____

A place where I have felt older OR younger than my age is...

_____

_____

_____

_____

_____

A place where I have felt like an outsider is....

_____

_____

_____

_____

_____

PART II. Choose one of the places you wrote about in Part I that has a strong memory associated with it. Answer the following questions:

What and where is this place? What memory do you associate with it?

_____

_____

_____

_____

Describe this place without mentioning the actual memory. Instead, allow your memory to influence your description. What details do you remember about it? Pay attention to the senses as you describe this place. What does it look like? What does it smell or sound like?

_____

_____

_____

_____

FREEWRITE: Now that you've described the place, tell us what happened. Build out the narrative through character, action, and/or dialogue. Who was there with you? What was the main event, conflict, tension, or emotion in this scene? You can include your descriptions from the above to flesh out the scene.

_____

_____

_____

_____

_____

_____

_____

_____

_____

_____

_____

_____

_____

_____

_____

_____

_____

_____

_____

_____

_____

_____

_____

_____

_____

_____

_____

_____

_____

_____

_____

_____

_____

_____

_____

_____

_____

_____

Bonus: Reflect on what your relationship to this memory is today. Are your feelings the same now as they were then? Has time given you insight into this memory? Imagine that you are coming back to this place and memory ten years from now. Would you write about this memory differently?

RECOMMENDED READING

See Fareena Samad's "Bedroom Voices" for an example of a piece that focuses on place (p. 233).

Fun Home: A Family Tragicomic, Alison Bechdel

The House on Mango Street, Sandra Cisneros

The Liars' Club, Mary Karr

Without You, There Is No Us: My Time with the Sons of North Korea's Elite, Suki Kim

The Woman Warrior: Memoirs of a Girlhood Among Ghosts, Maxine Hong Kingston

POETRY: PERSONA POEMS

*Use the following prompts to write a poem in which
you embody the voice of someone else.*

OPENING LINES: PART I. Start brainstorming characters (real or imaginary)
you might use as inspiration for your poem.

Someone you admire:

_____

Someone who disgusts you:

_____

Someone you saw on the subway or bus:

_____

Someone you used to know:

_____

A historical figure:

_____

PART II. Pick one of the people you listed in Part 1 and start to think more deeply
about her character.

What is the "essence" of this person's character?

If your character were an animal, she would be a:

_____

If your character were a mode of transportation, she would be a:

_____

If your character were a musical instrument, she would be a:

_____

If your character were a type of weather, she would be:

_____

If your character were a texture, she would be:

_____

FREEWRITE: Write a poem from your character's point of view. Put this person in a situation where she is compelled to speak, for whatever reason. Consider what event has compelled this character to speak, as well as to whom she might be speaking.

Bonus: Share your poem with someone else and ask them to give you a question about what remains unanswered in the poem and/or what they want to hear more about. Return to your poem, and write a few more lines, another stanza, an addendum, or an entirely new poem answering the question.

RECOMMENDED READING

See Rumer LeGendre's piece "Why I Run" for an example of a persona poem (p. 115).
The Wild Iris, Louise Glück
Mule & Pear, Rachel Eliza Griffiths
Lunch Poems, Frank O'Hara
Mirror, Sylvia Plath
Citizen, Claudia Rankine

SCREENWRITING: ADAPTATION

Use the prompts below to transform your favorite story into a screenplay.

OPENING LINES: Many popular movies were adapted from fiction, plays, or memoirs because there is something about the story that lends itself well to the screen. Choose your favorite story or a piece of your own writing to adapt into a screenplay.

One of the most important parts of screenwriting is thinking visually about the story you want to tell. Using the story you've chosen to adapt, think about the key scenes in it. Write a short description of each scene using the beat sheet below. A beat sheet is an abbreviated version of scenes that don't contain dialogue.

Scene 1:

_____

_____

_____

_____

_____

Scene 2:

_____

_____

_____

_____

Scene 3:

_____

_____

_____

_____

Scene 4:

_____

_____

_____

_____

_____

FREEWRITE: Choose one of the scenes from your Opening Lines beat sheet that you want to expand. Write it as a screenplay and add dialogue. Don't worry about getting the formatting perfect for now, but use the example below as a guide.

Formatting Example:

INT./EXT. LOCATION – TIME OF DAY
Action...   CHARACTER 1
                                   (parenthetical)
                                   Dialogue...
Action...   CHARACTER 2
                                   (parenthetical)
                                   Dialogue...

Write your scene below:

_____

_____

_____

_____

_____

_____

_____

_____

_____

_____

_____

_____

_____

_____

_____

_____

Bonus: Think about the characters in your story and imagine them performing the lines you have written. Then, recruit a friend to join you in reading several lines from your screenplay aloud. Ideally, assemble a few people as your "audience" and get their feedback.

RECOMMENDED READING

See Mennen Gordon's piece "I Think Best/Worst in the Dark" for an example of a screenplay (p. 75).
To Kill a Mockingbird, adapted by Horton Foote
Persepolis, adapted by Marjane Satrapi
Sense and Sensibility, adapted by Emma Thompson
The Namesake, adapted by Sooni Taraporevala

THE
GIRLS WRITE NOW
2015 TEAM

STAFF

Maya Nussbaum
Founder & Executive Director

Tracy Steele
Director of Operations

Katie Zanecchia
Communications Manager

Molly MacDermot
Communications Advisor & Editor

Nalini Edwin
Digital Program Manager

Chelsea Fonden
Writing & Mentoring Program Manager

Aarti Monteiro
Senior Program Coordinator

Sarah Hubschman
Program Coordinator

Christina Drill
Senior Program Coordinator

Amber West
Senior Grant Writer

Suhaila Meera
Operations Coordinator

INTERNS

Emily Becker
Wellesley Boboc
Madison Campbell
Rachel Cloyd
Rachel Flanders
Sara Heegaard
Jocelyn Jacoby
LaTroya Lovell
Megan Malloy
Nina Menchicchi
Emely Paulino
Sandra Pons
Devan Tierney

BOARD OF DIRECTORS

Chelsea Rao
Board Chair

Sandra Bang
Vice Chair

Ellen Sweet
Secretary

Justine Lelchuk
Treasurer

Sang Lee
Board Development Chair

Erica Mui
Finance & Audit Chair

Gloria Jacobs
Marketing/Publicity Chair

Laura Scileppi
Fundraising Chair

Marci Alboher

Faiza Issa

Michelle Levin

Nancy K. Miller

Maya Nussbaum

Kerry Smith

Elaine Stuart-Shah

Kamy Wicoff

YOUTH BOARD

Taysha Clark
Co-Chair

Natalia Vargas-Caba
Co-Chair

Nishat Anjum

Misbah Awan

Swati Barua

Tuhfa Begum

Sophia Chan

Nyasiah Colon

Mariah Dwyer

Teamare Gaston

Mennen Gordon

Jennifer Lee

Bushra Miah

Idamaris Perez

Tema Regist

Tiffani Ren

Sade Swift

Eda Tse

Roberta Yadira Nin Feliz

Sharon Young

Samantha Young Chan

PROGRAM ADVISORY
COMMITTEE

Rachel Cohen
Mentee Enrollment Chair

Demetria Irwin
Mentor Enrollment Chair

Alice Pencaval
Curriculum Chair

Heather Graham
Pair Support Co-Chair

Kate Jacobs
Pair Support Co-Chair

Kirsten Reach
Anthology Chair

Pamela Osbey
Readings Chair

Ella Morton
Digital Exhibition Chair

Ashley Howard
Web Chair

CURRICULUM COMMITTEE

Alice Pencaval
Curriculum Chair

Allison Adair-Alberts
Heather Graham
Claudia Parsons
Kate Schmier
Juliet Werner

WORKSHOP TEAMS:

Fiction
Allison Adair-Alberts
Jan Alexander
Nicole Counts
Heather Graham
Claudia Parsons
Chana Porter

Memoir
Allison Adair-Alberts
Linda Corman
Stacie Evans
Morayo Faleyimu
Catherine LeClair
Mary Pat Kane
Juliet Werner

Screenwriting
Elizabeth Irwin
Claudia Parsons
Kate Petty
Chana Porter
J M Stifle
Juliet Werner

Poetry
Allison Adair-Alberts
Bria Cole
Nicole Counts
Iris Cushing
Nicole Gervasio
Lia Greenwell

Journalism
Erica Moroz
Caitlin Rimschnick
Kate Schmier
Shara Zaval

Web Presence
Alex Berg
Elizabeth Decker
Katie Gemmill
Channing Hargrove
Sara Polsky
Kate Schmier

THERAPY PANEL
Erin Baer
Chelsea Grefe
Rashida Latef
Diane Rubino
Farrah Tassy

COLLEGE PREP PANEL
Corrie Driebusch
Robert Gulya
Mindy Liss
Luvon Roberson
Ruth Sullivan
Josleen Wilson
Yana Geyfman
Tom Rabbitt
Nicole Rothwell

POETRY AMBASSADORS
Mya Watkins
Bre'Ann Newsome
Calayah Heron
Kirby-Estar Laguerre
Sally Ferris
Chenelle Agnew
Rumer LeGendre
Kiara Kerina-Rendina

CRAFT TALK AUTHORS
Alexandra Kleeman
Hasanthika Sirisena
Suki Kim
Nicole Y. Dennis-Benn
Laura Maria Censabella
Gillian Robespierre
Rachel Eliza Griffiths
Vanessa Jimenez Gabb

CHAPTERS READING
SERIES KEYNOTE
SPEAKERS
Tiphanie Yanique
Emily St. John Mandel
Roxane Gay
Quiara Alegría Hudes